NUEVOS PASOS:
Chicano and Puerto Rican Drama

Nicolás Kanellos and Jorge A. Huerta
Editors

Nuevos Pasos: Chicano and Puerto Rican Drama was first published in 1979 as a special issue of *Revista Chicano-Riqueña*. The present reprint edition is made possible through support from the Ford Foundation.

Arte Público Press
University of Houston
Houston, Texas 77204-2090

ISBN 0-934770-98-0

Nuevos pasos: Chicano and Puerto Rican drama / Nicolas Kanellos and
    Jorge A. Huerta, editors.
        p.   cm.
    ISBN 0-934770-98-0 : $12.50
    1. American drama--Mexican American authors. 2. American drama-
-Puerto Rican authors. 3. Mexican Americans--Drama. 4. Puerto
Ricans--Drama. I. Kanellos, Nicolás. II. Huerta, Jorge A.
PS628.M4N84 1989
812'.008'086872073--dc19   89-361
                                                              CIP

CONTENIDO

Illustrations for *The Interview* and *Brujerías* by Alejandro Romero, Mexican expressionist painter whose works have been exhibited in various countries.

Nicolás Kanellos and Jorge A. Huerta

INTRODUCTION

Background

It can be said that Spanish American theatre was born somewhere in the sixteenth century when the Spanish missionaries wed their evangelical theatre to the dramatic performance of the indigenous peoples of America.[1] From there the basis was laid for the development of a "legitimate" theatre in the Western tradition as well as a folktheatre that was truly mestizo in nature.[2] Both theatrical traditions survive to this date in Spanish America and parts of the United States and have witnessed the birth of a third: a professional theatre that is truly Spanish American. From those times when Spanish religious plays were first translated to the indigenous languages up to the present, Latin America has seen the rise and fall of Spanish cultural hegemony and the growth of the United States as the dominant cultural influence not only in the Hemisphere, but in the world.

While both Mexico and Puerto Rico were in the process of creating their own national identities as separate and distinct from Spain and Europe, the great North American giant intervened and altered that process forever. Mexico saw the major portion of its northern territory devoured by its hungry neighbor and shortly thereafter Puerto Rico became his captive child. After the United States occupation, however, the cultural ties to Spain and Mexico were never completely severed, even while English became the official language of public education in Puerto Rico and Spanish was prohibited on school grounds in some Southwestern states. As more and more Puerto Ricans and Mexicans were drawn to labor in the factories and fields of the continental United States, interior colonization of the Mexican and Puerto Rican peoples became a reality.

While often uprooted from their native lands and converted to minority status in the belly of the giant, the Latinos of the United States never gave up their cultural institutions. Theatre, whether commercial or amateur, professional or folkloric, is one of the most important of those institutions and has been essential in maintaining a sense of identity and community solidarity throughout the last one hundred and thirty years. At each turn, an appropriate theatrical expression has responded to the historical, linguistic, economic, and spiritual circumstances of the Latino communities. During the second half of the nineteenth century, Spanish-language theatrical expression in the Southwest accomodated the populations scattered in ranches, towns and cities: folktheatre,[3] tent theatres, and professional companies that performed romantic melodramas traveled by horse-drawn wagon.[4] There was even at least one company that toured the major cities up and down the California coast by ship, from San Francisco to Mazatlán.[5] Even before the Mexican Revolution of 1910 professional companies from Mexico performed lyric and dramatic works along the border from Laredo to Los Angeles.[6] For them and the groups to follow their routes during the twentieth century, the advent of rail transportation was a boon. After 1910, the establishment of large colonies of Mexican immigrants throughout the United States was followed by the development of extensive, coast-to-coast theatrical circuits[7] and nation-wide tours. In fact, some of the Spanish and Mexican companies not only toured from New York to Los Angeles via the Southwest, but also made tours that included on their itineraries Cuba and Puerto Rico, as well as Mexico.[8] The great Mexican actress, Virginia Fábregas,[9] took her company on hemispheric and world tours that also included Spain, the Canary Islands, Cuba and the Philipines. New York, San Antonio and Los Angeles became theatrical centers that supported theatre houses with their own repertory companies, as well as establishments that hosted the touring lyric and dramatic groups. On another level, variety shows and tent theatres were still making the rounds and attracting great crowds.

In New York, the Hispanic community was made up of diverse Hispanic nationalities and thus Spanish, Cuban and Puerto Rican groups were to be found performing a variety of stage entertainments,[10] but quite often the same *zarzuelas* and dramas were being performed in the Southwest, Mexico and the Caribbean. In fact, the newspapers of the time tell us that the communities were very interested in seeing the latest hits from Mexico City and Madrid and touring companies often boasted that they were bringing those very works to the U.S. communities.

As the Depression approached, Spanish-language vaudeville began to displace serious theatre and the talking picture industry also delivered a serious blow to the professional stage. But all was not lost as the former professional artists continued to practice their craft as an avocation and fund-raising enterprise for numerous community projects. Along with the inroads made by the Depression, Mexican repatriation also took its toll of both artists and audiences and World War II followed on its footsteps. But the war also brought mass migrations of Puerto Ricans to the mainland and this prepared the way for the growth of cultural life in New York during the post-war period. As life stabilized again after World War II, the Hispanic communities began to reestablish themselves and amateur and sporadic professional performances began to appear. Of course this was followed up in the late sixties by the birth of Chicano theatre as a labor theatre and its development in the seventies into a professional theatre under Luis Valdez's leadership. And New York is witnessing today a flowering of Hispanic theatre that includes professional and community performances by the various Hispanic nationalities.

Chicano Theatre Today

No individual has been as important to the evolution of Chicano theatre as Luis Valdez, for he developed teatro from its humble beginnings as an organizing arm of the 1965 Delano grape strike into a nationally and internationally renowned theatrical form and, in turn, his own talents have widened from theatrical director and innovator to the leader of a movement and, most recently, to nationally acclaimed playwright. It can be said that Luis Valdez is the inspirer of a national theatre for the Chicano people.

When Valdez went to Delano in 1965 he had much to offer, besides his childhood experiences as a farmworker and his love of Mexican culture: he had written two successful plays while in college and had learned the ropes of agitprop theatre while working with the San Francisco Mime Troupe. With the struggling farmworkers union, Valdez was able to organize some of the workers into a theatre by and for the farmworkers who improvised agitational and propagandistic skits that Valdez labeled "actos." These actos were the predecessors of later works that would form the basis of all Chicano drama to follow. To the present the acto has been the backbone of Chicano theatre. It is a short, one act exposition of a social or political problem and uses the language and culture of the Chicano grass roots as its point of departure. The form seems to have been successful in combining aspects of Brechtian dramatics, commedia dell' arte, agitprop, Mexican tent theatre and Cantinflas.[11]

When El Teatro Campesino took to the road performing on campuses and in communities outside of Delano, the group carried a growing repertoire of actos that dealt with the campesino experience.[12] These early actos became models for the many groups that sprung up around the country to follow the example of Valdez's company. Soon the movement spread from the fields to the universities and local communities, with teatros forming everywhere from Los Angeles to Detroit, San Antonio to Seattle. In 1970 Valdez and his troupe gathered the new, fledgling teatros in a festival for performances, workshops and a general sharing of problems and materials. The festival became an annual event and in 1971 a national organization of teatros (TENAZ) was founded. TENAZ continues to administer the festival and today also serves as a communications network and overseer of the artistic and political growth of teatro.

Today Chicano theatre has gone beyond the acto which, with its simple plot, clearly defined antagonist and protagonist, and usually uncomplicated solution, remains the basic unit for the majority of community and student groups. Because the acto is collectively created or written, it is the product of many minds and relies heavily on the spontaneity and talent of its interpreters. Perhaps this collectivity has in the past surpressed the development of the individual playwright. But finally a strong core of Chicano playwrights and professionalized companies to perform their works has now appeared. In some instances, the writers have emerged from the most disciplined and experienced of the theatres: El Teatro Campesino, El Teatro de la Esperanza, El Teatro de la Gente and others. Some of the playwrights have reenforced their practical experience with university study. Adrián Vargas, Carlos Morton and Rubén Sierra have each obtained Master's degrees in playwrighting. The emergence of the Chicano and Puerto Rican playwright, which this anthology celebrates, is capped by a momentous event: Luis Valdez's play, *Zoot Suit*, produced with an equity cast and premiered at a major Los Angeles theatre, not only received great critical acclaim and national publicity, but also will make its New York premiere on Broadway in early 1979. With the Broadway production of Valdez's play Chicano theatre enters a new era. *Zoot Suit* has broken the barriers; publishers, producers and directors will be looking for other plays that depict the Chicano experience. There will probably be some exploitation on the stage just as Hollywood is currently churning out a score of gang movies that do little to erase the stereotypes of Latino violence and crime, but it will be the responsibility of the playwrights to create visions of the Chicano that are honest, sensitive and relevant.

New York Puerto Rican Theatre

There are easily over twenty-five Hispanic theatrical companies performing in New York City today. The majority of them produce works in Spanish and continue the tradition of ethnic foreign language theatre established in New York at the beginning of the century. Of the various nationalities, the Puerto Ricans dominate in population statistics as well as in theatrical activity. But it should be noted that there are very important and successful professional companies that perform bilingually and are made up of a cross-section of Hispanic groups.[13] The New York experience, unlike the Southwestern, is not characterized by one personality unifying and helping to create one distinctive theatrical expression. The Puerto Rican theatrical experience on the mainland is especially characterized by diversity. Although there are a few grass-roots based teatros that work in a style similar to and influenced by Chicano collective style, today's Puerto Rican theatre has continued to produce individual playwrights whose works are eagerly sought for production by the numerous companies that have sprung up since the 1950's. Furthermore, when one considers the impact of Miguel Piñero's *Short Eyes* garnering the New York Drama Critics Circle Award for Best American Play of the 1973-1974 season, and the stimulus provided by Joseph Papp's New York Shakespeare Festival, it is easy to understand why so many New York Puerto Rican theatres and playwrights exist.

Puerto Rican theatrical activity in New York has two focal points: the Puerto Rican Traveling Theatre and the Nuyorican theatre movement on the Lower East Side. The Puerto Rican Traveling Theatre was founded by actress-director, Miriam Colón, who since the 1950's has been active in developing Hispanic theatre in New York. As an actress, she first worked with La Farándula Panamericana where she participated in introducing René Marqués' *La carreta* to New York audiences. She later founded El Nuevo Círculo Dramático with playwright-director, Roberto Rodríguez. Then in 1967, with assistance from the Shakespeare Festival's Mobile Unit, Colón founded the Puerto Rican Traveling Theatre, a professional bilingual theatre which produces works by Puerto Rican and Nuyorican writers as well as other Latin American playwrights. The company today has its own theatre and also operates a traveling unit and a drama school.

The center of Nuyorican theatrical expression, nevertheless, is the Lower East Side of Manhattan. There such groups as the Nuyorican Poet's Café, Aquarius, the Latin Insomniacs, the Family, Teatro Otra Cosa and the Puerto Rican Bilingual Workshop address a widerange of issues in varied styles as they relate to the generation of Puerto Ricans born and/or raised on the mainland. But it should be emphasized that from the very creation of many of these groups, playwrighting was encouraged as central to theatrical work. Such was certainly the case when in 1974 Miguel Algarín, a key figure among Nuyorican writers, began conducting the Nuyorican Writers' and Actors' Workshop in conjunction with Joseph Papp and Raymond Barry, formerly of the Open Theatre. The workshop later grew into the Nuyorican Theatre Festival which featured works like Lucky Cienfuegos' *America Congo Mania* and Miguel Piñero's *Side Show*. At one point, however, Algarín and Piñero became heavily involved in writing for the "Realidades" television series and in Algarín's words, "the Nuyorican Theatre Festival went into t.v. production." Today the festival has been reestablished as part of the program at Algarín's Nuyorican Poets' Café[13].

Founded in 1973 and directed by Carla Pinza, the Puerto Rican Bilingual Workshop represents another key theatrical institution on the Lower East Side. The workshop, while at first producing only Puerto Rican works in Spanish, today features works in English by Hispanic playwrights of varying backgrounds, including Osvaldo Dragún, Guillermo Gentile, Jaime Carrero, Carlos Morton, Pedro Pietri and Jesús Papoleto Meléndez. In 1975 Carla Pinza and Woody King Jr. produced a salsa musical, *Mondongo,* by Ramón Ramírez, that was presented at the New Federal Theatre and the New York Shakespeare Festival's Mobile Unit. The play is presently in rehearsal for a Broadway opening in 1979.

It is easy to see that the experience provided by workshops like Algarín's and Pinza's, along with the opportunities for production provided by Joseph Papp, is leading directly to professionalization and access to the theatrical mainstream. Perhaps solely because of the proximity of the Great White Way and its current revitalization, Puerto Rican theatre in New York is bustling with activity. Today one cannot only hear Spanish spoken and see integrated casts in plays like Swados' *Runaways,* which deals with the problems of street youth, but it is also possible to see Puerto Ricans in the leading roles of tremendous box-office successes like *Dracula. Raúl Juliá,* who could be found in 1965 acting with Miriam Colón in *La carreta,* is the male lead in that play. And writers like Miguel Piñero are today achieving wide recognition not only through theatre but also television and cinema.

With both the Puerto Ricans and the Chicanos closing in on Broadway, the future for Hispanic drama in the United States looks very bright indeed. But it must also be noted that this success is probably a result of greater assimilation into the mainstream of American society and a willingness of the writers and artists to address their works to a wider audience than before. While theatre groups that direct their works to local barrio audiences continue to employ a bilingual Spanish-English or just monolingual Spanish format, Chicano and Puerto Rican playwrights today are relying more and more on the English script in their attempts to reach the greatest number of people and achieve the recognition that only comes from mass media. The present anthology cannot but reflect that reality. It will be the task of the historians and critics to evaluate the social and political significance of this latest step in the evolution of the theatrical expression of Chicanos and Puerto Ricans.

---

[1]See Pedro Henríquez Ureña, "El teatro de la América Española en la Epoca Colonial," *Cuadernos de cultura teatral,* 3 (1936).

[2]Francisco C. Lacosta, "El teatro misionero en la América Hispánica," *Cuadernos Americanos,* 142 (Sept.-Oct., 1965), p. 175.

[3]Hispanic folktheatre in the Southwest has attracted more attention from scholars than any other form of Latino theatre in the United States. See Bonnie Stowell, "Folk Drama Scholarship in the United States: A Selective Survey," *Folklore Annual,* 2 (1970), 51-66.

[4]See John G. Bourke, *On the Border with Crook* (New York: Charles Scribner's Sons, 1891), pp. 84-86, for a description of one such theatre (a "Mexican strolling heavy-tragedy company") that was performing in Arizona during the 1870's.

[5]The San Francisco newspaper, *Nuevo Mundo,* on December 12 and December 20, 1864, notes the departure of "D. Gerardo López del Castillo, primer actor y director de escena" to perform in Mazatlán.

[6]Even such minor population centers as Las Cruces, New Mexico, supported their own theatre houses, like the Teatro Juárez, that hosted these companies. See the Las Cruces newspaper, *El Labrador,* December 9, 1904.

[7]In Southwestern newspapers there are occasional references to formalized theatrical circuits like "el circuito Hipodrome" (*Hispano Americano,* San Francisco, April 1919); "el circuito Chataqua" that contracted Los Hermanos Llera, a vaudeville singing act for 125 performances across the United States (*La Prensa,* San Antonio, December, 10, 1925); "el circuito Interstate" (*La Prensa,* October 3, 1924); and New York agent Walter O. Lindsay who booked the Compañía María Guerrero from New York to Los Angeles and back via New Orleans and the Southwest as a trial run for other national tours by Hispanic artists that he had under contract (*La Prensa,* November 21, 1926).

[8]For example, *La Prensa,* San Antonio, February 2, 1928, notes the local appearance of the vaudeville act, Dorita Ceprano y Enrique Areu, after their return from an extended run in Puerto Rico and a tour of Central America and the Caribbean.

[9]*La Prensa,* San Antonio, November 28, 1926, and June 8, 1928.

[10]See John C. Miller, "Hispanic Theatre in New York, 1965-1977," *Revista Chicano-Riqueña,* 6/1 (1977), 40-59.

[11]For a complete discussion of the acto and how it differs from the traditional realistic play, see Jorge A. Huerta, "Where Are Our Chicano Playwrights?" *Revista Chicano-Riqueña,* 3/4 (1975), 32-42.

[12]See Betty Diamond, "'Brown Eyed Children of the Sun:' The Cultural Politics of El Teatro Campesino," unpublished Ph.D. diss., University of Wisconsin-Madison, 1977, pp. 50-128; and Jorge A. Huerta, "Chicano Agit-Prop; The Early Actos of El Teatro Campesino," *Latin American Theatre Review,* 9/2 (Spring, 1977), 45-58.

[13]See Miller, pp. 45-49

Illustration by Alejandro Romero

Ron Arias

THE INTERVIEW

This brief one-act comedy was scripted by Ron Arias, with the help of his students, Kathy Avila, José Garza, and Tony Mena, while Prof. Arias was teaching creative writing at a junior college in California. Though Mr. Arias is best-known for his short stories and most recently for his book, The Road to Tamazunchale, which was nominated for the National Book Award, this brief venture into the realm of teatro displays the author's theatrical creativity as well. The script provides the actor with characters that do not have to be stereotypical, though any barrio resident can envision their local "winos" and some of the more universal characteristics of this type. The student/interviewer, TONY CHAVEZ is also a readily identifiable character, the Mexican-American college student who has lost touch with his community or who might never have been a part of it.

Though this play can be performed economically, it does require minimal set-props, and most importantly, lighting. As denoted in the script, there are two specific areas onstage, the first indicating the "street," and the second representing JESS' imagination. The fact that the audience gets a glimpse of JESS' past through flashbacks that are carefully interwoven, suggests an expressionistic device used by Arthur Miller in Death of a Salesman and A View from the Bridge, and can be very effective. But the ability to light different areas of the stage interchangeably requires a dimmer, lights, and an operator, thus limiting production to a space that is equipped with these accoutrements. The play can be produced without these devices, but optimum effect demands more than bare necessities.

This is a comedy of ideas and situation, with the humor created by the juxtaposition of the Anglocized Chicano and the barrio derelicts as we watch the student ironically come to his own conclusions about the people he is interviewing, reminding us possibly of our own experiences with erroneous interpretations of barrio life. This is serious business, yet it is treated in a humorous manner to capture our attention and cause us to listen more carefully as TONY misinterprets his interviewees. His principle informant, JESS, is an imaginative character who decides to take this kid for a ride, either for the fun of it, or possibly to distract him while his buddy buys their wine with TONY'S money. The comic irony is complete when we and TONY discover that each of JESS' vivid flashbacks are pure invention. TONY has been duped, but his realization causes him to discard his project and join the men in drinking their wine.

This mixture of comic elements includes the ever-popular farce which sees its peak in the fight between JESS and his wife, his recreation of spray-painting a racist, giving the finger to his teacher, artificially inseminating "lady turkeys," as well as in TONY'S inability to withstand the heat and fainting. Played with sincerity rather than exaggeration, this play can effectively present a slice of barrio life and leave us with the question: "Who's fooling who?"

1

The Interview

CHARACTERS:
TONY CHAVEZ, *college student and interviewer*
PETE, *a wino*
JESS *or* JESUS, *a wino, nicknamed Chuy*
WIFE
OLD WOMAN
ANGLO WOMAN, *teacher*

SETTING: *Vacant lot.* TONY, *dressed casually in Ivy League style, notebook clutched to chest, he wanders around center stage, gesturing, muttering to himself. It's noon, hot and occasionally he wipes sweat from face.*

TONY: ¡Buenos días! No, stupid, it's late. ¡Buenas tardes! Antonio Chávez, a sus órdenes . . . Smile . . . keep your back straight . . . Good afternoon. My name is Tony Chávez, and I'm interviewing persons of Mexican descent . . . Oh, you're Cuban? Sorry. (*Walks away, as if from house.*) Somos Cubanos (*Mocking, then clears voice, prepares for delivery, as if approaching another house.*) Good afternoon. My name is Tony Chávez, and I'm interviewing persons of Mexican descent . . . Are you . . . yes? (*Walks, wipes sweat off brow, sighs, prepares again.*) Now then . . . Sex? . . . Marital status? . . . Occupation? (*While speaking, he marks squares in notebook.*) Religion? . . . Catholic? . . . Protestant? . . . Other? . . . (*Clears throat, looks up and curses under breath, shuffles as if about to faint from heat.*) You call yourself Mexican? Mexican American? Chicano? Latino? Hispano? Latin American? Spanish American? Spanish? Good afternoon. I'm Tony Chávez and I'm . . . (*Gasps, nearly faints.*) I'm . . . I'm thirsty. (*Stoops to pick burrs out of socks.*) Goddam stickers . . . spines . . . Shit! (*Stands, continues interview.*) . . . Have you ever felt discriminated against? . . . No? . . . Seldom? . . . Often? I see. Tell me, what's your usual response? (*Pauses, looks up, wipes neck with handkerchief.*) Fucking heat!

Shuffles toward JESS *and* PETE. PETE *wears no shirt. The two have a brown paper bag between them, twisted at the top. Light focuses on them seated on a mattress.* TONY *notices and straightens up.*

PETE: Hey, ese! What you got? (TONY *hugs notebook.*)

JESS: You give us forty-five cents? (*Pulls empty bottle from bag.*) T-bird cost forty-five cents.

(TONY, *suspicious, looks around for possible escape.*)

PETE: What's your hurry, man? Sit down.

TONY: I'm looking for . . . (Flips through notebook.) Tomás López. You know where he lives?

PETE: Tomás López?

JESS: What you want him for? You don't look like no cop.

TONY: I'm taking a survey . . . you know, questions . . . and I want to talk to him.

PETE: Well, talk to us. A ver, ask me a question. (*Boasting.*) ¡Órale! I've got all the answers.

JESS: Leave him alone, Pete. He don't want to talk to no winos. Mira, he's all nervous.

PETE: (*Stands, angry.*) Hey, you think we're winos? Huh?

TONY: I didn't say that.

PETE: But you think we're winos, no? (*Holds up bottle, threatening.*) Winos, huh? (*Drops bottle.*) Well, that's what we are. ¿Que no, Chuy? Just two jodidos trying to get the feria for a little juice. (*Scrutinizes* TONY.) Hey, ese! (*Smiles, puts arm around* TONY.) Relax. We ain't gonna hurt you. Sit down.

2

TONY: (*Hesitates.*) Yeah, okay. (*Drops heavily onto mattress.*)

PETE: (*Still Standing.*) Now how 'bout a little wine? You lend us something to buy a pint?

TONY: (*Removes wallet from pants pocket, pulls out dollar bill.*) Yeah, get me a beer. (PETE *starts to leave.*)

JESS: Hey, baboso! They won't let you in the store without a shirt. (*Throws him his T-shirt.* PETE *leaves, putting on shirt.*)

TONY: (*Moaning, rubbing forehead, about to faint.*) Jesus!

JESS: Yeah?

TONY: Christ! (*Gasping, rolls eyes toward sky, faints.* JESS *watches, puzzled, then becomes alarmed.*)

JESS: (*Slapping* TONY, *who slowly revives in a fog.*) Hey, man come out of it. What's the matter? You sick?

TONY: (*Sitting up, face in hands.*) Huh?

JESS: What's the matter with you?

TONY: I guess it's the sun, too much sun. I'll be alright.

JESS: (*Staring at* TONY.) You go to school, don't you? (*Sneers.*) That's why you can't take a little pinche sun. Man, you're in poor shape . . . College! Shit, I used to do twelve hours in the sun . . . y nada! All I got was a better sun tan.

TONY: (*Shaking off daze, stands, walks to one side and speaks as if he's writing interviewer's comments.*) Respondent brags a lot. Macho complex.

JESS: You got that clean look. But you don't look too sharp now.

TONY: Hey, what if I talk to you instead of Tomás López? (*Thinks to himself.*) Screw Tomás López! I'll talk to this guy. One name's as good as the next. Who's going to know the difference?

JESS: Orale, vato. What do you want to know?

TONY: (Still thinking to himself.) What do they expect for two-fifty an interview?

JESS: I said what do you want to know?

TONY: Wait a minute. (*Removes interview form and places it on top of notebook.*) First, your age. (*Takes pen from shirt pocket.*)

JESS: No! Don't write nothing down.

TONY: But that's not how you do an interview.

JESS: How do I know what you're writing? (*Grabs notebook and closes cover.*) Don't write nothing down!

TONY: Hey, give me that!

JESS: Later, ese. I'll give it to you later.

TONY: If it makes you feel any better, I don't even know your name.

JESS: How do I know you don't? Come on man. Everybody knows me.

TONY: Alright, but later on I'll write it down anyway.

JESS: Sure, you write it down, but later. I ain't as dumb as you think.

TONY: I didn't say you're dumb.

JESS: Okay, what do you want me to say?

TONY: Everything. Like what you do, where you from, your age . . .

JESS: Forty-one . . .

TONY: Forty-one?

JESS: No, make that forty. I ain't that old.

TONY: Okay, what else?

JESS: Like I was in the Navy, man . . . Watcha! (*Jumps up, clicks heels, salutes.*)

TONY: (*To himself.*) Navy veteran.

JESS: I ain't been here all my life. Chale, man! I got in the Navy when I was sixteen. Alright, don't believe me but I did. They sent me to Oakland, and you know what I did? (*Proudly.*) I painted those big ships. Yeah, me . . . ?

TONY: Occupation: painter.

JESS: (*Painting imaginary ship, turns to audience.*) Hey, ese, I had some good times. I even got this tattoo in the Navy. (*Shows tattooed arm proudly.*)

TONY: Decorated.

JESS: But they kicked me out after I beat some mother over the head with a spray gun. (*Acts out fight.*) I sprayed him good. Real good! (*Sprays for good measure, then turns to explain.*) He called me a little wetback, and I can't take that from no one. So I sprayed him real good. (*Chases victim around stage.*)

TONY: Dishonorable discharge.

JESS: When I got back to El Paso I got married. But that was the wrong thing to do . . . 'cause my old lady wanted everything. Like she wanted a new car. Man, I couldn't buy no new car . . . (*Light focuses on table at other side of stage.* WIFE *enters, sits, opens makeup kit and begins to tweeze eyebrows. Wears beehive hairdo.* JESS *strolls over.*) Hey, goodlookin. ¡Ya estuvo! Your daddy's here!

WIFE: (*Tweezing.*) Don't touch me!

JESS: Hey, it's me, chula. Your old man. (WIFE *ignores him, finishes tweezing, starts to put lipstick on.*) Come on, give me a little kiss. (*Tries to kiss her and she pushes him away.*) Que chingao. You work your ass off all day, and what happens when you get home? Your old lady, ni un beso te da!

WIFE: It's Sunday, Chuy.

JESS: It is?

WIFE: Where were you?

JESS: Uh . . . around . . . you know, around. (*Looks pleadingly to* WIFE.) Well, can't a man work on Sunday?

WIFE: In a bank . . . ? You sweep the floors on Sunday too?

JESS: Lay off me, okay? I've been thinking.

WIFE: Yeah? (*Stands, approaches* JESS.) About what?

JESS: Money.

WIFE: (*Sweetly.*) Chuy?

JESS: Yeah?

WIFE: Are you going to buy a car like you promised?

JESS: What?

WIFE: A car! You know, with wheels.

JESS: Don't push me!

WIFE: You think I like walking to the store all the time? Mira, Lupe's got a car. What about me?

JESS: (*Fiercely.*) ¿Qué quieres? Blood . . . ? I ain't got that kind of money.

TONY: Low income.

WIFE: (*Pouting, arms outstretched, as* JESS *walks toward* TONY.) But, Chuy, you promised!

JESS: I must have been crazy getting married. All she ever did is bitch about that car. So you know what me and my compadre did? We went out and stole one! That was the easy part. We just picked one out and drove off. (*Gestures and makes sound of engine.*) The vato even left the door unlocked. But you know what she did after all that? ¿Sabes qué? She called the police. Now what kind of ruca is that? I was just doing what she said. (*Walks to* WIFE, *who is crying, head on table.*)

TONY: Adjusts well to environment.

JESS: ¿Qué pasa? ¿Ahora qué quieres? I got you the car, didn't I? I even got the color you wanted. Your favorite color. (*Waits for answer.*) Why are you crying? ¿Qué te pasa?

WIFE: You stole it.

JESS: What?

WIFE: (*Pounds table, stands angrily.*) You stole it!

4

JESS: Where'd you hear that?

WIFE: Lupe told me. She said you and Raul went out and stole the car. Why, Chuy, why?

JESS: Qué chingado . . . why's he gotta tell his wife for? That's the last time I . . .

WIFE: (*Timidly.*) Chuy? Chuy, you better go.

JESS: (*Looks at her sharply.*) Why? This is my house, ¿qué no? I make the payments . . . No! You get out!

WIFE: Chuy . . . ?

JESS: ¡Andale! Go on! Take the kids too. Go tell your mother about your dirty old man.

WIFE: Chuy, I called the police.

JESS: You what?

WIFE: I called the police . . .

JESS: (*Grabs her, shouting, hits and pushes her to the floor.*) ¡Vieja pendeja! Ya verás . . . Ahora, sí . . . sonofabitchi . . .

(WIFE *trips him, stands and kicks him, he groans, crawls toward* TONY, *escaping.* WIFE *turns, straightens clothes and hair, looks in kit mirror, closes top, picks up kit and walks briskly toward stair at other end of stage.*)

WIFE: ¡Carmen! ¡José! ¡Vámonos! (*Stops beside* JESS, *gives one more kick.* JESS *grunts in pain.* WIFE *exits head held high.*)

JESS: (*Struggles to seated position.*) I beat her up good. Real good. (*Shakes head.*) ¡Cabrona! She turned me in. Me, her husband. I got her the car, ¿y qué? They put me in the bote for six months . . . six months. But that's how I got here. I never seen her again.

TONY: Permanent residence: Los Angeles.

JESS: But I got another old lady. See that house over there? The blue one? That's mine. (*Proudly.*) I painted it myself. Took me two days.

TONY: (*Complementing.*) Looks real professional.

JESS: And I got four kids. No, five. All of them boys.

TONY: Children: five.

JESS: But they ain't like me. They're going to stay in school and be something like you maybe . . .

TONY: Encourages education.

JESS: The bitch...

TONY: What?

JESS: I hate her...(*Walks over to table, slumps in chair.*)

TONY: Who?

TEACHER: (*Female teacher, an Anglo, enters stiffly and faces* JESS, *who appears to be asleep.*) Jesus! Jesus, wake up! (*Raps* JESS *on head with pointer.*) Do you hear me? Wake up! (JESS *lifts head, feigning boredom.* TEACHER *paces before class.*) Class, look at Jesus. He is an example of rudeness. Can you spell it? R-u-d-e-n-e-s-s. Look at him, class. You'd think with a name like Jesus he'd pay more attention.

JESS: Go to hell.

TEACHER: Class, did you hear that? Did you hear what Jesus said?

JESS: Pinche gabacha...

TEACHER: Jesus! What did I say about speaking Spanish in school? I don't want to hear that language. Young man, do you understand? (JESS *lays head on table.*) Jesus! Look at me when I talk to you.

JESS: Leave me alone.

TEACHER: (*Pulling his arm.*) Jesus, you're disrupting the class...Class. Class! Stop laughing. (*Turning back to Jess.*) Young man, go to the principal's office. Come on, get up! (JESS *stands, playing cool, starts toward center stage, casually removes comb from back pocket, strokes hair.*) Tell the principal I'll be there when the bell rings. (JESS *finishes combing hair, still defiant, turns and gestures to* TEACHER *with middle finger.* TEACHER *gasps, light dims on her and she exits.*)

JESS: (*Sits next to* TONY.) Pinche Huevona...Man, did I hate her.

TONY: Culturally deprived.

JESS: See, you thought I was a bum, puro wino nomás, just sitting on my ass all day. Well, I got a family...and a job.

TONY: (*Skeptical.*) Sure...

JESS: I do! This is my day off.

JESS: Well...actually I got laid off. I was gonna quit anyway. A turkey farm. You know what they had me doing? How do they say it...un...arti...artificially inseminating turkeys. Yeah, you know, puttin' it to the lady turkeys. It wouldn't have been so bad if I'd done the easy part...you know, the vato with the squirt gun. But I was the vato who picked up the lady turkeys (*makes grabbing motion.*)....chasing them all over the pen, then when I got one I had to flip her upside down and open the legs. ¡Híjole! Qué asco, it made me sick...all the shit and feathers...You try pickin' up forty-pound turkeys all night. Fíjese, 200 lady turkeys.

TONY: Ambitious, but lacks steady employment.

JESS: So what do you say about that? You got more questions, mister college?

TONY: Naw, that's good. (*Rises and points.*) Here comes my beer.

JESS: No, go on. Ask me a question.

TONY: Okay...Are you...(zsnapping fingers.) are you religious?

JESS: Orale, I was going to be a priest. Te juro, I was that close (*Gestures with palms.*) to being a priest. But I got in the Navy instead.

TONY: Yeah, sure...(*Starts to walk toward center stage.*)

JESS: (*Follows, drops to knees.*) It's true...(*Prays*) Padre nuestro que estás en los cielos, sanctificado sea tu nombre...

TONY: Okay, okay, I believe you. Devout Catholic.

PETE: (*Enters excitedly, waving quart bottle.*) Hey, ese, I got a quart!

TONY: Wait a minute! What about my (*Anglo accent.*) my... cerveza?

PETE: (*To* JESS, *with a shrug.*) ¿Qué dice?

JESS: (*Deadpan.*) He thinks you forgot his beer.

PETE: Hey, that's right. I did forget. But don't worry, ese. We'll give you some of our wine...(*Uncorks bottle, swigs some.*)

TONY: No thanks.

PETE: You don't have to thank us. We didn't give you nothing.

TONY: That's an understatement.

PETE: Under . . . ¿qué?

TONY: Never mind.

PETE: Oye, Chuy. Let's go. The old lady says she's going to call the placa if we don't get out of here.

TONY: Who's that? (*Confused.*)

PETE: (*Motioning.*) The vieja that lives in that house, the blue one. ¡Vieja metichi! She's always after us.

TONY: Isn't that where Jess lives?

PETE: (*Smiles.*) What's he been telling you? Shit, he ain't got no old lady. (PETE *and* JESS *laugh and start to leave, trading bottles.*)

TONY: (*To* JESS.) But you said . . .

JESS: (*Turns sharply, facing* TONY.) I said nothing!

TONY: What about the Navy . . . and . . . ?

JESS: Sure! And my uncle was Pancho Villa! (*Laughs, again starts to leave.* OLD WOMAN *enters hurriedly.*)

6

WOMAN: Get out of here, you bums! Andale. All you do is sit out here and throw your bottles all over. ¡Borrachos! ¡Atascados! ¡Cochinos! I'm calling the police! (*Exits.*)

JESS: (*At far end of stage, turns and shouts.*) Hey, mister college! You know that vato Tomás López? The one you wanted? He died two years ago. (JESS *and* PETE *exit, laughing.*)

TONY: (*Wipes sweat from eyes, sighs, picks up notebook, stares at it for a moment, then throws it down. Rises and follows the two men hurriedly.*) Wait! Let me have some of that wine. (*Exits.*)

Illustration by Alejandro Romero

Rodrigo Duarte-Clark

BRUJERIAS

Brujerías *was first produced by El Teatro de la Esperanza of Santa Barbara in the spring of 1972, under the direction of Jorge Huerta.* *Esperanza's original production was a collectively revised version of the original play by Rodrigo Duarte-Clark; however, in 1976 the teatro returned to this, the playwright's original script, once again to the delight of many audiences.*

Written as a comment on superstitious foibles, *Brujerías is one of the most delightful comedies to come from a Chicano playwright's pen. The interaction between* PETRA *and* RAFAEL *is rife with humor, as we witness* PETRA'S *transformation from doubter to believer in witches, ghosts, and things that go bump in the night.*

---

*The revised version which included an additional character, the allegorical "Espíritu de la Superstición," was published by Esperanza in their book of actos, *El Teatro de la Esperanza: An Anthology of Chicano Drama,* edited by Jorge Huerta in 1973, and was also produced as a thirty-minute motion picture in 1973 (available from El Teatro de la Esperanza, P.O. Box 1508, Santa Barbara, CA 93101).

Unlike the typical acto, which demands a strong delineation of Good versus Evil, this play gives us two basically good people who find themselves with metaphysical opponents rather than an evil grower, brutal police, or the like. PETRA sparks this conflict with her somewhat greedy desire for another person's house, and can certainly be censured for the action she takes to get the house, but she is still a very sympathetic character. Indeed, when she negates the existence of witches and spirits while her husband tries to convince her that they do exist, many in the audience might side with her, thinking themselves more rational than RAFAEL. But as PETRA slowly loses her confidence and succumbs to the rigors of her imagination, those same people who saw themselves in her might change their minds.

Although the playwright says he never intended to write a political comment with this play, two institutions known to all Chicanos and Mexicanos are exposed: the Church and La Migra or the Immigration and Naturalization Service. References to the Roman Catholic faith and all its accoutrements abound, and though there are few allusions to the Migra, it is PETRA'S call that initiates RAFAEL'S fear of supernatural reprisal. Lines such as TIA OLGA'S "le tienes que pasar la mordida (al cura) o no sirve el agua" need no further explanation, and always generate laughter in the audience. Irreverent remarks such as the latter make their point without added commentary and the knowing laugh that accompanies them underlines the absurdity of the statements. Whether university or community audiences, the spectators always enjoy these little barbs at the world's largest religious body and its dogma, even though many of them believe it all. The satire is complete when the audience recognizes it.

In the day of "Illegal Alien Threats" and tactics aimed at blaming Mexico's expatriots for the ills of the economy, the role of the Migra in this play cannot be overlooked. Though we never see any representative of this bureaucracy, the characters believe that PETRA'S collusion with the Migra will surely bring disaster. You cannot turn a person in to the Migra and walk away unscathed, RAFAEL tells us, and PETRA soon realizes the folly of her ways as she, too, begins to doubt the morality of her actions.

Ultimately, Brujerías is a comment on our easily aroused supersitious fears and the attendant humor that arises when we have to face the unknown, armed with notions and potions from the past. Though they are comic figures, the three viejitos in this play must appear to be as real as the aunt or grandfather who first told us about La Llorona or El Cuco: with sometimes magnified fear, but always with respect for the inexplicable.

Brujerías

CHARACTERS:
DOÑA PETRA
DON RAFAEL
TIA OLGA

The play will shift from the home of RAFAEL and PETRA to that of TIA OLGA. S.L. is RAFAEL and PETRA'S living-bedroom combination, and S.R. is TIA OLGA'S living room. In RAFAEL and PETRA'S house we have a bed and a chair or small table for a phone and their coats. To the left of the bed is a door leading outside, and to the right of the bed is a door leading to the next room, the kitchen. The table for the phone is D.S.L. If an actual set is to be constructed, it should give the appearance of a very humble "shack," well lived-in and worn down. TIA OLGA'S house is located S.R. and needs nothing more than three chairs facing the third in a sitting room arrangement. Again, if a setting is to be used, this house, too, is small and humble, full of religious figures, etc.

SCENE ONE

Lights come on S.L. only, illuminating RAFAEL *and* PETRA'S *house. The two viejitos are in the bed:* RAFAEL *is reading* LA OPINION *and* PETRA *is sitting there, thinking.*

PETRA: You know, viejo, I sure like old Juana's house.

RAFAEL: (*The newspaper lowers just slightly and the mumbling stops, his head turns slightly.*) Old Juana's house?

PETRA: Tú sabes, the one over there behind the orchards on the way to the cemetery.

RAFAEL: (*Warily.*) Old Juana's house?

PETRA: (*Looks at him.*) You know. La vieja esa que vino when the floods came? Don't you remember el viejo Mendoza used to live there, but they couldn't find him after the floods? And after that esa Doña Juana moved in to that house.

RAFAEL: Chea, I know wizh house you mean it. You mean you wanto livet there? You coo-coo?

PETRA: ¿Cómo que coo-coo?

RAFAEL: Coo-coo (*points to his temple.*) in the head!

PETRA: No soy coo-coo. It's a nice house. Tiene un jardín y hay árboles. Y la casa está purdy.

RAFAEL: You are coo-coo! Don't you know que esa vieja es bruja, una witch?

PETRA: (*Annoyed.*) No es bruja.

RAFAEL: Sí es. She talk to the dead people, los muertos. Why do you think nobody go there en la noche? Because they havit scare. Hay espíritus allí.

PETRA: ¿Sabes qué, viejo? You're the one who's coo-coo. ¿Cómo que es bruja? There are no witches. Con razón the gabachos say we are backwards.

RAFAEL: Sí es witch. Why do you think she live close to the cemetery? Para estar cerca de sus familiares, los espantos.

PETRA: Estás loco, Ghosts. You know what I think? You are cheeken.

RAFAEL: (*Throws the paper down.*) ¡Mira, vieja, eso sí no soy! ¡Yo no soy cheeken! No tengo miedo de nada. De Nada. You understand? Na ting! (*Pause.*) Pero brujas no son lo mismo. They not like people. Son diferent. They friends with the (*Whispers.*) devil. (*Crosses himself.*) They friends with you-know-who, y no se debe meter uno con el (*Whispers.*) diablo.

PETRA: Vieja, I'll prove it to you. We'll ask the priest. El te dice that there are no witches. Es superstición de viejas.

RAFAEL: Ah Ah-Ah! (*Raising his arm with an open hand as if to warn her.*) Don't speak it no more. Los padres no saben nada. Sí, hay brujas y es todo. ¡Ya cállate! Let me read it the newspaper. (*Picks up the newspaper.*) A ver, ¿dónde estaba?

PETRA: (*Derisively.*) Eh. Y tan machote. (*He grunts, but continues to read.*) After all these years I find out I'm married to a chicken, a superstitious chicken.

RAFAEL: Síguele, síguele.

PETRA: Well it's true.

RAFAEL: (*Puts the paper down.*) ¿Y qué? You aren't going to get the house de todos modos. Doña Juana is living there . . .

PETRA: Quién sabe she moves.

RAFAEL: Who told you?

PETRA: Nobody.

RAFAEL: (*Looks at her suspiciously as if to read her mind.*) Nadie. Entonces why you say it?

PETRA: Porque me dio la gana.

RAFAEL: Hmph. I think you thinkin something.

PETRA: ¿Quién sabe?

RAFAEL: Pos dime. (*She ignores him.*) Told me ahorita! (*No response.*) Me lo dices o

10

te lo saco a chiflazos, vieja mensa.

PETRA: Tan persuasive que eres, ¿verdá? Chiflazos, it cures everything.

RAFAEL: Bueno, vale más que no hagas nating. Y ya cállate. Don't think it no more. ¡Acúerdate que no te pago por los pensamientos!

PETRA: (*Angrily.*) You'll see. I'll get that house one way or other.

RAFAEL: (*Surprised.*) ¿Qué?

PETRA: You heard me.

RAFAEL: Mira, vieja, I told you, esa casa es casa de witch. Y Doña Juana es witch. No te metas con ella porque es amiguita de you-know-who.

PETRA: You're old fashioned, viejo.

RAFAEL: Forget it that house. De todos modos, this is a fine house. Is the best house we ever have.

PETRA: Y la única.

RAFAEL: Ni tenemos ratas como last year.

PETRA: They moved out when the heater broke.

RAFAEL: Estás crazy. Mira, the techo doesn't even leak.

PETRA: The clouds had mercy.

RAFAEL: Bueno, if you no like it, ¿por qué no te mueves con tu madre o alguién?

PETRA: She's dead, like if you didn't know!

RAFAEL: We forget the good things that happen to us, ¿no?

PETRA: Maybe I will move! Twenty years ago you used to talk about a new house.

RAFAEL: Twenty years ago. Han cambiado las cosas en veinte años. Dale una mirada al espejo, vieja pachichi.

PETRA: You're not exactly Casanova, palo seco.

RAFAEL: You know, you just don't know how to appreciate a good house like this one.

PETRA: Entonces we move?

RAFAEL: ¡No! ¡Y no! ¡Y no!

PETRA: ¡Apretado!

RAFAEL: Be quiet.

PETRA: You be quiet. And keep this old shack, tu palacio francés, Not me. (*She walks over to the phone.*)

RAFAEL: Te voy a comprar una chupaleta para que no ande tu boca dioquis.

PETRA: (*Angry.*) You'll see. (*She begins to dial the phone.*)

RAFAEL: (*He notices her calling.*) Hey what you doing? (*No answer.*) ¿Vieja? (*Warily*) Vieja, who you calling?

PETRA: Is this the Immigration Bureau? Yes I know its night.

RAFAEL: ¡La migra! (*Gets up and goes over to her.*)

PETRA: I want to report an alien without papers.

RAFAEL: Vieja, ¿qué haces?

PETRA: On Schilling Road here in San Martin, it's the only house on the road from San Martin.

RAFAEL: ¡Doña Juana!

PETRA: It's an old lady.

RAFAEL: ¡Ya para! ¿Qué, estás loca?

PETRA: Yes we are sure.

RAFAEL: ¿Cómo que we?

PETRA: (*Puts her hand on the phone.*) Shh. I can't hear.

RAFAEL: Hang up, por favor. No nos metas en líos.

PETRA: Our names?

RAFAEL: ¡Nó, no le digas! ¡Te pido!

PETRA: Do we have to say?

RAFAEL: Oh my got.

PETRA: We prefer not to. Yes, thank you. Goodbye.

RAFAEL: (*Looking at her in disbelief.*) ¿Cómo que no?

PETRA: Well, how will she find out? We didn't give our names.

RAFAEL: ¡Porque es bruja! They know it when alguien les hace lo malo. The ghosts they tell her because they can sense it. Saben todo. Didn't nobody told you? Dios mío, ¿qué vamos a hacer?

PETRA: She won't find out, viejo. They'll send her to México tomorrow and she'll be gone for good. Then we can have the house.

RAFAEL: The house? Are you crazy? Of course you crazy, what a stupid question. You can have the house, pero yo me quedo aquí. ¡Ni a patadas me meto en esa casa! ¿Crees que los espantos te dejan? The ghosts they stayit there, cuidando la casa.

PETRA: There's nothing there. We'll see tomorrow when we go see the house.

RAFAEL: We? You! (*Gets up on the downstage edge of bed.*) ¡Ni con Pancho Villa a un lado, y la Virgen de Guadalupe al otro, me metiera allí!

PETRA: ¡Qué cobarde!

RAFAEL: (*Getting down from the bed.*) In the morning, we go see mi Tía Olga. Ella sabe de brujerías. She told us what to do. (*Sits on edge of bed.*)

PETRA: (*Crosses to him and sits on edge of bed also.*) Ay, Viejo.

RAFAEL: You know what? Doña Juana ya sabe what you done. Maybe we should pray.

PETRA: You don't even know how.

RAFAEL: Entonces you pray. You did it.

PETRA: Nothing will happen.

RAFAEL: You don't know what you say. Mi padre siempre me dijo nunca me metiera con brujas. We have to watch out now, or she gonna get us. Ahora sí nos echastes a la chiflada. (*Crosses himself.*)

PETRA: Maybe we should go to sleep.

RAFAEL: (*Rising.*) I'll try. Maybe la bruja nos deja esta noche. (*Crosses to light switch.*) I'm gonna chut the light. ¿Estás lista?

PETRA: (*Coyly.*) ¿Lista para qué?

RAFAEL: (*Turns off light. If dimmer is available, lights should dim to show a change.*) ¡Ay si tú, chistosa!

Wind begins to blow outside.

RAFAEL: (*Has climbed in bed: Is looking out the "window" directly in front on the bed.*) Está bien fea la noche. Mira los árboles. The wind is blowing real hard. ¡Puchers!

PETRA: Qué funny. It wasn't blowing a while ago.

RAFAEL: (*Suspiciously.*) Yo sé. Maybe we should get under the covers. (*The two get under the covers like two children hiding from el cucuy. After a few seconds a scratching sound is heard. The two come out from their hiding place slowly and apprehensively: After RAFAEL is seen at head of bed, PETRA'S head slowly comes out at the foot of the bed.*)

PETRA: Did you hear that too?

RAFAEL: ¿Qué?

PETRA: You know, that noise like scratching.

RAFAEL: ¿El Ruído? Chea, I heard it.

PETRA: I think it was a cat.

RAFAEL: ¿Un gato?

PETRA: Don't you think?

RAFAEL: (*Lyrically.*) I don't know. Pero I'm gonna get my rifle. (*He gets up out of the bed and pulls his rifle out from under it. He slowly starts to walk to front door.*)

PETRA: (*Unsure of herself.*) It's only an animal viejo.

A loud "bang" outside.

PETRA: ¡Ay, Dios mío!

RAFAEL: Cállate mujer. Don't be afraid, remember, you don't believe in witches.

PETRA: ¿Qué vamos a hacer?

RAFAEL: I don't know.

PETRA: You don't think . . .

The wind blows real hard, making a "woo" sound.

RAFAEL: I think so.

PETRA: Really? Well, maybe we better do something.

RAFAEL: Dicen que if you have a rosary or a crucifix the bruja won't touch you.

PETRA: You know what? Está en el otro cuarto, on the wall. I mean the crucifix: you
    go get it and I hold the rifle.

A sound like shuffling feet.

PETRA: What was that?

RAFAEL: Santa Virgen, ¡llegaron los espantos!

PETRA: Are you sure? Maybe it was something else?

RAFAEL: ¿Por qué les preguntas? (*Quiet.*) You know what? We have to get the
    crucifix, porque si no, the ghosts won't leave us. Es la única cosa que nos salva.

PETRA: Don't look at me.

RAFAEL: Well, era tú culpa.

PETRA: But that was because you didn't get us a house.

RAFAEL: Si hubiera oído mi padre. (*Pause.*) Pos vale más que lo agarre. (*He takes a
    big breath.*) Allí voy pues. (*He gets out of bed with the gun ready. He turns to her.*)
    Entonces wait here.

PETRA: Did you think, maybe I was going somewhere?

RAFAEL: No es tiempo para ser chistosa. (*Rifle in hand, he starts tiptoeing toward the
    kitchen to the right of bed.*)

PETRA: Open the light!

RAFAEL: (*Jumps, scared.*) Shhh!

PETRA: OK, nomás quería ayudar.

He walks into the kitchen. PETRA *is at the edge of the bed. There is a gunblast.*
    PETRA *screams, and* RAFAEL *comes running into the bedroom without the gun,
    but with the crucifix in his hand. He jumps into the bed.*

PETRA: What happened?

RAFAEL: Shh.

PETRA: (*In a loud whisper.*) Pero what happened?

RAFAEL: I don't know. First I hear something, then I get the crucifix. I bump into the
    chair and then I hear a big crash and I turn around. Vi un bulto. Mis manos
    apretaron y el rifle descargó.

PETRA: (*Pauses.*) What else happened?

RAFAEL: I can't tell. I fall and then I coming here.

PETRA: And the gun?

RAFAEL: I dropped it.

PETRA: What do you think it was?

RAFAEL: Un bulto. Maybe Juana sent it.

PETRA: Is it still there?

RAFAEL: I think it went away. Pero I got the crucifix. I think que nos proteja.

Dogs bark offstage.

PETRA: You hear the dogs?

RAFAEL: ¿Ladrando? (*She nods.*) Los espantos están afuera, maybe. (*Pause.*) In the
    morning, we go to see mi tía Olga. Ella nos ayuda.

PETRA: Maybe we should go tonight.

13

RAFAEL: In the night? You crazy? You think the bruja will let us? She put it curse on the car and make it crash.

PETRA: (*Surprised.*) ¡No!

RAFAEL: Sí

PETRA: Que feo.

RAFAEL: We have to wait till the mañanita.

PETRA: (*Whispering.*) Holy Mary, mother of God, pray for us sinners now and at the hour of our death. Hail Mary, etc.

RAFAEL: Now you pray. (*She ignores him.*)

The two fall asleep. Sound of cock crowing. Lights come on. It is morning.

RAFAEL: (*Waking quickly.*) ¡Lavántate! We have have to go!

PETRA: Where?

RAFAEL: A ver a mi Tía Olga. Hoory!

They jump out of bed, and throw their coats on over their night clothes. General adlibbing about going out in their nightclothes, etc. They exit S.L. through front door. Blackout.

SCENE TWO

Lights come up on TIA OLGA'S house. S.R. She is seen napping in a rocker in her living room, when a knock is heard at the door. She begins to awaken with the first knock, but quickly falls back asleep. Second knock. She mumbles something, then again falls back asleep. Third knock, louder. She awakens with a start.

TIA OLGA: ¿Quién será? (*Fourth knock.*) Allí voy, pues. Espérense. Soy viejita. Si me apuro, se me para el corazón. (*She opens door, or pantomimes a door at the backdrop, and* PETRA *and* RAFAEL *rush in bien espantados.*) Ah, Petra y Rafael. Entren niños. Hace mucho que no los he visto. (*Noticing their night clothes under their coats.*) ¿Pero por qué vienen vestidos así?

PETRA and RAFAEL: Pues, es que estábamos en a hurry.

TIA OLGA: Bueno. No importa. ¿Cómo están, eh?

PETRA and RAFAEL: Pasándola.

TIA OLGA: (*To* RAFAEL.) Y tu mamá, ¿cómo está?

RAFAEL: ¿Mi mamá? Ella murió hace cuatro años. ¿No te acuerdas, tía?

TIA OLGA: Ah sí, con razón no me visitaba. Y ya me enojaba con la pobre.

RAFAEL: Y tú, tía, ¿cómo estás?

TIA OLGA: Bueno estoy bien; purty gut, como dicen los americanos. Lo más posible con tantos años que traigo encima, ¿verdad?

PETRA: You look good, señora. No sé cómo lo haces, pero sigues bien y sana.

TIA OLGA: Es el miedo do morir. Pero told me what brings you para acá? ¿Quién se murió?

RAFAEL: Oh No!!! No es eso. Is something more difficult.

TIA OLGA: ¿Que la muerte?

RAFAEL: Es que . . . Ah . . . is like this . . . Well, va así la cosa . . . Ah . . . Bueno, Petra will told you. Díle Petra.

PETRA: ¿Qué? Mejor tú, you know it better.

TIA OLGA: ¿Qué quieren, dinero?

RAFAEL: No, no. No es eso. ¿Verdá Petra? (PETRA *nods.*) es something serio.

TIA OLGA: Pos eso lo sabía.

RAFAEL: Somebody told you?

TIA OLGA: ¿Es escandaloso?

RAFAEL: No, pero . . .

PETRA: What he means es que we don't want anybody to know about this.

14

TIA OLGA: Is secret?

RAFAEL: Sí.

TIA OLGA: Pos dime, ya me interesaron.

RAFAEL: Bueno es así. I thinkin we in big trouble. Is about brujerías!

RAFAEL: Sí.

TIA OLGA: Entonces si están en trouble.

PETRA: I didn't believe in witches until last night. Then I change my mind.

TIA OLGA: El drecho de la mujer.

RAFAEL: We think a witch is trying to get us. Anoche she try to get us. Por eso we coming here for help. So you can told us que podemos hacer.

TIA OLGA: Y ¿por qué she wantit to get you?

RAFAEL: Porque she (*Pointing to* PETRA.) callit la migra pa que la agarraran so she could havit the house of a witch.

TIA OLGA: (*To* PETRA.) You wantit a house of a witch?

PETRA: No anymore.

RAFAEL: Tía, quién sabe you could tell us some consejos about what we should do to protect ourselves.

TIA OLGA: Bueno, no soy bruja, pero maybe I tell you somethings. ¿Tienen crucifix?

PETRA: Sí. It saved us last night.

TIA OLGA: Tuvieron suerte. Eran lucky. Un crucifix protect you against ghosts, espantos y los espíritus de los muertos que los comanda el diablo. Pero para las brujas you need it more.

PETRA: Señora, can I ask you one question? Where did you learn all this stuff? I mean who told you about ghosts and brujas?

TIA OLGA: De mi prima y de mi amá. Mi prima era monja. Me contó las cosas de los muertos que the devil havit en su poder. The espantos they mean, you know. Because the devil treat them bad. Pero they have to do what he say. Pos anyway, brujas they talk with devil and makit a deal. He, el diablo, he give her some ghosts and poder to do bad things to people. Pero her power coming from the devil.

RAFAEL: Entonces, ¿cómo you stop her?

TIA OLGA: Bueno, si eres santo they not hurt you. If you go to church many times then the santos they send angels to protect you from the ghosts. If you givet money to the cura then he askit the santos to take care of you.

RAFAEL: Oh no.

TIA OLGA: ¿Qué pasó?

RAFAEL: Bueno the last time we go to church hace muchos años y esa vez en lugar de dar, agarré.

PETRA: You did? Why did you?

RAFAEL: Cuando pasaron la canasta, estaba llena y yo estaba pobre, por eso le quité un little bit. Nomás para comer, tú sabes.

PETRA: Sin vergüenza.

RAFAEL: ¿Pero qué podemos hacer ahora, tía?

TIA OLGA: You have to getit holy water, una botella llena de la iglesia.

RAFAEL: ¿Del padre la agarro?

TIA OLGA: Sí, pero le tienes que pasar la mordida o no sirve el agua. Tiene que ser agua bendita. Vale más que la agarren today. Después you sprinkle, le echas a las puertas para que no entren los espantos. Y después echas around the bed pa que no te hagan nada en la noche. Si no, ni el crucifijo protect you.

RAFAEL: Entonces we go get el agua bendita.

TIA OLGA: Si no, la bruja no los deja.

RAFAEL: Dios mío. Vámonos Petra a la iglesia. Adios tía, y gracias.

TIA OLGA: Me llaman ¿eh? Mañana. De donde sea, tu casa o peor.

Blackout.

SCENE THREE

This scene takes place at PETRA *and* RAFAEL'S *home. They are getting in the door.*
PETRA *has a jar of holy water. It is getting to be night time. Wind blowing.*
RAFAEL: Apúrate, Petra. Se hace noche.
PETRA: Aquí estoy, right behind you. Don't worry.
RAFAEL: I didn't see you. A ver, you shut the door real tight and I'll shut the window.
PETRA: Mira, ya comenzó the wind again like last night.
RAFAEL: (*Crosses himself.*) Chea, let's hoory.
PETRA: Oh, pues.
He turns around to look out the window as she starts toward him. As she reaches him, he turns around abruptly, moving towards her without looking and bumps into her, knocking the open jar from her hands. As it falls, they both dive for it, but it is too late.
RAFAEL: ¡Babosa, look what you done! Oh no!
PETRA: Look what I done? It was your fault, suato!
RAFAEL: Is there any left?
PETRA: Oh my god, it's all gone! (*The two look at each other, frightened.*) Let's go back to the church and get some more.
RAFAEL: No, is not possible. Mira, is dark already. And I only had enough to pay for this.
PETRA: Pos we have to do something.
Wind sounds outside. Another storm is brewing.
RAFAEL: (*Pause.*) Pero what?
PETRA: Well, podemos usar the crucifix.
RAFAEL: Pues, ¿dónde está?
PETRA: I put it on the chair this morning.
RAFAEL: Pos get it.
PETRA: (*Crosses to the Chair D.L.*) No está.
RAFAEL: ¿No está?
PETRA: I left it here, right here. (*Pointing to chair.*) Did you get it?
RAFAEL: No.
PETRA: Humph? You know, maybe we should call tu tía. (*They both run to phone, grabbing at the receiver.*) Yo la llamo.
RAFAEL: No mejor yo. Quítate. (*Pushes her. He dials. They both listen.*)
PETRA: What's the matter?
RAFAEL: No contesta.
PETRA: Maybe she asleep.
RAFAEL: (*Pause.*) Nada. (*Thunder claps loudly. Lights flicker.*) Ah, ¡Dios Míos! ¿Qué es eso? (*Lights continue to flicker and finally go off. Dim lighting.*)
PETRA: Santa María, madre de Dios, ruega por nosotros los pendejos. ¿Qué vamos a hacer, viejo?
RAFAEL: I don't know. (*Noises.*) Pero no me quedo aquí por nada. Vámonos antes que nos maten.
They go to the door. He pushes, but it doesn't give.
PETRA: Come on, open the door.
RAFAEL: Estoy tratando, pero no abre. (*Loud banging.*)
PETRA: ¡Ábrela!
RAFAEL: ¡Empuja! Wait! Let's do this the right way. (*Steps back and opens door in and they exit quickly. Blackout.*)
(*Optional.*) *Two car doors slam, the ignition goes on but doesn't start until the third time and then the car goes.*

SCENE FOUR

This scene occurs at TIA OLGA'S *house. She is just about to sit down when a sound knock is heard.*

TIA OLGA: ¿Será el diablo? (Opens the door.) ¿Ahora qué (PETRA *and* RAFAEL *enter quickly.*)

RAFAEL: La bruja she still trying to get us!

TIA OLGA: El agua bendita, ¿la usaron?

RAFAEL: No, esta vieja babosa, she drop it on the floor.

PETRA: Because you ran into me, that's why.

TIA OLGA: ¿Y el crucifijo?

PETRA: Es funny. I left it on the living room, pero I couldn't find it. Y luego después I found it near the car. I don't know how it got there.

RAFAEL: She was going to get us, so we left the house así. (*Snaps his fingers.*)

TIA OLGA: Y ¿qué van a hacer?

RAFAEL: Pos, we can't go back porque esa casa está espantada. The bruja won't leave us alone.

PETRA: Won't she leave us alone, señora?

TIA OLGA: No, not until she getit what she wants.

RAFAEL: Y ¿qué es eso?

TIA OLGA: No sé. Maybe you have to make deal with her so she will let you go.

PETRA: How do you do that?

TIA OLGA: Bueno, I think you have to talk to her and ask her what she wantit from you.

RAFAEL: Talk to her?

PETRA: How do you do that, won't she hurt us?

TIA OLGA: I don't know it. Pero you have to do something or she won't leave it you alone. Dime, ¿quién es esta bruja anyway?

RAFAEL: Es una vieja del otro lado de San Martín.

TIA OLGA: ¿Vive en una casita cafesita?

PETRA: Yea, it's a real nice house!

TIA OLGA: ¿Cerca del cementerio?

PETRA: Yea, how did you know?

TIA OLGA: Y ¿cómo se llama?

RAFAEL: Doña Juana.

TIA OLGA: Doña Juana, ¿eh? Y who told you que era bruja?

PETRA AND RAFAEL: Todos, everybody knows she is a witch.

TIA OLGA: ¿De veras? ¿Pos saben qué? No es. Yo la conozco. Antes éramos amigas.

RAFAEL: Are you chur, tía?

TIA OLGA: Chur.

RAFAEL: Entonces what happened?

PETRA: La migra probably got her.

TIA OLGA: ¿La migra?

RAFAEL: Sí, remember Petra callit the migra on her.

TIA OLGA: (*Begins to laugh.*) ¿Pos sabes qué? She's a ciudadana. (*Laughs again.*) She a witch, y no está de alambre. She just an "oldie but goodie" como yo.

PETRA: See, I told you que no había witches.

RAFAEL: ¿Cómo? I told you que no había witches, ¡vieja mensa!

PETRA: ¿Qué? Viejo cobarde, que no te acuerdas . . . (*The two leave U.S.R. arguing vociferously.* TIA OLGA *is close behind them telling them to calm down. Blackout.*)

17

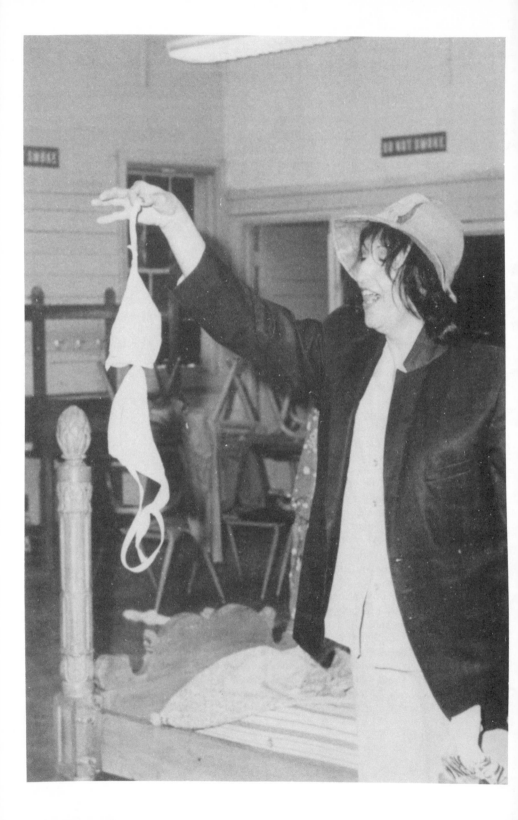

Estela Portillo-Trambley

SUN IMAGES

An anthology of Chicano and Puerto Rican drama would not be complete without a contribution by the multi-talented Estela Portillo. Best known in dramatic circles for her realistic drama, Day of the Swallows, *Ms. Portillo has left the realm of the serious play and tried her hand at musical comedy in* Sun Images. *This delightful piece was produced at the Chamizal National Monument, between El Paso, Texas and Juárez, México, in 1976, and received wide critical acclaim. Ms. Portillo wrote the lyrics for the songs and also composed the music, thus demonstrating her creative versatility. Noted Chicano film director, Moctezuma Esparza was so taken by this production, that he asked Ms. Portillo to adapt it for film, a project she is currently undertaking.*

Sun Images *is the first musical comedy to be published by a Chicano and represents a first step towards employing the style usually associated with Broadway and commodity theatre, a form of entertainment that does not attempt to be anything else. By creating a musical comedy that follows traditional stylistic development, Portillo is saying; "If the musical is successful on Broadway and in regional theatres all over the world, why not in the barrio — with a barrio theme? Spanish-language musical theatre was also a commodity and managed to flourish in the barrios and* colonias *throughout the United States during the first half of the twentieth century.*

Musical theatre was of great artistic and social importance to Latinos. Everywhere from New York to San Antonio to Los Angeles, it provided wholesome entertainment during the hard times of separation from the homeland while the Mexican Revolution was raging and during the rigors of the Depression. It also promoted community solidarity within the context of the dominant, alien culture by reflecting the life and culture of Latinos and by raising funds for the various community needs. Of the various types of musical theatre that were produced, the zarzuela *or Spanish light opera was the most popular during the first two decades of the century. Operas and operettas of the Germanic and Italian tradition were also well received, especially when performed by such touring companies as the Compañía Mexicana de Opera. During the 30's a genre actually called "comedia musical" included works by Mexico's famed composer-entertainer, Agustín Lara. But also during the 30's the popularity of the* zarzuela *was outstripped by vaudeville with its musical revues. And Estela Portillo's own twin cities of El Paso and Juárez not noly supported their theatre houses and professional and community players, but more importantly served as regular stops on the circuit of professional touring companies that performed everything from serious drama to vaudeville. Many of the companies would swing up along eastern Mexico and tour along the border making extended runs in the major cities of Laredo, San Antonio, El*

Paso and Los Angeles, with shorter stands at intermediate cities and towns. Thus El Paso often hosted such major dramatic companies as the Compañía Virginia Fábregas, zarzuela specialists like Compañía de Zarzuela Max Silva, and famous vaudeville troupes like the Cuadro Novel, Cuadro Iris, Campañía de Comedias y Atracciones "Don Chema" and the Revista de Toña la Negra.

Obviously this commerical theatrical tradition has been interrupted. Many of today's young Latinos are only familiar with West Side Story, a musical that is set in a New York Puerto Rican barrio. In fact, some high schools in the Southwest have carefully adapted the play to fit the Chicano milieu. But unfortuanately, like the recent spate of Chicano gang movies being produced by Hollywood, West Side Story deals with racial conflicts, thwarted romances and juvenile violence. And ultimately, West Side Story is a view of Latinos from the outside and includes many stereotypes.

Sun Images, on the other hand, is a perfect vehicle for younger audiences and players. Drama teachers at barrio high schools should take special note of the play as a very entertaining production that would enable young actors, singers and dancers to express themselves through situations and characters that are familiar to them. There is nothing objectionable in the play and it should therefore pass the high school censor's test with ease.

One possible shortcoming of Sun Images, however, derives from its following the example of commodity theatre: the absence of a strong social or political statement. Although the author's introduction of the "migra" may be seen as an attempt to suggest a political stand, by not openly committing herself to the issue of the undocumented worker the playwright has left the conclusions up to the audience. But since no one is harmed by the governmental forces, reaction among the uninitiated may be limited. On this matter Portillo has related that Moctezuma Esparza felt the play could have more political impact, and that she is presently revising the work for filming by including the theme of urban renewal and a politically involved Marcos.

Sun Images

CHARACTERS:

DON ESTEVAN	LA MALCOCHA
NENA	BETO
CHITA	ANA ESCOBAR SMITH
TENSHA	THE EXHIBITIONIST
DON ADOLFO	THE IMMIGRATION OFFICERS
DELFI	CROWD ON CAMPUS
MARCOS	CHUY
CARLOS	DR. REFUGIO SMITH

SETTING:

The stage is divided into three sections. Stage right represents a college campus. Up stage in this section is a door leading to a ladies room in a hall in the Student Union Building. There are some chairs and some artificial plants. At the end of this section is a signpost that acts as a divider between sets. It reads "Campus 30 miles this way." A huge arrow pointing towards hall. The second section is center stage. It is the cross-section of a bedroom in house of Don Estevan (called Don Estufas by the girls). Up stage are two doors. One leading to another bedroom. The other to the outside of the house. The bedroom contains a bed, a chest of drawers, a rocking chair, a small table, and a stool. The room is in total disarray. Clothes all over the place, dirty plates on the small table. It is obvious no one cleans the room very often. The third section of the *stage is set further downstage to separate it from the middle section. This section represents a guitar shop. This area contains a counter. There is a sign over the wall that reads "Guitars." There are some guitars standing up against the wall behind the counter on a shelf. In front of the counter are several chairs. There is a high stool behind the counter where Don Adolfo works on guitars.*

The guitar shop is in the barrio where Don Estevan lives. The barrio is a few miles from the border leading from El Paso, U.S.A. to Juárez, Mexico.

ACT ONE, Scene I

Time: the present: Saturday afternoon. Scene: the bedroom.
Lying sideways on the bed is Tensha, a girl about twenty-four. She is wearing street clothes. She seems exhausted as she stares at the ceiling. She reaches out for her purse which is laying next to her on the bed. She puts it on her stomach, opens it, takes out some money, and counts it high over her head. "Five-ten-eleven-twelve-thirteen-fourteen-fifteen," placing each bill in her chest. When she finishes, she just lies there. Nena comes in, glances at Tensha, then crosses to the rocking chair. She is about twenty-eight. She also wears street clothes. She slumps down into the chair and kicks off her shoes. Puts a box down on the floor.
NENA: What a life. My feet are killing me. What are you doing with that money on your chest?
TENSHA: It's my hope chest. Shall I buy goats for my dowry?
NENA: You'd be better off with straight cash.
TENSHA: By the time I go back to Zacatecas . . . (*She jumps up from the bed with the money in her hand.*) With all my dollars.
NENA: Ah! Méjico.
TENSHA: When I think about going back to Zacatecas . . .
NENA: All the fun in Zacatecas is one aqueduct.
TENSHA: But the boys from Zacatecas. They kiss so good.
NENA: You couldn't catch one?
TENSHA: That's why I'm here . . . you crazy.
NENA: You come here to catch a boy from Zacatecas?
TENSHA: (*Goes back to bed and counts the money again on her chest.*) No stupid, I come to get the bait.
NENA: Well, I have my man.
TENSHA: Does he know what you're up to?
NENA: Wait until Beto finds out, ¡Ay Dios!
TENSHA: What do you think he would do?
NENA: Kill me. He believes a wife's place is in the home . . .
TENSHA: There's a letter from your mother on the table. (*Nena goes to the table, looks through some mail and finds the letter. She opens it.*)
NENA: Ay, mamacita. I just bought her a new dress. (*Reads letter. Very alarmed.*) Oh . . . oh . . . oh . . . ¡Dios mío!
TENSHA: What's the matter?
NENA: Beto's coming!
TENSHA: He's found out!
NENA: He's coming to kill me!
TENSHA: He won't do it. (*Puts dress on end of bed.*)
NENA: Mama told Beto about Don Estevan.
TENSHA: I bet that made him feel good . . .
NENA: Mama told him about what a nice humane old man he is . . . taking us girls into his house . . . looking out for us . . .

TENSHA: Your husband knows about men . . .eh? Don Estufas, the philantropist!

NENA: He's bringing his horsewhip. Poor Don Estevan . . . Poor me! Poor me! Poor me!

TENSHA: Why don't you call him Don Estufas like Chita and I do?

NENA: I don't know him well enough.

TENSHA: You don't know him well enough? You have been here three weeks . . . he thinks he's one big furnace.

NENA: It's only in his mind.

TENSHA: Sí, hombre; a macho mind.

NENA: Macho do about nothing.

TENSHA: There's three of us . . .there's only one of him.

NENA: (*She looks around at the unkempt room.*) We could clean up the place.

TENSHA: After working for the gringa and fighting off Don Estufas?

NENA: He cleans up on Mondays, I think.

TENSHA: Well are you ready for a weekend with Don Estufas?

CHITA: (CHITA *enters. She looks at the girls and around the room.*) Hi . . . Who's our housekeeper?

NENA: We could clean.

CHITA: Huh!

NENA: Look what we do to him . . . and we don't even clean up.

CHITA: It's his idea.

TENSHA: He likes it.

NENA: Fooling him isn't right.

CHITA: You have a better idea? Go to bed with him!

NENA: No . . . I won't . . . but all those lies.

TENSHA: He's happy believing them.

NENA: Saturday nights are something else.

CHITA: He passes out, eventually.

TENSHA: Thank God, for that quirk of his.

NENA: One drink . . . Poof! He's out!

CHITA: Something to do with the body chemistry.

TENSHA: So we put him to sleep.

CHITA: Coffee and brandy . . . does it every time.

NENA: And the morning after . . . the lies, we tell.

CHITA: He doesn't suspect a thing.

TENSHA: The things we do for fifteen dollars . . . . . Imagine what we go through for fifteen dollars!

Song

Tres muchachitas, tres muchachitas
From South of the Rio Grand
Tres muchachitas, tres muchachitas
We really are heaven sent . . .
To the American gringa!

In spite of the fact
We don't speak the language
In spite of the fact
We hate the American sandwich,
we're tres muchachitas
Fresh and young from a foreign land
We wash and scrub

Defrost the meat
Cook and iron
Sweep out the street
Oh . . . what a fate
Oh . . . what a state
To spend all our youth
In hard labor
To live out our days
Without flavor.

We bathe their children
Feed them their food
And most times the Daddy
Is up to no good.

Oh . . . what a fate!
Oh . . . what a state!

To eat such tasteless meals
To work for gold-plated heels!

Oh . . . what a fate!
Oh . . . what a state!

We have no cars
No pretty clothes
No rich American husband
To play the boss

Oh . . . what a fate!
Oh . . . what a state!

No pretty money
Safe in the bank
No swinging parties
In the file and rank

And at the end of the week
If we're humble and meek
If no one complains and hollers
La gringa pays us . . . fifteen dollars

Oh . . . what a fate!
Oh . . . what a state!
To hide from the federales
For a measly fifteen dollars

NENA: We need the gringo's money.
CHITA: The whole world needs gringo money.
TENSHA: Only so much . . . then back to Zacatecas.
NENA: Chita . . . Beto's coming.
CHITA: To kill you, I bet.
NENA: What else?
CHITA: Me . . . I'm marrying my soldier boy.
NENA: You're going to marry a gringo?
CHITA: Maybe next week . . . maybe I quit my job on Monday.
NENA: Then you won't be coming back. You going to tell Don Estevan? (*Off stage they hear Don Estevan's voice. "Chiquititas . . .mis . . . gallinitas . . ."*)
TENSHA: Estufas is home!

Don Estevan walks in. Dressed smartly with a flower in his button hole. He has three boxes. The girls gather around him.

CHITA: You got me my blouse! You didn't forget the size, did you? In yellow?

DON ESTEVAN: (*Handing her a box.*) A yellow blouse.

CHITA: Oh, thank you! (*She kisses him on the cheek.*)

DON ESTEVAN: Nena, (*hands her a box.*) some chocolates.

NENA: Thank you, Don Estevan.

DON ESTEVAN: Sweets for the sweet! Tensha, (*He hands Tensha the last box.*) For you my dear.

TENSHA: What is it? (*She opens it.*) Perfume! (*She kisses Don Estevan.*)

DON ESTEVAN: Now . . . are all my little chickens happy?

CHITA: Where are you taking us tonight?

DON ESTEVAN: First we have dinner at Pancho's . . . nice chiles rellenos . . . or whatever you wish . . . then we go to a nice movie.

CHITA: No . . . we go dancing.

DON ESTEVAN: Again? We go dancing every Saturday night.

TENSHA: We like to dance . . . don't we girls? (*The girls all agree.*)

CHITA: (*Deliberately.*) You get tired . . . eh . . . Don Estevan?

DON ESTEVAN: Of course not . . . I am in my prime . . . and I am a superb dancer. (*Does a tango with* TENSHA.) Tum . . . tum . . . tum . . . tum . . . (*While they're dancing,* NENA *opens up the candy box and starts eating chocolates.*)

CHITA: I'll wear my new blouse.

TENSHA: Let's use the perfume.

DON ESTEVAN: Then after a night out on the town. (*He rubs his hands and twirls his moustache.*) We'll come back here and play . . . "Blind Man's Bluff." (*Pronounces it "Bluf."*)

CHITA: (*Pinching him on the cheek.*) You ol' devil you!

TENSHA: Let's go get dressed!

All the girls go into their bedrooms to get ready. Don Estevan goes to the chest, opens a drawer, takes out a mirror, looks for a comb. When he finds one, he combs his moustache and looks at himself in various postures. When satisfied, he walks downstage and talks to the audience.

DON ESTEVAN: It's not easy, being a great lover. It takes energy, money, intelligence. Look . . . now, you tell me . . . not everybody has these things. But if we do have them, ah! Look at me. I have three ladies. Three! What do you think about that? Even my son is jealous. He can't even handle one gal! When my wife was alive . . . God keep her in heaven safe and sound . . . and far away. I was a good husband. Walking a straight line. Now I take all the detours. Every man should do it once in his life. (*Girls return ready to go.*)

TENSHA: Here we are!

The girls parade before him for inspection; then he offers each of them his arms. With TENSHA *on one arm and* CHITA *on the other, he exits.* NENA *hesitates, goes back, picks up the box of chocolates and exits as she chooses a piece and pops it into her mouth.*

Scene 2

Place: The guitar shop. DELFI *is listening to* CARLOS *play the guitar. Another friend,* CHUY *accompanies* CARLOS *playing.* DELFI *comes in.* MARCOS *enters and approaches* DELFI. DELFI *struggles to keep her composure.*

MARCOS: Are you talking to me?

DELFI: (*Cooly.*) You do the talking.

MARCOS: See, I knew it . . . you're not talking to me.

24

DELFI: Don't you want to talk about Miss Ana Escobar Smith and your engagement?
MARCOS: It was a freak accident.
DELFI: Yeah . . . two freaks got together.
MARCOS: You're mad . . . you've been my girl a long time.
DELFI: Not any more. How long have you known her?
MARCOS: A month.
DELFI: A month! Did you sweep her off her feet or did she overwhelm you?
MARCOS: She tricked me. I think she tricked me.
DELFI: Don't you know?
MARCOS: I don't quite remember . . . I mean . . . how I got en gaged. Let's talk.
DELFI: I'm sorry but I have a date with Carlos.
MARCOS: Carlos! You can't have a date with Carlos. You're my girl.
DELFI: Two girls . . . eh? You're beginning to sound like your father.
MARCOS: Never mind my father.
DELFI: You want to have a harem . . . like him!
MARCOS: I don't want to fight. I just want to explain.
DELFI: You don't owe me any explanations.
MARCOS: You *know* you love me.
DELFI: Do I? Maybe you have the wrong tense. Maybe long ago . . . I *loved* you.
MARCOS: You still do.
DELFI: Oh! I don't *know.* All good things come to an end. (DELFI *walks to* CHUY.)
    Isn't that right, Chuy?
CHUY: Like love?
DELFI: Especially love.

Todo lo Bueno Pasa

Me diste corazón
Un rato de tu vida
Probaste mi pasión
Y bien que me querías

Pero, todo lo bueno pasa . . .
Se acabó, la meil de
La abeja
Se gasto el vino que festeja

La luna nos contaba
Cuentos elegantes.
Tu y yo
Pasábamos el tiempo
Soñando como amantes.

Pero todo lo bueno pasa . . .
Se acabó, la miel de
La abeja
Se gastó el vino que festeja

Ahora, quedo libre
Con alas pa' volar
Me ofrezco así al mundo
Con ganas de cantar

Porque todo lo bueno vuelve . . .
Ha! Ha! Ha! otra vez, aquí está, otra vez

La abeja pa' la miel
La uva pa' el vino
Y espero que también, me encuentre un nuevo
Amor divino

Así es la ronda
De la vida

¡VIVO!

(*When the song ends,* DELFI *takes* CARLOS' *arm and walks out.*)

CHUY: (*Walking up to Marcos.*) She's trying to make you jealous. How did it happen . . . with Ana?

MARCOS: Liquor.

CHUY: She got you drunk?

MARCOS: I woke up in her car the next morning . . . she said I had to marry her.

CHUY: That's dumb. Nobody has to get married now a days. That's a dumb line.

MARCOS: It's the way she said it . . . so innocent . . . so helpless. Before I knew it, she took me home, introduced me to her parents and told them we were engaged.

CHUY: You stupid! Didn't you say anything? Protest? Fight?

MARCOS: I had a terrible hangover. Now . . . I've got to get out of it . . . I got to make up with Delfi.

CHUY: That's some doing.

MARCOS: They say Ana's very fickle . . . that she changes boyfriends the way she changes shoes.

CHUY: It depends then, on how long it takes for you to become an old shoe. Alli te veo. (*Exits.*)

MARCOS: Todo lo bueno pasa . . . that's what she thinks! (DON ADOLFO *comes into the shop and notices that* MARCOS *is disturbed.*)

DON ADOLFO: Where's Delfi?

MARCOS: Your daughter went out with Carlos.

DON ADOLFO: So that's why you're looking so sad.

MARCOS: She's mad at me.

DON ADOLFO: She showed me the news in the paper about you and Ana. She couldn't stop crying.

MARCOS: She didn't seem to mind a little while ago.

DON ADOLFO: Women play the game better than we do.

MARCOS: Love can be a lot of trouble . . .

DON ADOLFO: What would we do in a problemless world?

MARCOS: I guess at your age, you see life different. It's a view from the end of things.

DON ADOLFO: End? No . . . no . . . it is not an end. In the spring I still shiver with the winter wind. Still, I feel the newness of spring. Just like you do . . . maybe I feel it in a different way. Always like the sun . . .

MARCOS: Time does change things. You're different from me.

DON ADOLFO: I see me in you. New image . . . old image . . . are we not all images of the sun?

MARCOS: If you want to put it that way, I guess we are.

Song

Spring came and went.
Carrying winds
But now, it's the
end of summer.
When roses die
When time must fly.
Yes, it's the end of summer.

Love came and went.
Restless in ways
Oh how I feel
the end of summer.
When roses die
When time must fly . . .
Oh, I feel the end of summer.

Remember the gift
and the giver.
Remember the young
and the free.
And if there's no dying.
Where did they go?
Are they waiting? Are they waiting . . .
Waiting for me?

Oh, carrying winds,
Show me the way.
To that one single
bright moment.
When all things are one.
and outlast the sun,
That single, shining moment.

Now I'm alone,
Tell me what's gone . . .
Now at the end of summer,
and I can tell
I can tell very well.
They are waiting!
They are waiting . . . waiting for me.
Roses and time.
Round and round and round.
roses and time,
Time, time, time . . .

Scene 3

Place: The bedroom. Time: Sunday morning before dawn.
DON ESTEVAN *is returning with the girls. He's singing a popular song. He opens the door and takes exaggerated bows as each girl enters. Then he dances into the room, snapping his fingers.* CHITA *places a finger to her lips and goes into the other bedroom to get to the kitchen. The girls know that she is preparing the special coffee for* DON ESTEVAN .
DON ESTEVAN: O.K., gallinitas, it's game time! Game time! Let's see who I catch
   tonight! It's time for *"Blind Man's Bluff"*
NENA: It's a dumb game. (TENSHA *nudges for her to keep quiet. Then she goes to a
   drawer and takes out a handkerchief.*)
TENSHA: I will cover your eyes. Sit! (DON ESTEVAN *sits on the bed and* TENSHA
   puts the handkerchief over his eyes.)
DON ESTEVAN: Where's Chita? Chita must play. (CHITA *comes through the door.*)
   Chita.
CHITA: Here I am!
DON ESTEVAN: (*Stands up.*) Minnie . . . Minnie . . . Miny . . . Moe . . . Who am I
   going to catch by her little toe? (*He starts feeling the air. The girls avoid him. They
   go over the bed, one by one making faces at him. He misses each one; then they
   pick up the covers and wrap him up in it.*) Get me out! Help! Help! (*None of the
   girls help him. He falls off the bed and unwinds himself. The girls giggle and
   laugh.*)
DON ESTEVAN: (*Huffing and puffing.*) Now, was that nice?
TENSHA: You're peeking! I can see your left eye.
DON ESTEVAN: Alright . . . alright . . . put the blindfold on again. (*Has a bright
   idea, suddenly.*) Why can't I chase you all around without the blindfold?
CHITA: No . . . we must play the game properly.
DON ESTEVAN: I'm tired after all that dancing.
TENSHA: One more try! (*He attempts to find them.* CHITA *pushes him towards*
   NENA. NENA *pushes him towards* TENSHA. *Then they turn him and turn him
   until he falls to the floor.*)
DON ESTEVAN: Enough! Enough! I'm out of breath.
CHITA: Rest a while. (*They all help him to the bed where he sits.*) I'll get you some
   coffee. It will wake you up. (CHITA *goes back to the kitchen and comes back with
   a cup of coffee.* TENSHA *takes off the blindfold.*)
CHITA: (*Handing him the cup of coffee.*) Good . . . eh?
DON ESTEVAN: (*Winking.*) I drink . . . then I catch. Ajúa! Ajúa! (*Cries like a
   rooster, then he drinks the coffee. Suddenly, his head drops to one side. He has
   passed out.*)
CHITA: (*With one finger, touches him, he falls into bed.*) There . . . another orgy for
   old Estufas.
NENA: (*Shaking her head.*) Never fails.
TENSHA: (*Yawning.*) It's morning and I need my beauty sleep.
CHITA: We all need our beauty sleep. Who's turn is it to tell him about the wonderful
   experience tonight when he wakes up?

NENA: It's my turn . . . but I don't want to. It isn't right. I'm a married woman.

TENSHA: You and your scruples.

NENA: I'm worried about Beto.

TENSHA: Don't worry 'til it happens.

CHITA: I'll do it, Nena. It will be my last grand performance. I'll be marrying my soldier.

TENSHA: You tell the best. Your orgies are just like the movies.

CHITA: That's where I get them from. (*They go towards their bedroom.* NENA *turns and looks at* DON ESTEVAN *on the bed.*)

NENA: Shouldn't we take off his shoes?

CHITA: Forget it! (*All exit.*)

ACT II, Scene 1

Place: Bedroom. Time: Late Sunday afternoon. TENSHA *appears from the other bedroom.* CHITA *and* NENA *follow. She looks at* DON ESTEVAN *who is still asleep.*)

CHITA: He's snoring.

TENSHA: He better wake up if he is going to drive us to work.

NENA: It's terrible going to work on Sunday nights.

TENSHA: It's better than staying here another night . . .

NENA: We're going to be late for work. (CHITA *goes into the bedroom to get suitcase.*)

TENSHA: (*To* CHITA.) You packed?

CHITA: Yes. This is goodbye. (*She goes back to the bed and practically shouts.*) Don Estevan! (*He wakes with a start and sits up on the bed with a dazed look on his face. There's a knock on the door.*) Who is it?

BETO: (*Voice from outside.*) I am looking for my wife, Nena Esquivel.

NENA: Beto! He's come to kill me and Don Estevan!

DON ESTEVAN: (*Hides under bed covers and peeks over covers slowly.*) Kill me?

TENSHA: What do we do?

NENA: He has a horsewhip!

DON ESTEVAN: (*Looking over the cover again.*) Horsewhip! Do something! Do something! (*The girls pull* DON ESTEVAN *out of bed.*)

CHITA: You got to hide.

NENA: Maybe he has a gun.

DON ESTEVAN: A gun! I'll hide in your room. (*He goes towards door. The girls pull him back.*)

NENA: No, he'll look in there. He'll look everywhere . . . he's very jealous.

TENSHA: Don Estufas, you're going to get it!

DON ESTEVAN: Who's Don Estufas?

TENSHA: You are, you dirty old man. Let's get him under the bed. (*They try to help him under, but it is not big enough for him.*) No, that won't do. I know, the dress you bought for your mother, Nena. Get it. (*The knocking starts again.*)

NENA: (*As she exits to bedroom.*) Beto's going to kill me, then him.

DON ESTEVAN: Maybe, maybe I can reason with him. I merely want to help the orphans of the world.

CHITA: Yeah . . . good looking orphans under thirty. You want to try?

DON ESTEVAN: Now that I reconsider, it is hard to reason with a madman. (*The knocking starts again.* NENA *comes back with the dress. Gives it to* TENSHA.)

TENSHA: (*To* DON ESTEVAN.) Okay, put this on.

DON ESTEVAN: A dress?

TENSHA: Don't argue. Don't you want to be saved? (*She puts the dress over his head*.) You're your own grandmother. You understand?

CHITA: The moustache! I'll get a razor.

DON ESTEVAN: No! No! No! You can't do that. (*The girls grab him and sit him roughly in the rocking chair. Chita comes back with the razor and a shaving mug. The others hold him down. He struggles to escape.* CHITA *lathers his face. He struggles again and escapes from them. They chase him around the room and over the bed. They catch him. The knocking becomes louder.*)

CHITA: There's no time to shave him. I know! A shawl. It will cover his face. (*She exits through the bedroom door to get the shawl. The girls lead the tired* DON ESTEVAN *to the chair again.*)

TENSHA: Alright, granny, sit down and behave yourself. (CHITA *comes back with a shawl and a rosary. They cover half the face of* DON ESTEVAN *and* CHITA *hands him the rosary.*)

CHITA: You keep your mouth shut and pray silently, you understand? You could stand a few prayers. (DON ESTEVAN *mumbles something from under the shawl.*) Shut up and pray! O.K., open the door and let me handle it. (NENA *hides behind* CHITA. *The knock is heard again.* TENSHA *goes to the door and opens it.* BETO *comes in. He carries a horsewhip. He hits the floor with it.*)

BETO: Where is he? Where is that defiler of women? (*He spies* NENA *hiding behind* CHITA. *Crosses to her and pulls her towards him.*) What have you done, woman?

NENA: Nothing! Nothing! I have not betrayed you as God is my witness.

BETO: Where's the lecher?

CHITA: Don Estevan is not here. He left town a few days ago.

BETO: (*Looking around suspiciously.*) Oh, yeah?

CHITA: Yes, look for yourself. He's not in the house.

BETO: That's what I'm going to do. (*He exits through the bedroom door to search the rest of the house. The girls cover* DON ESTEVAN'S *face. The shawl has slipped and his moustache shows. He has a petrified look on his face.*)

CHITA: Now, pray your beads off. Your life depends on it! (DON ESTEVAN, *with bent head, prays at a great speed.* CHITA *kicks him.*) Not that fast, you knucklehead! (DON ESTEVAN *slows down with the rotation of beads.* BETO *comes out, looks suspiciously at them, searches around the room; finally notices* DON ESTEVAN.)

BETO: Who's that?

CHITA: That's granny Estufas, Don Estevan's mother.

BETO: Why is she all covered up like that?

CHITA: She's very shy.

BETO: When does she breathe?

CHITA: Oh, she only covers up with strangers.

TENSHA: We girls are like her children.

BETO: She doesn't look as if she's good for much. (DON ESTEVAN *begins to pray on his beads faster.*) Where's your son? I'm going to whip him to an inch of his life! (BETO, *hits the floor around* DON ESTEVAN *mercilessly with the whip.* DON ESTEVAN *is now going around the rosary hardly touching each bead.* TENSHA *kicks him again.* BETO *looking suspiciously at* DON ESTEVAN.) What is she doing with that rosary?

TENSHA: She's a very devout person. She prays to a long list of saints every day. That's why she prays so fast.

BETO: (*Peering at* DON ESTEVAN.) She has shifty eyes. Listen, granny, how can you breathe with that shawl covering your face? Or is there another reason for covering your face?

CHITA: Of course there's a reason. She has a bad case of acne . . . very bad case. She won't let anybody look at her face.

BETO: Acne? At her age?

CHITA: It's a new disease in the U.S. . . . . old age puberty.

BETO: I think you're all crazy. Nena, you're coming with me. Now! (*He hits the floor with the whip.*)

NENA: Yes, dear . . . my things . . .

BETO: Never mind your things. Let's go. (*He grabs his wife by the hand and pulls her to the door. He turns and looks at them suspiciously.*) If I ever catch that old satyr, you tell him for me, I'm going to skin him alive.

CHITA: We'll tell him.

NENA: Nothing happened, Beto. I swear it. He's a harmless old man.

TENSHA: We'll send your things to you.

BETO: Come on. (NENA *and* BETO *exit.* DON ESTEVAN *slides down from the rocking chair onto the floor. He's all done in.*)

CHITA: Serves you right! We should have given you to him!

TENSHA: You have to pay for your sins in this life, you stink pot! (DON ESTEVAN *gets to his feet and musters all the dignity he can, under the circumstances.*)

DON ESTEVAN: You girls have no right to talk to me like that! I have taken you under my roof . . . fed you . . . entertained you.

CHITA: And made a fool of yourself. (DON ESTEVAN *immediately takes off the dress and shawl, throws them on the bed. He hesitates a moment and looks towards the door.*)

DON ESTEVAN: They're gone, aren't they? They're not coming back, are they?

TENSHA: (TENSHA *goes to the door and looks out, then returns.*) They're gone and it's late.

CHITA: You'll have to drive us to work tonight, exhausted or not.

DON ESTEVAN: Yes, my pidgeons . . . but last night . . . who did I catch last night?

CHITA: (*Shaking her head.*) You'll never learn will you? (*she thinks for a moment.*) No one.

DON ESTEVAN: But . . . I always catch someone.

CHITA: Not this time . . . so there's no tale to tell. No one can tell you what a great lover you were last night. You fell asleep and snored like a pig.

DON ESTEVAN: (*Confused.*) I fell asleep? (*He scratches his stomach, then his head, and then his moustache.*) My luck! I'm going to make some coffee. (*He exits through the bedroom door to the kitchen.*)

CHITA: Someone has to tell him the facts of life . . . one of these days.

TENSHA: No thank you . . . not me. (*They sit dejectedly on the bed.*)

CHITA: I'm splitting . . . for good.

TENSHA: (*Calls out.*) Don Estevan . . . hurry up . . . we're late! (DON ESTEVAN *comes out.*)

DON ESTEVAN: Here I am, little pidgeons! (*They exit.*)

Scene 2

Place: The College Campus. Time: One week later. Ana Escobar Smith enters stage right with an armful of books. She wears glasses. She sits on a chair in the hall of the Student Union Building and lays her books and purse down. Then she takes one and begins to read. Suddenly she becomes aware of the audience, slams the book shut, takes off her glasses, and walks down stage.

ANA: (*To audience.*) Hell, there! You know, it's very hard being a female. Especially now in 1976. Can I tell you a secret? Well . . . I'm still a virgin . . . and that's something that's hard to be . . . in 1976. I mean, I tell my friends, "I'm a Virgin." Some of them look at me as if I were a freak. Others look like they're sorry for me.

Some just advise me to keep it to myself. You know, I'm beginning to doubt if it's such a good thing to be. (*A college boy walks by. She follows him with her eyes, enjoying herself.*) My mother thinks being a virgin is a great thing. Who am I to argue? I came to college to consume the knowlege of the world . . . to liberate myself. (*Another boy passes by and she follows him with her eyes. He stops in the hall as if waiting for someone.*) But liberation and virginity don't mix very well, I think. Anyway, mother says that every girl is bound to lose her virginity and the best way to do it, is under contract. (*Another boy comes and begins to talk to the second boy.*) Well, I didn't come to college to catch a husband . . . of course not! I came to consume the knowledge of the world. (*She looks towards the boys and sighs.*) Anyway I got myself engaged recently . . . just for fun. (*Another boy comes in furtively looking from side to side. He goes into the girls' bathroom when no one is looking.*) Marcos, my fiancee, is a doll . . . but he's giving me trouble already. He's angry about our engagement. He says I should have asked him first, but I thought at the time it was all settled. The morning we got engaged, I told him we had to get married. He had a headache because he had taken one drink. One drink, mind you . . . and then . . . he passed out! (*Snaps her fingers.*) Just like that . . . one drink and he was gone. Well, the next day I told him we had to get married, and he assumed the worst just like a man. What I really meant at the time was . . . We had to get married because I felt like being engaged . . . but he never let me finish the sentence. What are we poor, defenseless, weak, tender females to do? It's a cruel, hard world for the likes of us . . . dainty and gentle as we are. Oh! I got to run! But first, I'll powder my nose. (*She picks up her books and purse and goes into the girls bathroom. Suddenly there are screams and shouts and bangings. The boy runs out with his pants half-falling.* ANA *chases him beating him with her purse, kicking him, biting him, etc. He screams for help attempting to put up his pants and run. He finally manages to escape from her and she runs after him, yelling.*) "Stop, pervert! Police! Sex-maniac! Stop him!" (*A crowd gathers exclaiming what happened. A young professor,* DR. REFUGIO SMITH, *joins the crowd.*)

DR. SMITH: What happened?

1ST STUDENT: You wouldn't believe it! Some chick was beating on a guy.

3RD STUDENT: An exhibitionist. He attacked her in the girls bathroom.

1ST STUDENT: That's not the way it happened.

2ND STUDENT: She attacked him.

1ST STUDENT: Yeah . . . did you see him run!

3RD STUDENT: He was in the girls bathroom!

DR. SMITH: Alright! Alright!

2ND STUDENT: The poor dude . . . he needs help.

3RD STUDENT: She needs help. (*Ana comes back on stage with vengeance on her face.*)

ANA: He went right over the fence and I couldn't find the campus patrol. They're never around, when you need them.

1ST STUDENT: Poor dude!

ANA: (*Angrily.*) Why are you sticking up for him? I'm going to carry some tear-gas in my purse. They ought to hang him.

2ND STUNDENT: Help!

Dr. SMITH: Are you alright?

ANA: (*Noticing him for the first time. She changes character immediately.*) Oh! I think so . . . I was so shocked.

DR. SMITH: I can imagine.

ANA: It's so hard, you know.

DR. SMITH: What is?

ANA: Staying a virg ----- oops!

DR. SMITH: You had quite a scare.

ANA: (*Taking his arm.*) It's so good to have someone around to protect you. Your wife must feel so safe.

DR. SMITH: I'm not married.

ANA: (*Elated.*) Not married . . . but how could that be?

DR. SMITH: (*Jokingly.*) It's been hard for me . . . too!

ANA: You're joking!

DR. SMITH: I'm joking.

ANA: What do you teach?

DR. SMITH: Philosophy.

ANA: All about truth and beauty.

DR. SMITH: About people.

ANA: I thought that was sociology.

DR. SMITH: It all concerns people.

ANA: I never thought of it that way.

DR. SMITH: Just imagine . . . a ball of fire . . . in the sky . . . the earth taking shape . . . waiting . . . for people. (Sings *"Before the People Came."*)

Before the People Came

Stone-fire, Sun-tides,
Red sounds . . .
To make an earth of love.
Before the people came.

Moon-child and mother
Round a nameless space.
Of spinning days.
Before . . . the people came.

Water flowing, rivers growing.
An ocean giving birth:
Before . . . the people came.

It's warm, it's bright,
This endless stream
of breathing life
Before . . . the people came.

Morning . . . Morning of life.
Everlasting life.
Before . . . the people came.

Star-field in the universe.
Waiting for the spoken work.
Before . . . the people came.

Light . . . could not be denied.
Sky . . . could not be defied.
Because of a growing Love.

ANA: Oh! I can see it! I can see it! Dr. . . .Dr. . . .You are a doctor aren't you?

DR. SMITH: Yes . . . Smith is the name.

ANA: Smith! Oh, my!

DR. SMITH: What's the matter?

ANA: I'm Smith, too! It must be fate. (*She hugs him and kisses him.*)

DR. SMITH: My, you're an impetuous young lady.

ANA: I am really a very nice girl. I take Mama's advice . . . but you're so wonderful, so full of the knowledge of the world. I would like to consume . . .

DR. SMITH: (*Clears throat.*) Well, I am already late for an appointment. (*Ana takes his arm as he starts to walk away.*)

ANA: You must come home to meet Mama and Daddy. Now, you can't say "no." I shall cook your favorite meal. Shall we say next Saturday?

DR. SMITH: I will have to look at my calender . . .

ANA: Don't do that! Just say "yes." Yes?

DR. SMITH: Well . . .

ANA: That will do, that's a good enough "yes."

DR. SMITH: Goodbye. (*Exits. Ana returning. Boys and girls gather around her.*)

1ST STUDENT: You have some nerve!

ANA: Is that what you call it?

2ND STUDENT: Aren't you engaged to Marcos?

ANA: I have been engaged many times . . .

2ND STUDENT: That figures. So Marcos is scratched . . .eh?

ANA: Oh, he won't mind! He wasn't too pleased about our engagement.

1ST STUDENT: Has love anything to do with all this?

ANA: But of course! I love them all madly.

1ST STUDENT: That's the word: "madly."

ANA: I know about love. Of course, I know about love! Don't you know about love?

What love Is

> *Love is opened wide*
> *Like yellow daisies*
> *Wanting sun.*
> *Love is a wild clash . . .*
> *Surf on rock*
> *lightning flash.*
> *Love is being only what you are.*
> *What makes a you?*
> *What makes a star?*
>
> *Love is as green*
> *As eyes that see . . .*
> *And then with joy.*
> *Let be! Let be!*
>
> *Now I know time*
> *Builds no walls*
> *No one dies . . .*
> *No one falls . . .*
>
> *I must be a well*
> *So deep*
> *That quiet things*
> *I'll learn to keep.*
> *I hold the gift*
> *You give to me . . .*
> *Roots so fierce*
> *The sky they pierce.*

I will climb
A hill to find
A place to be . . .
A world to see.

(This is a choreographed dance number.)

Scene 3

Place: Guitar Shop. Time: Two Fridays later. Carlos and Chuy are strumming guitars.
Don Adolfo is polishing a guitar on his stool.

CHUY: Hey, Carlos, how's it going between you and Delfi?

CARLOS: We're good friends.

CHUY: Is that all?

CARLOS: Marcos doubled-crossed her, and my girl doubled-crossed me. We console each other.

CHUY: Marcos is an old shoe now. He's off the hook. Ana's after some poor professor at the college.

CARLOS: Poor guy!

CHUY: Delfi knows, but I don't think she's about to forgive Marcos.

CARLOS: She will. I know that if my girl came back to town . . . I would still feel something.

CHUY: In spite of . . .

CARLOS: In spite of anything. Mistakes are mistakes.

CHUY: But your girl had . . . so many guys in . . . between.

CARLOS: When we were kids, she used to follow me around . . . all through school. Hasta que cambió . . . hasta que la perdí.

CHUY: ¿La quieres todavía?

CARLOS: Before the world took over. (*Carlos sings.*)

Choriada

Choriada, Choriada, Choriada.
Te recuerdo yo así.
Desde tu niñez
Compañera de
sueños y juegos.
Descubrimos el amor
Por primera vez.

Con tus lindas manos
La cara te lavaste
Lucías listón.

Corriste a la vida
Buscando alegrías
Entregando corazón.

Choriada, Choriada, Choriada.
Me dejaste a mí
por un nuevo amor.

Quizás fui no más que juguete,
Un ambiente

Que repente
Te dio calor.

Dejaste tus juguetes
Entre flores secas
Que ruegan amor.

Tan necia y orgullosa
arrancas de la vida
Sin pedir perdón.

Te buscas paisajes de amores
Tomas en lleno
Todo el placer,
Y dejas las flores marchitas.
Sueños perdidos al amanecer.

Dices que te quedas,
Niña de juguetes,
Con tesoros de amor
Pero eso es mentira.
Ya tus ojos hablan
De un gran dolor.

Choriada, Choriada, Choriada.

DON ADOLFO: ¡Las heridas del amor.(*Marcos enters and looks for Don Estevan around the room.*)

MARCOS: Don Adolfo, have you seen my father?

DON ADOLFO: No . . . not for weeks.

MARCOS: Some immigration men were looking for him. They've found out about the girls.

DON ADOLFO: Poor Estevan!

MARCOS: I bet he's over at the Green Parrot in Juarez.

CARLOS: Isn't that the place where your ol' man interviews the girls that answer his ad in the newspaper?

MARCOS: That's the place. He's probably interviewing again . . . maybe the federales saw the ad.

CHUY: No, I think it was that guy that came for his wife a couple of weeks back. The one with the horsewhip.

MARCOS: Chita ran off to marry a soldier and Nena went back with her husband. He'll advertise again. He was down, man, when I went to see him. He always gets that way when the girls run out on him.

CHUY: How many girls have run out on him?

MARCOS: Too hard to keep count . . .

DON ADOLFO: It's hard for Estevan to accept old age.

MARCOS: You have.

DON ADOLFO: When I lost my wife. I had this shop . . . my music . . . but when Estevan lost your mother, all he had was a pension, a house, and time on his hands. And, remember when he was young he was popular in the barrio with the girls.

MARCOS: That was long ago.

DON ADOLFO: He'll run out of wind . . . one of these days. Then he'll come over and we'll play checkers, remember our youth, and enjoy the peace in our lives.

MARCOS: When immigration catches up with him, he'll be off to jail or a fine. He's a poor man . . . though he tells it different.

CHUY: Want to drive over to the Green Parrot?

MARCOS: Yeah . . . let's scout around.

CARLOS: I'll go with you.

MARCOS: Kiko, the owner, might know where he is.

DON ADOLFO: Good luck. (*As they're about to leave,* DELFI *comes in and deliberately ignores* MARCOS.)

DELFI: Hello, Carlos, Chuy.

CARLOS: Hi Delfi.

MARCOS: (*Going to her.*) No "hello" for me?

DELFI: Oh . . . did I overlook you? Hello.

MARCOS: Hello again.

DELFI: Hello.

CARLOS: Hey, you two . . . break it up. Are we going or not?

MARCOS: I have to go now, but can I see you later . . . to talk?

DELFI: I'll be here. (*They look at each other for a moment, then* MARCOS *leaves with the boys.*)

DON ADOLFO: You know, he's not engaged any more?

DELFI: I heard.

DON ADOLFO: And you've already forgiven him.

DELFI: Oh, Papa, of course.

Act III, Scene 1

Place: The bedroom. Time: The same afternoon. DON ESTEVAN *comes in looking dejected. He misses the girls and is waiting for* TENSHA.

DON ESTEVAN: (*Calling out.*) Tensha . . . you home? (*No answer.*) All my gallinitas gone . . . Only Tensha . . . she's going to leave too . . . I know . . . when they start to go . . . they all go. I have to go to the Green Parrot when I feel a little better. (*He falls into the unmade bed. He just lies there and is unaware of a knock at the door. After a while the door opens and* LA MELCOCHA *enters. She's a woman about forty. She's wearing an old pair of army boots and an old hat. She wears a misshapen coat, sizes too big for her. She walks into the room and looks around, shaking her head. She sees* DON ESTEVAN *lying on the bed. She tip-toes over and looks down at him.*)

LA MELCOCHA: Are you awake? (DON ESTEVAN *sits up startled and looks at her.*)

DON ESTEVAN: Who are you?

LA MELCOCHA: Everyone calls me La Melcocha.

DON ESTEVAN: Melcocha . . . I hate the stuff.

LA MELCOCHA: It's good candy . . . sweet and long lasting.

DON ESTEVAN: What are you doing in my house?

LA MELCOCHA: Kiko at the Green Parrot gave me your address.

DON ESTEVAN: Kiko gave you . . . (*He gets out of bed with some difficulty, groaning and moaning. Then he looks her over.*) You look like something the cat dragged in . . . you're old.

LA MELCOCHA: What is old?

DON ESTEVAN: Kiko's not to send me prospects. I go there and choose them for myself. You say . . . he gave you my address?

LA MELCOCHA: Not exactly . . . a young girl answered your ad at the same time. We waited for you, but you didn't show up . . . so Kiko gave the address to the girl.

DON ESTEVAN: How did you get it? The newspaper ad says explicitly that I help young girls . . . not old scarecrows like you.

LA MELCOCHA: I paid the girl my last ten pesos for the address.

DON ESTEVAN: I should have gone yesterday. Look what happens when you don't do what you are supposed to. The girl, where is the girl?

LA MELCOCHA: She didn't know how to get across the bridge . . . so she gave up.

DON ESTEVAN: I usually bring the girls over in my car. Never been caught.

LA MELCOCHA: I waded across the river close to here. Look at my shoes.

DON ESTEVAN: You're one big mess. You waded across the river, eh? Well, now you can wade right back. This place is a haven for young girls.

LA MELCOCHA: Haven . . . looks more like a trap an old man, like you, would set.

DON ESTEVAN: Old! I'm not old!

LA MELCOCHA: They all leave you . . . eh? The girls fool you and then leave you, eh?

DON ESTEVAN: They leave because of extenuating circumstances. Now go!

LA MELCOCHA: You described yourself as a lover of humanity and you don't even let me catch my breath.

DON ESTEVAN: You talk too much! As soon as you catch your breath . . . vamoose! scram! vanish!

LA MELCOCHA: I'm hungry. I haven't eaten in a long time. Point me to the kitchen. (DON ESTEVAN *points and she goes through the bedroom door to the kitchen. Calls out.*) Poor man, your house is a mess! (*He sits dejectedly on the low stool, as* TENSHA *comes in. She sees him and crosses over to him.*)

TENSHA: What's the matter?

DON ESTEVAN: Oh, Tensha. Thank heavens you're here! I thought this would be the loneliest weekend of my life . . .

TENSHA: I'm going back to Mexico. I'm not staying.

DON ESTEVAN: Why . . . little pidgeon? Did you lose your job?

TENSHA: No, I quit! I have enough money for a dowry. I'm going back to Zacatecas to find myself a husband.

DON ESTEVAN: Dowry? Husband?

TENSHA: What do you care? All you ever did was chase the life out of us.

DON ESTEVAN: I gave you good times! Presents! I drove you around . . . anywhere you wanted to go. I was good to all of you.

TENSHA: I guess you were . . . in a way . . . but I'm leaving. It was hard enough for three of us to keep you in line. I'm not staying by myself.

DON ESTEVAN: But we had good times. Saturday nights, you remember. I am your passionate lover.

TENSHA: Never were! We put brandy in your coffee. Every Saturday, you passed-out cold.

DON ESTEVAN: (*Scratching his head.*) But, I remember . . .

TENSHA: You remember the lies we told you the next morning.

DON ESTEVAN: Lies?

TENSHA: Lies . . .

DON ESTEVAN: But my reputation . . . everybody in the barrio knows.

TENSHA: That was a long time ago. Why don't you wise up! Is life that bad when you get old . . . that you have to fool yourself?

DON ESTEVAN: Will you marry me, Tensha?

TENSHA: No, Don Estevan, I'm young and I want somebody young.

DON ESTEVAN: There are ready-made advantages.

TENSHA: I'd rather make my own advantages with someone my age. Listen, Don Estevan, you're a nice man. Find somebody your own age. I've got to go. I have to catch a bus to Zacatecas.

DON ESTEVAN: I'll drive you to the station.

TENSHA: You've been the best of drivers . . . I'll get my things. (*She goes into the*

38

other bedroom.)

DON ESTEVAN: (*To the audience.*) She's wrong, you know. I'm as great a macho as I ever was. There are many fish in the sea. Women are a nickle a hundred. I must have been crazy, asking that silly girl to marry me. Thank goodness she refused! (TENSHA *comes back with a bag.*)

TENSHA: I'm ready. By the way, there's a woman eating in the kitchen.

DON ESTEVAN: I must remember to throw her out when I come back. (TENSHA *looks bewildered as* DON ESTEVAN *pushes her out the door.* MELCOCHA, *still eating, opens the door of the bedroom, peeps out, watches them go. When they leave, she comes into the bedroom and looks at the room in despair.*)

LA MELCOCHA: Poor man! No wonder he's crazy! Living like this. Men are helpless! They bluster through life creating every kind of trouble. We take care of them, make them comfortable. What on earth would they do without us? (*While she is talking, she begins to pick up and straighten the room.*) I'll have him tame and manageable in no time. (*She continues her work.*)

Scene 2

This scene is played simultaneously in the guitar shop and on the campus. Action in the guitar shop is pantomimed, accompanied by a strobe light, to give the effect of a silent movie, while the characters in the campus scene act normally.

Campus: DR. SMITH *walks on with* ANA.

ANA: Tell me more! You're so wise. I want to consume the knowledge of the world!

DR. SMITH: So you've told me many times.

ANA: You say that the miracle of things is people because when they came upon the earth, they brought love. Weren't the other life forms doing well without them? I mean, the frogs and the deer and the dinosaurs couldn't care less if people were around.

DR. SMITH: Oh, but the frogs and deer and dinosaurs didn't know they were frogs and deer and dinosaurs.

ANA: You mean, they didn't have names.

DR. SMITH: Exactly! Nothing had names.

ANA: Oh, I see. Without the words, love, peace . . . there wouldn't be any.

Shop: Background music of "Before the People Came." MARCOS *walks in, catches* DELFI *flirting with* CARLOS *and* CHUY. *He goes up and pulls her away.* CARLOS *doesn't like it. He gets up and tells* MARCOS *to let her go.* MARCOS *refuses.* DELFI *pushes* MARCOS *away and* CARLOS *and* MARCOS *face each other; start circling each other posing with karate moves. Blackout.*

DR. SMITH: (*Scratching his head.*) That is a questionable syllogism . . . but yes, you could say that.

ANA: People made up the words . . . Love! Peace!

DR. SMITH: Or was it the other way around? Words were still energy, then the people came.

ANA: Words are important.

DR. SMITH: No, not really . . . when you think about it . . . silence is a good thing.

ANA: Silence . . . is that love and peace?

DR. SMITH: Creation . . . the den of creation is love too! Struggle . . . change.

ANA: It's confusing . . . but everybody strives for love and peace!

DON ESTEVAN *goes into shop with* TENSHA. *They sit down.* DON ADOLFO *comes to greet them. They shake hands:* DON ADOLFO *kisses* TENSHA'S *hand. Two immigration officers enter, cross to* DON ESTEVAN *and flash their credentials. Blackout.* DON ESTEVAN *is proclaiming innocence. One of the immigration officers grabs* TENSHA *by the arm. She steps on his foot, he grabs his foot in pain. She starts to run out. The other officer catches her. She hits him over the head with her bag; he falls to the floor.* TENSHA *runs out.* DON ESTEVAN *starts to follow her, trips over officers. They all get up.* DON ESTEVAN *runs out.* DON ADOLFO *follows. Officers chase them blowing whistles. Blackout.*

*   *   *

ANA: I feel guilty! Let's go apologize to Marcos and Delfi. (*They exit stage right, blackout campus set. They enter guitar shop.* ANA *ignores commotions, goes over to* DELFI *with outstretched arms.* DELFI *turns her around and kicks her in the behind.* DR. SMITH *goes to the rescue and gets involved in the fracas with the boys. The fight is in full swing, while very loudly, over the speaker, the voice of* DR. SMITH *sings out the last chorus of "Before the People Came."*)

Light could not be denied
Sky could not be defied
Because of a growing Love.
Before the people came.
And then! (*Clash of cymbals. All freeze onstage.*)
The People Came! (*Blackout.*)

Scene 3

This is also a dual scene, focusing on the guitar shop and ESTEVAN'S *bedroom. The shop is empty, except for* DELFI *who is sitting dejectedly on her father's stool. At the same time,* DON ESTEVAN *enters bedroom, and is greatly surprised to find everything in order. There are even flowers on the table.* MELCOCHA *comes in. She is dressed neatly. It is evident that she is an attractive woman.* DON ESTEVAN *is very surprised by the change in her appearance.*

DON ESTEVAN: You look . . . er different.

LA MELCOCHA: You poor man! Sit down. I heard about you being thrown in jail. (*She leads him to a chair. He doesn't resist.*) A man like you deserves so much! Life should be kinder.

DON ESTEVAN: You are right. A man like me deserves so much more.

LA MELCOCHA: You deserve everything. You have so much to offer . . . (*Sings.*)

Y dices que tú
Conoces tan bien el amor . . .
Ofreces tanto, amor,
Y quiero yo compartir . . .

Dejaste tu ayer
La luz final del amanecer . . .
Y tu compás
Ya sabe querer . . .
Que quieto es el merecer.

Toma mis labios
Toma mi suerte
Callada quiero
Quiero ofrecerte . . .
Amapolas,
Amorosas en todo color
Afroditas
Que se abren al sol . . .
El silencio es amor.

(*During the song* LA MELCOCHA *massages his neck muscles, makes him comfortable, puts her arms around him from behind the chair. When the song ends:*)

DON ESTEVAN: Ah! I need peace . . .

LA MELCOCHA: The girl, Tensha . . . she was sent back to Méjico?

DON ESTEVAN: (*Rather pleased.*) Ha! That's exactly what she wanted! (*Suddenly he jumps up in anger.*) They fined me five hundred dollars! Five hundred dollars! Me, a poor man!

LA MELCOCHA: That is the prize of sin.

DON ESTEVAN: What, you say?

LA MELCOCHA: Oh, nothing . . . I'm just wondering how you've been.

DON ESTEVAN: Oh . . . I have suffered, suffered, and my corns hurt.

LA MELCOCHA: Oh, sit down, let me look at your feet. (*He meekly does what she asks. She takes off his shoes, and looks at his feet. He reaches out and touches her hair.*)

DON ESTEVAN: Your hair is soft.

LA MELCOCHA: I'm going to get some warm water to soak your feet.

DON ESTEVAN: I smell something nice.

LA MELCOCHA: I'm cooking you your favorite dinner. Marcos told me what your wife used to cook you.

DON ESTEVAN: Wife! I don't want a wife!

LA MELCOCHA: (*Calming him.*) There! There! Who said anything about you wanting a wife! I'm just making you comfortable. Let me get the water for your feet. (*She goes to get water.* DON ESTEVAN *watches her as she leaves. At the shop,* DELFI *stands and walks around, touching guitars, etc.*)

DON ESTEVAN: Nice . . . nice . . . She still wiggles quite well . . . good figure. Oh! I like this . . . maybe tomorrow, I'll go interview some young girls. Wife! Who needs a wife!

LA MELCOCHA: (*Coming back with the water.*) Here, put your sore feet into this. (*She places the basin at his feet. He puts his feet in it and sighs with pleasure.*) Isn't that nice? Aren't you hungry? We'll start with some nice soup. I'll bring it, you just relax. (*She goes to get the soup. Again* DON ESTEVAN *watches her.*)

DON ESTEVAN: I got to watch out for that woman. She's setting a trap! I'm too smart for that. I always had a weakness for behinds. Fine . . . fine . . . figure of a woman. (*He closes his eyes and relaxes.*)

At the guitar shop, MARCOS enters. He walks up to DELFI and taps her on the shoulder. She turns and goes into his arms. They kiss as background music of "Gocé" is heard. After embrace, they walk downstage and sit on edge of stage. DELFI leaning on MARCOS as he sings.

Gocé

Gocé en tus brazos
Como gocé . . .
Para que te digo lo
que tú, ya sabes!

Dejamos tan lejos
Al hambre, a la sed.
Dejamos tan lejos
Al miedo sin fe.

Sentimos tan cerca
El humor de la paz.
Te siento, tan cerca
Silenciosa estás!

Y por eso, nunca
seremos solos,
Tú y yo.

Tomé los colores
De todo tu ser . . .
Y ahora, y mañana
Y siempre . . .
Ahora, mañana,
Y siempre,
Ya tengo tu pulso
Ya tengo tu canto
Ya tengo tu vida
En mi . . .
Estás, en mí . . .

In middle of song, MELCOCHA comes in with a bowl of soup. She feeds DON ESTEVAN a couple of spoonfuls as he sits relaxed and comfortable. Then hands him the plate, sits on stool and puts her head on his lap. He puts the bowl down on the floor next to the chair. Strokes her hair and leans back and closes his eyes. When the song ends the curtain falls.

Carlos Morton

RANCHO HOLLYWOOD

Carlos Morton is one of the most prolific and produced Chicano playwrights to date.
Rancho Hollywood *is Morton's thesis play, for his Master of Fine Arts degree at the*
University of California at San Diego. It represents a culmination of all that he has writ-
ten before, bringing together his broad comprehension of the differing styles of Teatro
Chicano from the acto to the documentary.

A study of Morton's published works begins with El Jardín[1] *and is followed by* El
Corrido de Pancho Diablo,[2] Las Many Muertes de Richard Morales,[3] *and* Rancho
Hollywood. *The first two plays are "super-actos" that are Chicano versions of the Fall*
of Man. Written in Morton's bawdy, farcical style, these plays employ song and narra-
tion to keep the action moving forward. Las Many Muertes de Richard Morales *is Mor-*
ton's only serious drama to date and displays his talents for a form that can be effective
in staging the many injustices that are occuring in barrios and ghettos throughout the
U.S. The play is a docu-drama which investigates the unjust murder of a Texas Chicano
by a local sheriff and the court's leniency towards the "Lawkeeper."

In Rancho Hollywood, *Morton returns to his distinctive style which is characterized*
by broad, farcical humor, an exaggerated and contorted history and characters. The
play is loosely based on historical facts and personages, but real names have been slight-
ly altered so that Pío Pico becomes RÍO RICO, *and Jedediah Smith is transformed into*
JEDEDIAH GOLDBANGER SMITH. *Chronologically, the play opens right before*
the Gold Rush of 1849 in California, and continues to the present in a series of quickly
changing scences that parallel historic events and documents.

As might be noted from its title, this play is a parody of the Hollywood vision of the
Latino, Black and Native American in this society. The metaphor of the Hollywood set
is always present, and as the play progresses, the vision of the "movie capital of the
world" is more and more on the characters and the situations in which they find
themselves. This is not a play about slowly evolving psychological transformations, but
a film onstage that can go fast forward, reverse action, single frame or slow motion as
the scene demands. Because anything is possible on the screen, anything is possible on
Morton's stage as we watch over one hundred years of history condensed into an even-
ing's entertainment and enlightenment.

Because this play is a statement about the false images Hollywood has created, the
settings, the costumes, the props must all be equally false and indicative of the one-sided
wall of a Universal Studios' set. The illusion, the fantasy and myth of the silver screen
must here be forced to bear the consequences of a vision that will not tolerate deceit any
longer. Thus, the less realistic the accoutrements, the better, allowing the designer great
freedom to exaggerate and comment upon the myth being shattered.

Rancho Hollywood *is the only play in this collection that has not yet been produced,*
but the exception was made because we are certain it will be seen onstage very soon. As

[1] *El Grito,* 7/4 (June-August, 1974), 7-37.
[2] *Grito del Sol,* 1/3 (July-September, 1976), 39-85.
[3] *Tejidos,* 4/1 (Primavera, 1977), 28-50.

43

of January 1979, Morton is one of the playwrights-in-residence for the internationally acclaimed San Francisco Mime Troupe, and if this multiracial troupe does not produce this multiracial play, another company will undoubtedly see the merits in this satiric statement and seek production rights.

Rancho Hollywood
"A California Dream"

CHARACTERS:

GOVERNOR RIO RICO, *the last Mexican Governor of California, a middle-aged mulatto or Mexican man.*

DOÑA VICTORIA RICO, *the Governor's fair-skinned "Spanish" wife.*

RAMONA RICO, *the Rico's young daughter, a brown mestiza.*

JEDEDIAH GOLDBANGER SMITH, *a Yankee trader-trapper-goldminer-soldier-capitalist with a vision.*

TONTA GERONIMA SINMUHOW, *an Indian maid, maiden.*

YALLER MARCUS MALCOM KUNTA KINTE, *a high yaller slave, worker, invisible man.*

SETTING:

A movie set. At first it looks like a stage setting done in traditional colonial style with patio, bedroom, living room, etc. However, after the Anglo conquest the set becomes a glowing neon film set with wagons and backdrops to facilitate the speeding up of time. Overture. Banjo on one side, Guitar on the other, Latino versus Anglo music. DON RICO and his wife, DOÑA VICTORIA, are seen dancing a fandango at rise, occasionally interrupted by the strains of a banjo or fiddle. As they finish their dance, they freeze, like an old painting. TONTA, their maid, who has been clapping and keeping time to the music, steps forward.

TONTA: Damas y Caballeros, Ladies and Gentlemen, bienvenidos a Rancho Madera Acebo, Pueblo de Los Angeles in Alta California. The year is 1830 and the land was Mexicana, when California danced fandangos until dawn — though lately they would soon hear another tune (*Banjo plays.*) which rivaled their own in intensity. And this is what our cuento is all about, the many different tunes men dance to. Behold, here is my Master, El Gobernador; he represents three generations of Rico's who conquered here. How proud, how dignified, how angry! Why? You'll see. And here is my mistress, Doña Victoria, a high born dame of pedigree Española. (*TONTA waves rag like flag.*) ¿Y yo? Soy su humble servant, Tonta, Indian by birth, para servirle. (*Putting her ear to the imaginary key hole.*)

RICO: You told her *what*?

VICTORIA: I couldn't help it, she kept badgering me.

RICO: But you didn't have to go and tell her *that*!

VICTORIA: I told you, I didn't tell her the whole truth, just partly.

RICO: I ought to slap your face for that.

VICTORIA: Don't you dare!

RICO: And where is she? It's getting late. In my day, youths had more respect for their parents.

VICTORIA: Don't put the bit too harshly against her mouth; give her a little play. The girl is headstrong, independent.

TONTA: (*To audience from the door.*) In short, una spoiled brat.

VICTORIA: I warn you, don't try to tie her down, she'll revolt. And for God's sake don't keep the truth from her, she'll only hate you for it later. (*As RAMONA enters, TONTA opens the door for her.*)

TONTA: (*To audience.*) Aquí está my little mistress; the beautiful, impertinent, Ramona!

RAMONA: (*Clicking her heels, Castillian Rose in her mouth.*) Olé! Olé!

VICTORIA: Ramona, take that silly rose out of your mouth. Can't you see your father's very angry? What took you so long?

RAMONA: Oh, I ran into my Cousin Lorenzo in the Plaza. Then we saw Edwardo, Silvia, José Luis, and María.

RICO: Besides staying out late, you associate with riffraff.

RAMONA: I do not associate with riffraff. Those are my best friends.

VICTORIA: Don't talk that way to your father; now, what were you doing?

TONTA: (*To audience.*) She was with those smart young blades, the ones who drink vino in the taberna.

RAMONA: I told you, I went for a walk in the plaza. Papá, what have you got against my friends?

RICO: They are not fit company. Why, they are barely gente de razón.

VICTORIA: Except for her Cousin Lorenzo, he's my sister's only child.

RAMONA: What else do you have against them?

RICO: They drink too much, swear, read suggestive books, shoot their guns in the air, duel, and plot insurrections. Is that enough!

RAMONA: Good God in heaven!

RICO: There she goes, using the name of Dios in vain.

RAMONA: Why don't you admit the reason you dislike them is because they are in the forefront of steering a new and independent course for us Californios . . .

RICO: There she goes, using that word again: Californios!

VICTORIA: But Rico, it's just a word the young people use to describe themselves these days.

TONTA: (*To audience.*) Not good enough to call themselves Mexicanos como sus parents.

VICTORIA: Don't remember how in our day we called ourselves "criollos" to distinguish ourselves from the Españoles?

RICO: Correct, but today we are Mexican, of the Mexican Republic, which is a political entity that extends from Guatemala in the south to Alta California in the north, of which I am the Mexican Governor of said territory!

RAMONA: Papá, the tutors taught me my history and geography well.

VICTORIA: Ramona. don't be so impertinent.

RAMONA: Papá, with all due respect, hear me out. You pretend to dislike my friends because they are not all upper class like us. Yet, mother has told me that your grandparents sprang from the humblest origins themselves.

TONTA: (*To audience.*) Now we're getting to the roots!

RAMONA: (*As DOÑA VICTORIA makes frantic "silencing" motions.*) Mother told me that your grandfather, Santiago Rico, was but a poor shepherd. Mother's family, on the other hand, were all Spanish merchants, rich and powerful.

RICO: Yes, can't you see how well bred, ladylike, and aristocratic your mother is. (*As he walks to the door.*)

RAMONA: Well, mother told me that your grandmother, Jacinta de La Bastida, was a full blooded Indian!

RICO: (*Opening the door.*) Unlike this illbred, gossip of a Tonta here!

TONTA: (*Falling.*) El skeleton está out of el closet.

RICO: What do you think you're doing? I ought to slap your face!

TONTA: (*Whispering.*) Don't you dare! I'll tell!

RICO: Lárgate de aquí! (TONTA *exits.*) So, Ramona, that's what your mother told you, uh?

RAMONA: Yes. Doesn't that explain why you are so dark like an Indio, mother white like a Española, and I . . . well, sort of café con leche?

RICO: Yes, the Indios say we drink so much chocolate we are becoming more like them each day.

VICORIA: Sí, ¡el chocolate!

RAMONA: Please, no more stories, I'm not a little girl anymore. I mean, just look at me. There's no denying it, I'm part Indian.

RICO: No, you are of pure Spanish blood, do you understand?

RAMONA: But Papá, I'm almost as dark as Tonta.

RICO: Only Españoles are worthy of becoming gente de razón in this society. Call yourself India or anything else, and no gentleman will ever ask for your hand in marriage. You would only be fit to keep their kitchens, like Tonta.

VICTORIA: Your father means well, Ramona, listen to him.

RAMONA: I can't stand it anymore, I am being engulfed by lies, deceit, and ignorance. I live in a world of shadows, half truths . . .

RICO: Silence! Do you want your face slapped?

RAMONA: Don't you dare, I've done nothing wrong! (RICO holds RAMONA.)

RICO: Oh, why can't you be like the little girl I once knew, who used to sit on my knee and listen, transfixed, to stories of why the sea is so salty, or why the full moon has the face of a rabbit.

VICTORIA: Go on dear, have Tonta fix you a light supper, and go to bed.

RAMONA: (*Exiting.*) Buenas noches.

RICO and VICTORIA: Buenas noches, hija.

TONTA: Do you want something para comer, niña? (*Meeting* RAMONA *at the door.*)

RAMONA: No gracias, I'm not hungry, for food that is. Only for Truth!

TONTA: (*To audience with her ear to the keyhole.*) Huh, if she only knew. They keep her like a caged songbird.

VICTORIA: I know what you're going to say! But I told you, I had to tell her something. She asks too many questions. Now, what if I had told her the truth? What if I had told her that your grandmother was, in fact, a mulatto.

TONTA: (*To audience.*) I knew it! That wooly headed old vieja was as dark as Cleopatra.

RICO: May she rest in peace. The poor woman worked herself to death.

VICTORIA: And you were cast in her image.

RICO: I am told that. But why trouble our daughter with inconsequential matters concerning the lineage of my grandmother.

VICTORIA: Because it is important, because it is nothing to be ashamed of. Why, your forefathers were the second wave of settlers who founded the city of Los Angeles.

TONTA: (*To audience.*) Es verdad, and over half were as black as Africa.

VICTORIA: If you don't tell her, it's just going to cause problems later on. What if one of her children decides to look like you?

RICO: I wouldn't wish that on anyone. Besides, Ramona will marry a caballero, and their children will be Español.

VICTORIA: Now I begin to see the method to this madness. Even though your grandmother was black, her children claimed to be mestizo . . .

RICO: Why not? My parents were mestizo, or at least the census taker took them as such.

VICTORIA: Then, as the status of the family improved, so did the lineage. Ingenious, where else but California could you begin life as a Negro and end it as an Español?

RICO: That's right! I'm proud that this sort of thing could happen under the Mexican system of government. I am the Governor of the Territory, and I am a black man.

VICTORIA: You should admit it more often.

RICO: Let me tell you something, woman. I have heard of places where one drop of black blood automatically makes you a slave, what they call a nigger. And I am no nigger!

TONTA: (*To audience.*) Well, is he or isn't he?

VICTORIA: Just look at you, dark as an Andulsian Moor, and thanks to your rank and wealth, you dare call yourself a Spaniard.

RICO: You think you're better than me, don't you, just because your skin is as white as the Sierra Nevada, and your blood as cold and blue as the streams that run through it.

VICTORIA: And is that the only reason you married me?

RICO: No, I think it is because I admire your mind and its outspokeness.

VICTORIA: And I, señor, think you are a proud and sensitive man.

RICO: Let us go to bed. (*As RICO and VICTORIA exit, TONTA steps downstage with a lamp in her hand.*)

TONTA: Just see how fast his darkness covers all her whiteness! But, it's true, Las Razas are so intermarried in California and all Latin America that most of us are a mix of colors. You'd be surprised, the mixing that goes on. (*Blowing out lamp.*) Me, I'm not married. Someday, perhaps. A strapping farm hand; just you see, we'll have our own little ranchito where I shall be the mistress of the casa, put on airs, hire a criada to cook and clean for me. Ven, Maruja, pick the vegetables para hoy! Ven, Maruja, cook the comida, set the mesa, serve us, don't forget the café. Now, clean up and wash. We'll have brandy in the study. Gracias, burp! Ahora, get my bed ready, it's time for sleep. (*Laying down to sleep.*)

VICTORIA: (*Off stage.*) Tonta! Tonta!

TONTA: (*Relighting the lamp.*) Oh God! Morning so soon! Time for Misa.

VICTORIA: (*As TONTA whirls around attending to her and RAMONA.*) Oh, in my day we lived like Kings and Queens. Tonta, fix my hair, dear. On Saints Days or religious festivals we had bailes, danced and sang. There were bullfights, cockfights, horse races, bearbaiting. My rouge, Tonta, my rouge. We ate and drank for days. Not that powder, this powder.

RAMONA: Did Papá join in the festivites? Tonta, pin my dress, will you?

VICTORIA: Oh, he ˈwas a demon! Running amok with his eyes ablaze. Tonta, Ramona's stocking's need mending. Gambling, drinking, flirting with all the women.

RAMONA: Tonta, I need my red shoes, the ones with the buckles. (TONTA *exits.*)

VICTORIA: I'll wear the brown shoes, Tonta! Oh, your father, let me tell you, he's settled down considerably. (RICO *appears behind a curtain, grabs* TONTA.)

RAMONA: So Papá was just as wild in his youth as my Cousin Lorenzo.

TONTA: Don Rico! Is there no Indian maiden safe from your advances?

VICTORIA: Your father was wilder. He probably sees himself in Lorenzo and it aggravates him that he can't womanize anymore.

RAMONA: I bet you've been a calming influence on him.

VICTORIA: I like to think so.

TONTA: Haven't you fathered enough wooly headed mestizos?

VICTORIA: After your father married me, he turned with the same fever to cultivating his vast land holdings, raising cattle, which we used for hide or tallow, and grazing sheep, horses, and goats. He also grew grain and fine grapes for wine. Hah, we always paid our debts then, unlike now, with hides, which the Yankees called California bank notes. Oh, where is that girl with my shoes. Tonta! Tonta!

TONTA: (*Behind the curtain, struggling.*) I'm coming!

RAMONA: Mother, I've been meaning to ask you about that. Is Papá in serious debt?

VICTORIA: No, not yet, but we can't afford to play around like we used to.

TONTA: (*Slapping* RICO.) You old fool!

47

VICTORIA: You see, dear, with the exception of soap, wine, and cloth, we rarely make finished products, depending instead on the Yankee Clipper ships. Our hides are sent to New England, manufactured into shoes, then shipped back here to be sold. It's a vicious cycle and we're losing, according to your father. (*A loud crash is heard.*) What was that!

TONTA: (*Running in, straightening herself.*) Here are your shoes, mistress.

VICTORIA: No, no, you got the wrong color. (TONTA *exits.*) What was that noise? (*As* RICO *appears at the door to their bedroom.*) Rico, what's the matter with you, are you all right?

RICO: Nothing dear, I just fell down the stairs.

RAMONA: Are you hurt, Papá?

RICO: (*Limping away.*) No, just a slight limp here in my leg . . . oh, but my back.

TONTA: (*Returning.*) A sail, a ship's been sighted in the harbor!

VICTORIA: Ramona, where are you going?

RAMONA: To watch the ship unload at the dock.

RICO: (*Still limping.*) No, I think not.

VICTORIA: Let her go, Rico, I will accompany her to see she gets into no mischief. Besides, I want to see the goods myself. Tonta can take care of things while I'm gone.

RICO: Very well.

VICTORIA: Your father does not want you parading back and forth among all those Yankee sailors, Ramona. (*They exit, leaving* RICO *and* TONTA *alone. He walks up to her, looks her right in the eye, they both laugh.*)

JED SMITH: (*Entering from the audience with his slave amidst the strains of "Oh Susana."*) "Oh Susana, oh don't you cry for me, for I'm bound to Californee with my banjo on my knee." (*Speaking to* YALLER *with a thick accent.*) Fina tela aquí, mercancías, muebles, bajas intereses de crédito? I know it's hard, but you're going to have to learn it.

YALLER: Fine tele aquí, merchandise, mueblas, bajas intereses de crédito.

JED: Not bad. What you're saying is "fine cloth here, merchandise, furniture, low credit terms available." Tell 'em we take Master Charge! Now, that's what you're going to say when we land in California, Yaller man.

YALLER: Yus suh, Massa Jed.

JED: We'll split up, make more money that way. Put the bright colors up in front, hide the drab ones. Fancy boots and trinkets; eyeball to eyeball with the customer. These Californians go in for ostentatious displays of opulence, my boy. You know what that means?

YALLER: Yus suh, dey is big spenders. I 'spect I'll have all mah goods sold widin a few days or so.

JED: Yaller, I want you to understand these people, so I'm going to read to you from a book written in 1840 by Richard Henry Dana, Jr. It's called "Two Years Before The Mast." Now then, "the Californio men are generally indolent, of a harmless disposition, fond of spiritous liquors, who care little for the welfare of their children. The women have but little virtue, the jealously of their men is extreme and the revenge deadly and almost certain."

YALLER: Don't mess wit dey women folk! Well, suh, some a dat dere sound what you say I is, especially de parts 'bout liquor.

JED: That's not all, Yaller, listen to parts of this other book. "There are very few white people; it consists principally of a mixed breed. That they should not be industrious is not surprising; their government does not encourage industry." (*Skimming through a book.*) "Indian character. Dull suspicious countenance, the small twinkling piercing eye, the laxness and filth of a free brute, using freedom as a mere means of animal enjoyment . . . dancing and vomiting."

YALLER: Whew, did a white man write dat, Massa Jed? Well, 'cause he shoo made them out to look like real no count niggers.

JED: That's right, you Yaller coon you, so figure 'em out and take their money away.

YALLER: Yus suh, I'se going to skin 'em alive!

JED: Because if you make me enough money this trip, I'll make you a free man! (*Lights out on* JED *and* YALLER.)

RICO: (*Lights up on* RICO *and* TONTA *leaning on his desk.*) Dios Mío, I've suddenly developed quite a splitting headache.

TONTA: Quieres que te rub your temples?

RICO: Ah, sí, you're the only one who knows how to do it.

TONTA: ¿Mejor que Doña Victoria?

RICO: Si, even better than her. Don't get me wrong, she's my lawful wedded wife and I love her dearly . . . pero, she has not the warmth, the passion that burns . . .

TONTA: Words, palabras, words! Tell that to her face!

RICO: You know I can't do that. How are nuestros hijos?

TONTA: Bien, the older boy tends to his flock, the younger is still in diapers.

RICO: I will come and see them this Sunday.

TONTA: That is what you said last Domingo. Dime algo, Rico: your wife, after seven years, are you sure she suspects nothing?

RICO: Hah! She thinks you sleep with a soldier in town.

TONTA: What if I am?

RICO: You better not be! ¡Eres Mía!

TONTA: ¡Déjame! Since when are we getting so possessive? What if I told the truth to Doña Victoria!

RICO: Tonta! She would banish you in an instant from Rancho Madera Acebo, and your children as well. Then what would you do?

TONTA: Drown them?

RICO: What are you saying. ¿Estás loca? Don't I give you enough money? Don't ruin things, you are better off than most Indios!

TONTA: Oh, Don Rico! Will our children become mestizos in the next generación?

RICO: Come on, don't be sharp tongued with me. I've got enough headaches as governor of this territory.

TONTA: (*Rubbing his temples.*) ¿Qué pasa? Tell me.

RICO: First of all, Mexico City acts as though we were in Siberia. The Russian Bear is fast advancing from Alaska. And since the secularization of the missions, some of your relatives are beginning to get out of hand! Then there is the difference between those of us in the south and those in the north. Add to that the plundering carried out in the treasury which I have failed to curb.

TONTA: Don't try to shoulder todos esos burdens. They are more than enough for un hombre.

RICO: And now, the latest ill to befall us is the sudden and rapid influx of Yankee trappers, traders, and ruffians into Alta California.

TONTA: Estos Yankees, what are they like?

RICO: I'll tell you; they are opportunistic, greedy, pushy, offensive and racist. In general, they are a lazy people of vicious character who treat their slaves badly.

TONTA: Tienen slaves?

RICO: That's right; whereas your people were set free over twenty years ago. And why do you think they are that way? It is because of what they eat. Imagine, they eat only salted meat, corn bread, homemade cheese, and coffee. Oh, and strong liquor.

TONTA: No chile?

RICO: None whatsoever. Not only that, they're Protestants!

TONTA: (*Aside.*) Little did we know that soon all of California would be overrun with

Yankees. (*Lights out on* RICO *and* TONTA.)

JED: (*Almost at the apron of the stage.*) Here we are, Yaller, California!

YALLER: Lawd 'a mercy!

JED: Fine cloth here! Tele fina! Merchandise, mercancía!

VICTORIA: (*Entering with* RAMONA *from the side.*) Oh, Ramona, look at that beautiful chest of drawers. Wouldn't it look good in my bedroom?

RAMONA: And Mamá, may I buy this fine Calico cloth to make a dress with?

TONTA: (*As she comes downstage with* RICO *behind her.*) Don Rico's hospitality was renowned throughout the territory. No matter what his shortcomings, he turned no man away from his casa.

RICO: (*Greeting the Yankees at the entrance to his home.*) Bienvenidos a Rancho Madera Acebo.

RAMONA: My father, Governor Río Rico, welcomes you.

RICO: Mi casa es su casa.

RAMONA: Our house is your house.

YALLER: Massa Jed, de Gubner, he's a nigger!

JED: Nah, can't be! These Californios just git real dark. (*To* RAMONA.) Why, thank you, I think I'm going to like this casa very much. (*Overjoyed.*) "Already, the señoritas speak English with finesse. Kiss me, say the Yankees, the girls all answer YES!"

YALLER: Massa, now you be careful wit dem hot tamales!

RICO: (*Stepping in between* JED *and* RAMONA.) Señor, ésta es mi hiija, Ramona, y mi esposa, Doña Victoria.

JED: Mucho gusto. (*With a thick accent.*) Yo soy Jedediah Goldbanger Smith, at your service.

RICO: Bienvenido a Rancho Madera Acebo. (*Showing them into the patio.*)

JED: Gracias, Don Rico, I think I'm going to enjoy my stay here in Rancho Mad Era Azebo. Yo bringo unos presentos. (*Signaling to* YALLER *who pulls out a six pack of Coors, Coca Cola, Frisbees, other objects of colonialism.*) Cerveza para Don Rico. A little something for the ladies. We hablar negocio later on.

TONTA: (*Aside.*) My master does not have the slightest idea of what the Yankee is saying, so Mistress Ramona will translate hasta que Don Rico aprenda English, which should be any momento now. (*As* RICO *orders* TONTA *to fetch something.*)

RICO: Señor, ¿cuál es su misión aquí en California?

RAMONA: My father would like to know what your mission is here in California.

JED: Tell your, uh, Padre, I am here in search of goldo!

RICO: Goldo? ¿Qué es eso! ¿Cómo la de Calafia?

RAMONA: Excuse my father's laughter, Señor, it's just that he is reminded of the old Spanish myth of Calafia, Queen of the Amazons, whose tribe was reputed to have worn breast plates of solid gold. Of course there was no gold, but the name, California, derives from that myth.

JED: Much interesante! Pero, I know there's gold in them thar hills! I even brought my nigger along to help me find it.

YALLER: Massa says us niggers, specially us *Yaller* niggers, gots magic powers to finds de gold.

RAMONA: (*As her father "speaks" Spanish to her.*) My father wants to know why you have not beaten your slave.

JED: What, me beat Yaller! Why, he's like my own son. Tell your Padre I appreciate his adviso, pero will continue to seeko el gold, entiendo?

RICO: (*As* TONTA *re-enters with food.*) You querer eater? Whiskey? Carner salted? Corn pan?

JED: No, but I could go for some tacos or a margarita. Got any of them mariachis? I hear you folks dance fandangos until dawn and leave bowls of loose change in each guest room to use as one pleases.

RAMONA: Sir, my father would like to know how long you plan to stay.

JED: (*Looking at his wrist watch.*) What year is this? 1842? Oh, a couple more years oughta do it.

RICO: Señor, one cosa . . . very importante.

JED: Sir, I thinko you ready to speako el English.

RICO: Y you el Español.

JED: Claro, yo hablo Spanish perfecto. Six weeks Berlitzo.

RICO: If you stay aquí . . . deber ser citizen of Mexico. ¿Comprende? Very importante.

JED: OK. OK. But let me take una siesta to thinko on it. After all, isn't this the land of mañana?

RICO: OK. I show you tu roomo. Tonta, el granero para el negro! (TONTA *and* YALLER *exit.*) My maid show you slave sleep in barn. (*As* RICO *and* JED *exit.*) Mañana you decide become citizen Mexicano. OK?

JED: Bueno. (*Exit.*)

RAMONA: What a strange man, do you think he will stay?

VICTORIA: I have a strange suspición that we shall be seeing him for some time to come.

RAMONA: Hmmmm, I'd like to talk to him, about his country I mean.

VICTORIA: Just make sure there is a chaperone present.

RAMONA: Oh, Mother, don't be so old fashioned. What's so bad about two adults holding a perfectly innocent conversation without a chaperone?

VICTORIA: Don't let your father hear you talking like that; he'll have a heart attack. (*Kissing her.*) Now, be a good girl and run along to bed.

RAMONA: Buenas noches, Mamá. (*They exit.*)

TONTA: (*On another part of the stage.*) This way to your cuarto, Mister Nigger.

YALLER: Say, girl, you ain't got to be putting on dem fancy airs wit me. You and I in a same situation.

TONTA: What do you mean, same situation? I'm no slave.

YALLER: Sure, you just cooks and cleans for dem Californios from morn till night 'cause dey treat you so good.

TONTA: I earn my keep. I'm a free woman.

YALLER: If'n you're so free, why ain't you living wit your own people 'stead a working for dat Mexican nigger man. Is that your name, Tonta?

TONTA: (*Avoiding his question.*) Don Rico is no nigger man, he's Español.

YALLER: Sho, and I's pure blooded English. Tonta, what's dat mean? You Injun woman?

TONTA: Sabes qué, Mister Nigger, you're whiter than Don Rico.

YALLER: Obviously, I'se a high yaller nigger. Dats why dey calls me Yaller, Yaller Smith.

TONTA: Smith. Your name is the same as the white man.

YALLER: Nigger ain't got no choice, Tonta. Last name be what your Massa's name be. I been bought and sold three times and I be but twenty years old. Last name was Jackson. Before dat Jefferson. Born wit de name Washington. Come to think of it, I may be the great grandson of de fadder of the United States!

TONTA: Say, Yaller, porque you no stay here in California and become Español like Don Rico. Maybe even be Governor!

YALLER: Yes, Mam, I think I will. So, what kind of Injuns 'round here?

TONTA: Yo soy Kemyia. Born south of here in San Diego Mission. Orphaned. Brought to Rancho as a young girl by Don Rico. Why you ask so many questions, Yaller?

YALLER: Just naturally curious. You got to ask questions if you ever wants to get ahead. Don't you think I gonna be a slave the rest of my life, no Mam! Matta a fact, after dis trip, if'n I make Massa Jed a whole pile a money, I'se gonna be free. He promised.

TONTA: (*Pointing to the wings.*) Aquí you sleep, with the mules.

YALLER: I ain't gonna be sleeping in barns all my life, no suh. After dis trip, he promised . . . (*Getting his blankets out.*)

TONTA: Don't believe a word they say, Yaller, don't trust none of them. I worked seven years for Don Rico, have two of his children, but I just a dumb maid to him. You know what "Tonta" means? I tell you. "Tonta" means "dumb." Don't let them make a "Tonta" out of you, Yaller. (*Running off.*)

YALLER: No, I won't. I'll kill him first, I swear. I'll kill him! (*Lights out.*)

VICTORIA: (*Entering from the side, followed by* RICO.) Is something wrong, querido, you seem preoccupied.

RICO: It was something the Yankee said. He asked why there were so few white people in the territory like myself and my family. And I couldn't help but note a tone of derision in his voice.

VICTORIA: Are you certain it wasn't your imagination?

RICO: And then I asked him if he was from New England and he said Texas.

VICTORIA: Texas!

RICO: Yes, the same Texas the Yankees stole from Mexico in 1836. The same Texas which is now a slave state. Dios Mío, time is moving by so quickly, it seems as though we conquered California just yesterday.

VICTORIA: (*As though they were looking out a window.*) Sí, and Mexico the day before. (*Blackout.*)

JED: (*Out on his balcony, next to* RAMONA's *balcony. Looking at her covetously.*) Buenas tardes, Señorita Ramona.

RAMONA: Buenas tardes, Mister Smith.

JED: Looks like it's going to be a beautiful sunset there on the sea. (*She nods but does not answer.*) What do you call those mountains to the north?

RAMONA: Las Moñtanas de San Bernardino.

JED: And the valley?

RAMONA: El Valle de San Fernando.

JED: A little too much smog today.

RAMONA: Smog? What's that?

JED: Smog is what you get when General Motors, Firestone, and the Oil Companies buy up the Electric Trolley Car system.

RAMONA: Oh. (*Not wishing to appear ignorant of the latest inventions.*) We are very isolated from the rest of the world here in California. We have no electric trolley car systems like you do back East. We do have El Mar del Pacífico.

JED: Oh yes, there's Marine Land. Say, which way are the pyramids from here?

RAMONA: Oh, Señor, we have no pyramids here in La Cuidad de La Reina de Los Angeles del Río Porciúncula.

JED: Is that the full name of this city? Isn't it rather long? Why don't you just call it Los Angeles, or L.A.?

RAMONA: El Lay? Sounds obscene! But Los Angeles, the city of the Angels, sounds heavenly.

JED: My God! I've suddenly been struck with a vision!

RAMONA: What, what's the matter?

JED: The city, it's burning! It's the city of the Lost Angels. We're in Hell!

RAMONA: I see nothing; no smoke, fire, hell.

JED: Look, the freeways! The Pomona, San Diego, Santa Monica, Santa Ana! Millions of automobiles snaking along, exhaust fumes trailing. There, the Harbor Freeway, Golden State, Long Beach! Endless miles of concrete!

RAMONA: Señor, where do you see this?

JED: My God! It's enough to curdle your blood. Look there, tall buildings, scraping the skies! Airports; with planes stacked up like saucers in holding patterns! Marinas glutting the shoreline! Stadiums, with millions of sports fans growling in unison! And slums, slums everywhere! East L.A.! Watts! It's burning, it's burning!

RAMONA: Señor, Señor, what can I do?

JED: My mind is burning! Give me some water!

RAMONA: (*Dousing* JED *with a flowerpot.*) Are you all right?

JED: Yes, yes, just a momentary burst of apocalyptic prophecy. I'm all right. I have fits, er, visions. I'll be OK.

RAMONA: Do you see any vision or future for yourself here in our city?

JED: Yes, I'd like a little piece of land. Say, Orange County. I'll develop, but modestly, in harmony with the environment. A few condos, 7-11's.

RAMONA: We have a very liberal immigration policy, there being but 6,000 of us and so much land for the taking. My father is the Governor, he could give you a land grant.

JED: Your father, does he like Yankees?

RAMONA: Only Mexicanized Yankees. We have quite a few, you know, who have come here and adapted our ways, intermarried with our people.

JED: Tell me, your father, how does he feel about an independent California?

RAMONA: Don't let him hear you say that! He's a staunch Mexican all the way. But I know that we must leave the Fatherland some day.

JED: There you go! Join our Union! Go the American Way!

RAMONA: What can you offer us Californios?

JED: Protection from foreign encroachment, for one thing. Those Russians are sneaky, just look how fast they got into Cuba. Besides security, I can give you undreamt of wealth, and a future with a vision never before seen on earth. I can give you apple pie and motorboat races, hamburgers and Disneyland! (*Kneeling.*) Marry me!

RAMONA: Señor, please, this sort of thing is not done here in Rancho Madera Acebo. There are proper channels, traditions. Besides, I will not marry outside my race, my class.

JED: Rancho Mad Era Azebo. What does that translate to?

RAMONA: Literally, it means Rancho of the Wood Holly.

JED: Hollywood! Hollywood! Hollywood and Vine. Groman's Chinese Theatre, the Brown Derby. The Film Industry! Television!

RAMONA: Are you having a fit again? Look at your eyes, they are like shooting stars.

JED: I'll open a string of porno shops. I'll do snuff films. Life is cheap in Latin America. No, just kidding. (*Pulls out photograph.*) Look, see this photograph of my mother, let me explain. See, someday, we'll be able to run thousands of these together into moving pictures which will be projected on a screen and be able to reach an audience of millions. Well, here, I'll make you a camera. (JED *fashions a little box, climbs over into her balcony.*)

RAMONA: Un momento, por favor. Slow down. This is your mother? What's her name? Where is she from?

JED: Her name is Goldie. This was taken in Europe. She's dead now, of a broken heart, but that's another story. I am her son, her only son. Promised I would carry her picture with me forever.

RAMONA: Are you Anglo-Saxon?

JED: Yes, yes, of course, isn't everyone? Except for you, who are Spanish.

RAMONA: Yes, of course. But with a dash of Indian, for spice.

JED: Your father, he is very dark.

YALLER: It's going to be a free state, you promised! For Tonta as well!

JED: Liberty and justice for all. (*As* TONTA *joins* YALLER, JED *swears* RICO *in.*) Do you swear to uphold the laws of the United States, so help you God!

RICO: Sí, I mean, yes.

JED: You are now a citizen.

RICO: I didn't ask to be.

JED: Furthermore, I would like to ask for your daughter's hand in marriage.

RAMONA: Oh Papá, he's already taken me!

VICTORIA: ¡Mi hija!

JED: I trust you will perform the marriage ceremony.

RICO: Yes, just let us have a few moments alone with our daughter.

VICTORIA: (*The three of them together.*) Rico, you're going to have to tell her now, before she marries this white man. You see, dear, your father is . . .

RICO: I am mulatto, hija, part Negro. My grandmother was Black.

RAMONA: Now you tell me, just as I am about to marry this Gringo.

VICTORIA: Your father did it to protect you, mi hija, or so he thought.

RAMONA: What am I going to say? What am I going to do?

RICO: It's up to you. We just wanted to tell you the truth.

JED: Let's get on with it; California's joining the union!

YALLER: Say, as long as you all are marrying people off, why not hitch me and this Injun girl up.

RICO: No, don't go, stay with us!

YALLER: Get someone else to sleep with you on the side, you no count black mothafucka! (*Going for* RICO, *the two men grapple.*)

RAMONA: Papá!

VICTORIA: I knew it, I suspected it all along!

RAMONA: (*Stepping in between the two men.*) Don't fight, there's nothing (*Motioning to* JED.) he'd like better. Besides, it's all over.

JED: Ramona's right, it's time for reconciliation, time for marriage. Let's get on with the ceremony!

RICO: (*Acting as priest with his wife as a witness, crying.*) Do you?

JED and RAMONA: We do.

YALLER and TONTA: We do.

RICO: (*Giving the sign of the cross.*) You are!

YALLER: (*Turning with* TONTA, *to leave.*) Thank you, and goodbye!

JED: Not so fast, I need both of you to help me build this country. I'll pay you more money than you ever made in your lives.

TONTA: (*To* YALLER *as he hesitates.*) But what about our little Ranchito?

YALLER: We gonna need some capital; do you know what a home costs now-a-days?

JED: (*Handing them some coveralls.*) Here, put these on and move that set, things are going to be mighty different around here! (JED *and* TONTA *start moving sets around, revealing Rancho Hollywood's new facade, sign, neon, glitter.*)

RICO: And, if you'll excuse us, my wife and I must go and start our lives anew.

JED: Not so fast, there's still a few more papers to sign.

RICO: (*Reading the papers* JED *hands him.*) What does it say? You know I can't read English.

JED: You better learn. (*As* RICO *signs.*) This is the law of 1851 under which the burden of proof is placed on the landowner to defend the title to his land.

VICTORIA: Doesn't that mean much time and money spent in court defending our rights to Rancho Madera Acebo?

JED: (*Snatching the paper away.*) Correct, and by 1880 the Mexican will be relatively landless in California. (*As he shows the* RICOS *to the door.*) But don't worry, Ramona and I will make good use of Rancho Hollywood.

THE RICOS: Rancho Hollywood!!

JED: (*As he takes out his camera.*) Yaller, Yaller!

YALLER: My name's not Yaller any more, it's Marcus Garvey.

JED: (*Handing him the camera.*) That's a nice name. Here, take a picture of Ramona and me kissing in front of the Rancho. Fiery, impetuous Señorita with handsome Yankee soldier, heal those old war wounds, that sort of thing.

RAMONA: (*Forcing a smile.*) Jed, those are my own flesh and blood. You just can't throw them out in the cold.

JED: Tell 'em to pull themselves up by their bootstraps. Tell 'em to get organized, they got the vote.

RICO: That's it! I'll run for public office.

JED: Have you registered this year? Do you own property in this country?

RICO: No property, but tell me where I register to vote. (*As JED hands RICO another form.*) Another one, in English.

JED: How do we know you're qualified to vote on the issues, especially if you don't read English? And by the 1880's people with Spanish surnames will no longer be found in public office in California. (*Snapping his fingers.*) Hey, Tonta! (*Pointing to RICO'S shirt.*)

TONTA: That's not my name. (*As she rips RICO'S shirt off his back and hands it to JED.*) The name is Geronima! (*She returns to the set work, setting up for the next scene.*)

RICO: My shirt!

JED: I'm so sorry. (*Tipping his hat and exiting with RAMONA under his arm.*) Good day!

RAMONA: Bye Mamá, bye Papa!

RICO: I'm ruined; I've lost everything, my land, my daughter, my career, and most important of all, your respect.

VICTORIA: No, you haven't, I forgive you. And don't be despondent, we are still very much alive. Let's go and look for that gold, remember? The gold we always searched for in our myths and dreams?

RAMONA: Calafia's gold! You're right, we still have time. Why, the Gold Rush hasn't even started yet.

VICTORIA: (*Pointing to the stream being layed down by the workers.*) Look, in that stream, something glitters! (*The workers scatter gold nuggets as RICO and VICTORIA pan for gold. JED and RAMONA enter from the opposite end, dressed like gold miners.*)

JED: The miners came in forty-nine . . .

RAMONA: The whores in fifty-one . . .

JED: And when they got together . . .

RAMONA: The produced the native son! (*Pointing to JED.*)

JED: Camera! (*The workers wheel a large tripod camera out from the wings. Then they go off to the side and take a break. Smoking and watching the show.*) All right! The Miner Forty-Niner and his Darln' Clementine run the claim jumpers off their stake.

RICO: Gold, gold, I've found gold!

JED: Hey there! What the blazes you think you're doing? This here's our claim!

RICO: I beg your pardon, Señor, but we've been here for over three generations.

JED: You're not even supposed to be working unless you paid the Foreign Miner's Tax.

RICO: I just told you, I'm an original Californio.

JED: You look like any other greaser from Sonora or Chile to me. Now, I told you, only 100% red blooded 'mericans can dig for gold. All others got to pay a tax of $300 per month.

RICO: But then I wouldn't be able to make a profit.

JED: Exactly.

VICTORIA: No, it's ours, we found it first.

JED: Are you going to leave, or am I going to have to persuade you? (*Pulling out his gun and shooting wildly.*)

RICO: (*Returning fire.*) We've been pushed around long enough.

RAMONA: Help, help, help! It's an insurrection!

JED: No, don't give it any legitimacy! You're line is, "help, the bandidos are *robbing us.*" Jeez, now you made me forget my line. Oh yes, bring me the head of Joaquín Murietta! I said, bring me the head of Joaquín Murietta! (YALLER *and* TONTA *change into their cavalry clothes.*) Or any other spick, for that matter. Oh, watch that diabolical sneer turn into a cowardly whimper on his dark moustachio'd face as I call for the vigilantees to "lynch the greaser bastards!"

RAMONA: No, that face! I recognize that face . . .

JED: (*Charging out and then retreating.*) We're pinned down, there's too many of them! This is a job for the United States Cavalry! Troopers, mount up, "Boots and Saddles!" (YALLER *and* TONTA *as conscripts shuffle in, very apathetic.*) Sgt. Garvey, you and Indian Scout Geronima circle around and surprise them from the rear. But wait until I blow the bugle, then attack! (*They do not move.*) Well, what are you waiting for?

RAMONA: (*Stopping the fight.*) No, don't shoot! It's my father! Papá, it's me, Ramona!

JED: Get down, it's the Frito Bandido!

RICO: (*Rising up from the other side.*) I'm no bandido, I'm a guerilla fighter!

JED: It's Pancho Villa, the terrorist.

RICO: That's General Francisco Villa, hero of the Mexican Revolution.

VICTORIA: ¡Viva Villa! (*Moving slowly to the middle of the stage.*)

RAMONA: Mamá, Mamá! You're trying to kill my parents! (*Going to meet them.*)

JED: See, that's not your father, it's a Negro!

RAMONA: But my father is part Negro. (*Hugging and kissing her parents.*)

JED: (*To his soldiers.*) I don't like the looks of this, men. We are surrounded!

YALLER: What do you mean "we?"

TONTA: Paleface. (*Guns casually pointed in his direction.*)

JED: (*Crossing to* RAMONA.) Uh, Ramona, what did you just say?

RAMONA: My great-grandmother on my father's side was Black, which makes me part Black.

JED: (*Not really listening to her.*) She was an Indian Princess, how nice!

RAMONA: Of course I'm part Indian, but I'm also part Black.

JED: You should be proud of your Indian heritage, it's good karma.

RAMONA: Jed, you're not really listening to me. I'm all the colors of the land, even white, like you. And I'm proud of it. But you look down on people with darker skin.

JED: Who me? Oh no, I'm not going to be accused of bigotry, no way. Why, we're much more enlightened now-a-days. Why, I'm a minority just like all of you. I'm part Jewish!

YALLER: Next thing you know, he's going to tell us he's got a flick of the tar brush.

JED: Someday, Marcus, I'm going to help you form the NAACP.

YALLER: The name's not Marcus anymore; (*Shouldering his rifle.*) it's Malcom!

JED: My mother left Poland to escape the persecution. Why, that part of my family has been discriminated against for over 2,000 years. And all because they think we killed Jesus Christ!

TONTA: Your forefathers may have suffered, but you never have!

RAMONA: Mamá, did you hear that, Jed's not really an Anglo . . . he's part, uh

Slavic. Jed, don't ever let my mother know I married outside the church; she'll disown me.

JED: Oh, I don't believe in God.

RAMONA: Jesus, Joseph and Mary! Worse yet, an atheist.

JED: Well then, since we've all made our little confessions, since we've gotten much more liberal here at Rancho Hollywood, why not let bygones be bygones. After all, it's the Twentieth Century, time to usher in a new era of human understanding.

RAMONA: Do you really mean that?

JED: I swear, I'm going to change my image.

YALLER: A wolf in sheep's clothing!

RICO: The twentieth century, already? It seems as though we just conquered California yesterday.

VICTORIA: And Mexico the day before.

JED: You already said those lines. We're going to have to get you some new ones.

RAMONA: Jed's right, Mamá, we Mexican-Americans can't be living in the past. We gotta get modern.

RICO: Mexican-*American* is it now!

RAMONA: That's right, Papá, I'm a child of both cultures now.

VICTORIA: Oh, I wish we could go back to the old days! It was a veritable Jardín de Edén with all the fiestas and dances and fairs . . .

TONTA: For her it was!

JED: Yes, it would be nice to go back to the good old days, but . . .

YALLER: The hell it would!

JED: Wait, the thought suddenly struck me! We could use the past to help the present. Why don't we have us an Old Spanish Days Fiesta, complete with fandangos and horsemen, just like the good old days? We could celebrate your Spanish heritage! See those old adobe houses and missions; we'll preserve and restore all of them, start a Native Sons of the Golden West Chapter. What do you say?

RAMONA: (*Getting all excited along with her mother.*) Mamá, doesn't that sound like a great idea?

JED: We'll start off with a big parade, with Don Rico as the Grand Marshall.

RAMONA: You can wear your charro suit, Papá.

JED: Yes, and Doña Victoria can ride side saddle in her mantilla.

VICTORIA: Oh, but we never wore mantillas; those are Spanish, from Spain.

JED: We need lots of local color . . .

YALLER: Watch out!

JED: Mariachis, piñatas, sangría, Taco Bells! We'll haul the tourists in by the bus loads, real estate values will soar. Think of the jobs it will bring. (*Signalling the workers to help him with the cameras.*) We'll even film it.

RAMONA: Rancho Hollywood!

JED: Ramona, I'm going to make a big star out of you. Places everybody!

YALLER: Wait, it's all an illusion! (*Trying to stop the* RICO *family.*)

TONTA: It's just another trick! (*No one listens or even sees them.*) They're not listening to us, they've forgotten.

YALLER: I might as well be invisible. You might as well be a Wooden Indian.

TONTA: Let them play this scene out, they'll see the real picture. (*Sitting and watching.*)

JED: (*Donning beret and sunglasses, ala Hollywood director.*) Let's shoot the Spanish Grandee Balcony Scene. The fiery, impetuous Ramona is pacing nervously on her balcony waiting for her demon lover, Cisco. She is being fanned by her faithful Victoria. Yes, that's you, Vicky.

RICO: And who is playing the part of Cisco?

JED: To tell you the truth, Rico, we're having a little problem with central casting. The part calls for your typical Spanish Grandee Latin Lover Don Juan Cisco Kid Zorro type. Granted, you could pass for the worldly, debonair graying Ceasar Romero type, if only you weren't so (*Patting* RICO *on the stomach.*) portly. Look, Rico, I can overlook the paunch even, but, quite frankly, you're a little too old. Today's audience would not find a love affair between you and Ramona *credible*. Unless it was a Lolita scene, with lots of kinky sex.

RICO: Heaven forbid!

RAMONA: He's right, Papá, after all, you are old enough to be my father.

RICO: I am your father, you silly girl, or have you forgotten so soon? Well then, who is going to play my part?

JED: (*Donning* RICO'S *sombrero.*) I am!

RICO: I knew it! You're going to hear from my agent!

JED: (*Tying a black cloak around his shoulders.*) Besides, you're too dark. But wait, don't go! I do have a part for you. (RICO *stays, shoulder's bowed.*)

JED: Quiet, quiet on the set! (*Adjusting camera.*) Role 'em! The gay caballero, that's me, leaps off his Arabian stallion and hands the reins to his faithful sidekick, Pancho. That's you, Rico. Stand over there.

RICO: A non-speaking role!

JED: Your accent's too thick. Meanwhile, Ramona, dark eyes flashing, blood red lips pouting, waits anxiously with her maid.

VICTORIA: Her maid!

RAMONA: Do you want the line with or without the accent?

JED: From you I need an accent because you sound too Anglo.

RAMONA: Ayyyyyyy, is he not bold and dashing, my Cisco?

RICO: (*Tripping* JED *up as* JED *alights from the horse.*) I quit! Come on, Victoria.

JED: Ramona, I come to you. (*From the floor.*) Cut! Cut!

VICTORIA: Get someone else to play the maid! Ramona, are you coming with us?

RAMONA: But Mamá, this is my big chance, I'm going to be a star!

VICTORIA: It's up to you, you are a grown woman.

RAMONA: But where will you go? What will you do?

RICO: We'll go back to the land, that is where you'll find us.

JED: And the land belongs to me! Go ahead, become a Farmworker.

RICO: At least it's honest work. (*They exit.*)

RAMONA: My parents, they're gone! (*In tears.*)

JED: There, there, try a little of this, it will make you feel better. (*Offering her a white vial.*)

RAMONA: What is it?

JED: Cocaine. (*She declines. He takes a few snorts.*) And I was going to give Pancho and Vicky a Coors distributorship in Montebello. Well, let them go pick their grapes . . . of wrath. You see, Ramona, everybody works for me, there's no getting around it. There's thousands of players in this town who would die for a part in a Jedediah Goldbanger Production. Take those two over there (YALLER *and* TONTA *walk over.*) walking in for an audition. (*To* YALLER *as* RAMONA *sits and wipes her eyes, consoled by* TONTA.) What's your name these days, Mohammed?

YALLER: Kunta Kinte.

JED: Any experience?

YALLER: Slave, worker, invisible man.

JED: This part calls for a Mexican, but, you'll pass.

YALLER: Hah, they're worse off than we are!

JED: (*Handing him* RICO'S *sombrero.*) Put this sombrero on, it will cover your Afro.

YALLER: Just what kind of reality do you think you're showing here, anyway?

JED: This is a non-speaking role, Kunta, do you want it?

RAMONA: (*As* YALLER *stares at her.*) Please stay, I need help with this scene.

JED: (*As* YALLER *steps back,* TONTA *steps forward.*) Who's next?

TONTA: I am. My name is Sinmuhow, Spirit Woman, woman who knows many things.

JED: I'm sorry, but we don't need a woman like that. The part calls for a silent Latina.

TONTA: My first role was a maid. I also played concubines, Wooden Indians, and loyal scouts for the U.S. Cavalry.

JED: You're perfect! Try this shawl on. Very authentic. I love it! You're both hired.

TONTA: Wait a minute, what kind of audience are you trying to reach?

JED: A paying one.

TONTA: A white middle class audience, whose fantasies you need to titillate?

JED: What's wrong with that? Everybody needs a little escapism. Remember, during the Big Depression of the Thirties, the movie houses were always packed. Besides, *Ms.* Sinmuhow, I didn't ask for a marketing analysis. (*As he motions them to their positions.*) O.K. A hot and torrid tango is playing in the background. Ramona is steaming, the maid is trying to cool her down, and Pancho is, well, sleeping. Lights, camera, action!

RAMONA: Cisco!

JED: Ramona! My hot and sultry little Spanish spitfire, run away with me, your gay caballero, to the Rancho Grande of Ecstasy!

RAMONA: Ohhhhhhh, keeeeees me, I hear castanets crackling.

JED: I would smash my guitar, drink my blood for you. (*Kissing and feeling her all over.*)

YALLER: No plot.

TONTA: And X-Rated.

RAMONA: Ohhhhhh, it's no use, my heart isn't in it!

JED: What the hell does the heart have to do with it? (*Snorting some more coke.*) Want some?

RAMONA: No. You see, that's not the way the Californios really were, all that Spanish stuff.

JED: Look, I want you to go even more Spanish. We'll put some Flamenco music in, have Mario Lanza sing "Granada," put roses in your mouth.

RAMONA: But don't you see, you're distorting the Californio reality.

YALLER: Hey, girl, don't forget who you are, that's your shit he's messing with.

JED: Can't you just play it my way, for the cameras?

RAMONA: And another thing, I'm sick of playing these shallow, shadowy parts. As a Chicana and as a woman, you leave me with nothing, man.

JED: (*Pointing to audience.*) It's what *they* want, change their taste and I'll cast you as the first Chicana President of the United States. But until then, you'll play the parts I give you, otherwise go back to the Safeway and check out groceries.

RAMONA: I don't need your shit, man, there are other parts to play.

JED: No! Unless you play it my way, I'll have you black listed in every house, in every studio in town.

RAMONA: Just what is it you want me to do?

JED: The scene has got to be jazzed up. I want you to do it in the nude!

TONTA: He wants to prostitute you!

YALLER: Now the motherfucker is going to die!

RAMONA: You are out of your mind.

JED: Come on, you said you wanted to live in Beverly Hills.

RAMONA: All I said was I wanted to get out of East L.A. I didn't say anything about having to do a porno movie. Or are you going to tell me it's your "Art."

JED: I don't care what you call it. You do it my way or I'll get a gringa to do it! I'll have you deported back to East L.A. Then I'll build a wall between here and the west side. How would you like that, you chile pepper!

RAMONA: You can't do that. You can't turn me into something I'm not. It scares me to think that I might even be acting your way off camera.

JED: Ramona, you know my powers. I can etch your image forever on the diamond screen of time. Or I can rub your face into the mud.

RAMONA: I would tell you to go to hell, but you are already in it.

TONTA: (*Handing her a gun.*) Ramona, here is your father's gun . . .

JED: (*Back tracking.*) Hey, the scene calls for the maid to shed salty tears which fall like a gentle shower on Pancho's wide sombrero . . .

YALLER: Blow him out of your mind . . .

JED: And Pancho's supposed to be curled up against the wall fast asleep.

RAMONA: (*Advancing on* JED; *backed up by* YALLER *and* TON- TA.) They're right! I have to rid myself of twisted images. (*Pointing gun at* JED.) You have poisoned me and all my generation!

JED: Hey, wait, this is just a play! Come on, cut, cut! The End! (*Lights low,* JED *drops to the floor.*)

RAMONA: And yet, it's not entirely your fault. (*Pointing gun at audience.*) Them, out there, they're also to blame. For all those little children whose minds and emotions have been eaten away by the venom that spurts out of the screens and tubes and stages. (*Dropping the gun, holding her head in her hands.*) Ohhhhhhhh God, the stereotypes, they had me believing them! (*She exits.*)

JED: Ramona, wait, don't go, don't leave me alone. Oh Jesus, is it really as bad as she says?

YALLER: That's right, motherfucker, and you better get hip to it. Those Superfly Superstud Baaaaaaad Asssss ghetto spectaculars are not what's happening, dig? Don't you go laying that shit on us! (*Standing over* JED.)

JED: OK. Man! OK! But there's also Roots, Sanford and Son, The Wiz, Baraka! Ed Bullins! Raisin in the Sun! (YALLER *exits.*)

TONTA: What about me, aren't you going to ask me to play Cowboys and Indians with you?

JED: Dustin Hoffman did Custer's Last Stand the real way. Marlon Brando refused an Oscar, gave it to the Indians.

TONTA: You owe us a lot more than that. (*She exits.*)

JED: All right, I'll make it up to you, I'll make it up to all of you. (*Walking all over, looking for them.*) Only don't leave me alone, I need you! Hey! (*Downstage, to the audience.*) What more do they want? Is it my fault what my ancestors did? I wasn't there. So now it's my turn to go through this big guilt trip, right? Hey, look, forget the past. Let's talk about right here and now. (*Turning around, he notices the players putting a new set together. A long table with chairs, steaming plates of food. There is a gate to the entrance of the dining room.* RICO *stands guard.*) I better go and see what they are up to.

RICO: (*Blocking* JED'S *way as he tries to enter. The players are about to sit down for dinner.*) You can't come in here.

JED: Why not?

RICO: You weren't invited.

JED: But I live here too!

RICO: We don't have any room, it's getting very crowded.

JED: Don't give me that, I'm in the majority around here.

RICO: Taking all of us so-called colored people into account, you are in the minority, not only here, but everywhere!

JED: Says who?

RICO: Says us. We just rewrote the script. Not only that, we have our own director, and we are playing all the parts.

JED: There's no part for me? But I have a lot to offer: technology, commerce, art. Please, I'm hungry.

RICO: Let me go and ask the rest of the people. (RICO *confers with the others, they nod approval although there are a few dissenters.*) Yes, there is a place for you, although the vote was close.

JED: (*Entering and sitting at the center of the table.*) My name is Jed. I'm from Los Angeles, California. (*Everyone surrounds him; it is like a scene from The Last Supper.*)

RICO: You are welcome.

RAMONA: Yes, that is our goal, we want *everyone* to like it here.

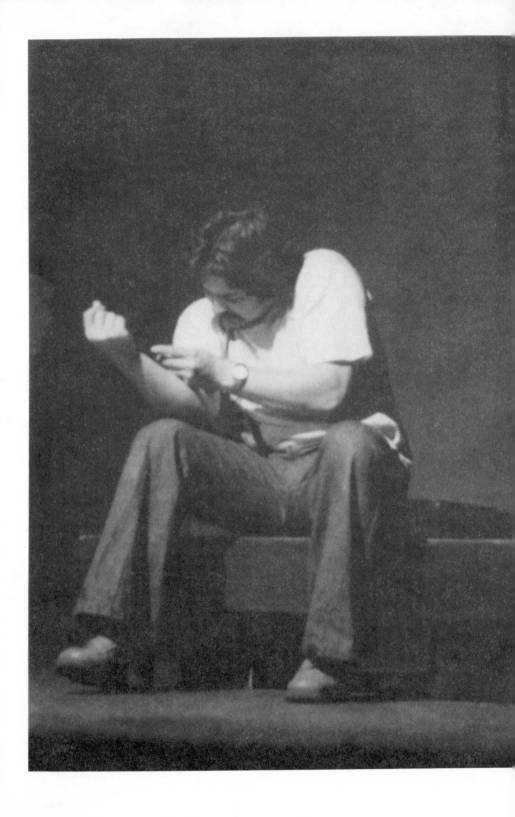

Rubén Sierra

MANOLO

Manolo *is Rubén Sierra's second published work, preceded by* La Raza Pura, or Racial, Racial *published in 1976.*[1] *Whereas the first play was a multi-media piece which dealt with racial intolerance and discrimination on both sides of the color line,* Manolo *is the first Chicano play to deal with the drug addiction of a Vietnam veteran. More significantly, the play is written in a realistic style and presents a series of conflicts and confrontations in the tradition of good melodrama. Of course, El Teatro Campesino's* Vietnam Campesino *and* Soldado Razo *were written during the apex of that war and exposed the inequities of the economic system, the draft, and the war itself from within the* acto *format.*[2] *But niether of these* actos *extended beyond the time-space of the war, both ending with the death of the Chicano on Vietnamese soil.*[3]

A veteran of Vietnam himself and a careful observer of life in his own San Antonio barrio, Sierra has created well-rounded characters, figures that internalize the very contradictions that the war and life in the barrios represent. The protagonist, MANOLO *is inherently good, yes, but we find him at his lowest point, unable to cope with his situation and thus under the control of psychological and physical addiction. Some might call this a tragic flaw, but the play is not a classical tragedy, and as a contempory statement on one man's condition, we can simply say that* MANOLO *is heir to human weakness. We are told that* MANOLO *did good deeds for the barrio, although these acts are never fully explained, leaving the audience and reader to discover for themselves what* MANOLO *might have done in their community. By not listing* MANOLO'S *contributions to the barrio the playwright has avoided too much concern with his protagonist's past deeds, focusing on his present struggles.*

---

1. See: Roberto J. Garza, *Contemporary Chicano Theatre,* University of Notre Dame Press, 1976, pp. 60—101. For a review of that play, see: Jorge A. Huerta, "From Quetzalcoatl to Honest Sancho"; A Review of *Contemporary Chicano Theatre,* in *Revista Chicano-Riqueña, V, No. 3 (Verano, 1977), pp.38-40.*

2. See: Luis Valdez, *Actos,* Cucaracha Publications, 1971, pp. 104-44. *Vietnam Campesino* also appeared in Henry Lesnick, *Guerilla Street Theatre,* Avon Books, 1973, pp. 225-249.

3. Luis Valdez's *Dark Root of a Scream* is an extension of his teatro's two actos on the war, bringing the veteran's body home. See: Lilian Faderman and Omar Salinas *From the Barrio,* Canfield Press, 1973, pp. 79-98. Another play which brings a Chicano Viet-Vet home is *A Barrio Tragedy,* scripted by Raúl Estrada, Joe Olvera and Leo Rojas and published in *Caracol,* IV, No. 7 (March, 1978), pp. 16-22. In this brief dramatization the veterano is not a heroin addict, but through a series of circumstances is shot by the police and dies. For an analysis of this play see: Ricardo D. Aguilar's review in *Caracol,* IV, No. 11 (Julio, 1978), pp. 20; and Jorge A. Huerta's review in *Tenaz Talks Teatro,* I, No. 2 (Spring, 1978) pp. 6-7.

Because MANOLO *is so human, and so forlorn, we cannot help but sympathise with him. His interactions with his friends, his childhood sweetheart, and his enemies, demonstrate a compassion that we can respond to emotionally. Everybody likes* MANOLO *for differing reasons, but they all unfortunately lie in the past—what* MANOLO *used to be before the war. We only saw him once—the opening scene—before he was thrust into his living nightmare, but that glimpse of a happy, sensitive young man being sent to a war nobody understood must remain in our minds as a constant reminder throughout the play that any of us could experience what* MANOLO *did. Ultimately we come to realize that one of the tragic results of the Vietnam conflict was the depriving of the barrio of the strong and dedicated young men who could bring about the progress of its people.*

Manolo *presents us with characters that are drawn with a careful eye, with proper shading of light and dark areas, giving full-bodied people rather than flat cartoon figures. While stereotypes are limited by the playwright in his attempt to present us with living beings,* LOUIE *is perhaps the only one-dimensional character in the play.* LOUIE *is evil and he believes that no one is incorruptible. But unlike his two henchmen,* BIMBO *and* TANK, LOUIE *is very smart. He knows what he wants and will stop at nothing to get it. But because of* MANOLO'S *complexities, the typical good versus evil scenario has been avoided when* LOUIE *is pitted against the protagonist.* LOUIE *represents the Evil that* MANOLO *could have been addressing had he not been struggling with his own interior conflicts.* MANOLO *is at his weakest and has found an adversary even greater than* LOUIE: *himself. Such is the effect of his addiction.*

Set in a barrio and employing barrio types, this play is quite a challenge to its production staff, demanding careful designing and acting in order to be most effective. If overplayed, Manolo *can resemble a typical soap opera or telenovela; acted with a realistic freedom, the play can hold its audience until the final curtain. As indicated in the stage directions, the setting can be very sparse, and lighting should be an important element in the quick transitions or movement from one locale to another. A sound designer would also find broad avenues for creativity, adding to the scene changes and blackouts with sound effects and musical transitions. The playwright has purposely left the design staff a great deal of freedom by indicating scenes as "somewhere in the barrio."*

Teatro Quetzalcoatl, directed by Rubén Sierra himself, opened Manolo *in 1976 and toured it through the barrios of Aztlán from Texas to Washington state. The tour began in a Mexican restaurant in Brownsville where, in the playwright's words, "We moved the tables back, set up our props and ran it. The people loved us and we were off and running." From there the teatro went to San Antonio, then to Colorado where the mayor and city council of Pueblo made the troop honorary citizens, and proclaimed Drug Awareness Day in honor of their performances there. Wherever the teatro toured the play, it received standing ovations from the community audiences. A realistic production like* Manolo *is certainly new to most barrios and the appreciation of the community was the group's greatest reward.*

MANOLO

CHARACTERS:

Manolo, *a drug addict*
Domingo, *his best friend*
Teresa, *Manolo's girlfriend*
Dr. Shain, *a psychiatrist*
El Louie, *drug pusher*
Sgt. Jiménez, *police detective,*
   narco

María, *Teresa's friend*
Carmela, *María's younger sister*
Bimbo, *one of Louie's henchmen*
Tank, *one of Louie's henchmen*
Chano, *low-riding cat burglar*
Joey Boy, *María's younger*
   brother

SETTING:

The play takes place in the barrio of a city in the Southwest. Two scenes are flashbacks to Manolo's past. The set can represent various locations such as the street, the park, the interior of Manolo's small apartment. Much can be done with lighting and a minimal number of properties and set pieces to suggest different locales. It is important to keep the set flexible and not attempt any kind of super-realism within it. It should be simple.

ACT ONE, Scene 1

Somewhere in the Barrio. When the lights rise, we discover MANOLO *and* TERESA.

TERESA: I'm afraid, Manolo . . .
MANOLO: (*Holding her in his arms.*) Por favor . . . please don't be.
TERESA: (*Trying to fight back tears.*) Anything could happen to you, you could change . . .
MANOLO: Come on, you know me better than that. (*Looking into her eyes.*)
TERESA: (*Holding him tightly.*) Te quiero tanto.
MANOLO: (*Comforting her.*) I know . . . I know . . .
TERESA: You could get shot.
MANOLO: No way. I'm too fast.
TERESA: Stop making dumb jokes.
MANOLO: Dumb jokes? Me?
TERESA: Sí.
MANOLO: Okay mamasita, whatever you say.
TERESA: Manolo!
MANOLO: I can't help it if you're a mamasita.
TERESA: Will you write me?
MANOLO: Only if you write back.
TERESA: I'm going to miss you, you big tonto.
MANOLO: Who's tonto?
TERESA: You are.
MANOLO: Cut me some slack, mujer.
TERESA: Tonto.
MANOLO: I may be a lot of things, but I'm not tonto. (DOMINGO *enters on the last line. He is* TERESA'S *older brother and best friend of* MANOLO. *He is medium height and build and is an optimist by nature.*)
DOMINGO: Whose tonto?
TERESA: Manolo is.
DOMINGO: This is true.
MANOLO: You've got room to talk.
DOMINGO: Genius runs in my family.
MANOLO: ¿O sí?
DOMINGO: Look at my sister, Teresa.

MANOLO: Her only drawback is being your sister.

DOMINGO: That's not a nice thing to say . . . pero considering the source, I will let it slide.

MANOLO: All the way up your nose.

TERESA: Stop acting like niños!

MANOLO: Mingo can't help it. He never grew up.

DOMINGO: That comes from following you around.

TERESA: You interrupted our conversation.

DOMINGO: Excuse me please one time too manys!

MANOLO: I've been drafted, dummy!

DOMINGO: What?

MANOLO: D-r-a-f-t-e-d. Drafted.

DOMINGO: (*Laughing.*) Look out Uncle Sam here comes Super- MEX! Private Chicano . . . after a week he'll probably organize a huelga.

TERESA: Sí, chistoso, I'm sure.

DOMINGO: Can you see it? During bayonet practice Manolo will probably pull out a switchblade . . . "Sí señor, Mr. Drill Sgt. But Mr. Drill Sgt. that is my bayonet . . . barrio style." (*Laughing*)

TERESA: You're as tonto as Manolo.

MANOLO: Por eso somos amigos.

DOMINGO: Right on, ese!

TERESA: This is nothing to laugh about! Try to be serious for a change.

DOMINGO: Yes, man.

TERESA: Mingo!

DOMINGO: I'm just agreeing.

(CHANO *enters. He is thin and of medium height. A low riding cat burglar who speaks with his own kind of slang.*)

CHANO: Boogie . . . boogie . . . boogie! ¿Pos qué pasa, batos? Hello, bros and sister.

MANOLO: What's cooking, Chano?

CHANO: Zipping down the street, over buildings, over fences, through windows and doors, taking what I can, when I can, if I can. Chano número uno is here. Manolo my bro, grapevine has it that Uncle Ding Ding is ringing on your doorbell.

MANOLO: Simón.

CHANO: Uh! uh! uh! Cut down in your prime.

TERESA: He hasn't been cut down.

CHANO: Humble apologies, sis, just meant it as a figure of speech. (*Pause.*) Grapevine is saying some other things, Manolo, my bro.

MANOLO: What, Chano?

CHANO: Barrio is due for a re-vamp.

MANOLO: What d'you mean, Chano?

CHANO: Dudes is moving in.

MANOLO: What kind?

CHANO: Nothing but heavies, my bro, nothing but heavies. El Louie is out of the joint.

DOMINGO: He's a punk.

CHANO: Word has it that his new racket is junk.

MANOLO: Junk?

CHANO: Simón, my bro . . . junk!

DOMINGO: From pimp to pusher. Just like that bastard.

MANOLO: So what else is coming down in the barrio, Chano? Any good news?

CHANO: Right on, bro! Let me check out my memory bank . . . oh yes, Elsa Sánchez gave birth to cuates last night.

TERESA: To cuates?

CHANO: One macho and one girl.

DOMINGO: I bet Pete is unglued about that.

CHANO: He went out and got so drunk it took him three hours to get home.

TERESA: Typical.

MANOLO: The guy must be overwhelmed, Teresa.

TERESA: Sí, I'll bet he was.

CHANO: To continue my report, Jiménez was shot last night.

DOMINGO: ¿La jura, Jiménez?

CHANO: ¡Simón! Took a bullet in the chest during a drug bust on the northside when some white dude tried to make a run for it.

TERESA: Is he alright?

CHANO: He'll be okay but the white dude got blasted by a shotgun and was killed.

MANOLO: At least it didn't happen in one of our barrios.

CHANO: This was rich city, bro. The white dude turned out to be the son of some rich businessman on the north side.

DOMINGO: Let 'em kill themselves off for all I care.

MANOLO: Let's hope it never happens here.

CHANO: Right on, bro! All them fuzz hanging around could be bad for business.

MANOLO: Bad for the barrio.

CHANO: (*Looking at watch.*) My Mickey Mouse says I got to make tracks, but I will catch you before you split, bro. By the way, when are you splitting?

MANOLO: Una semana.

CHANO: So soon?

DOMINGO: El tío wants him bad.

CHANO: No envy on my part, bro, I'm just glad I got my 4F.

MANOLO: Want to trade?

CHANO: Like I said, bro, I think I hear my mother calling and so I'll make like the wind and smoke away. Later, bros and sister! (*He exits and they laugh and say goodbye.*)

DOMINGO: That Chano's a nut.

MANOLO: He sure is, but he's one helluva guy.

TERESA: He's a thief.

DOMINGO: A cat burglar.

TERESA: He steals, doesn't he?

MANOLO: His standing motto is never hit the same place twice and only steal from those who gots.

TERESA: A modern Robin Hood.

DOMINGO: Or Joaquín Murieta.

MANOLO: He's a good guy with a big corazón.

DOMINGO: Speaking of corazón, I've got to get to the store and pick up a Valentine card for Mom. (*He exits.*)

MANOLO: (*To Teresa.*) What can I give you for Valentine's Day?

TERESA: Promise me you'll come back safe.

MANOLO: That's a promise.

TERESA: Hold me, Manolo. (*He does so.*) Te quiero.

MANOLO: Y yo también te quiero.

The lights fade out and in the distance the sound of wind. Several seconds pass to the next scene as machine-gun fire is heard along with men marching to the cadence of: "I want to be an airborne Ranger . . . I want to live a life of danger . . . I want to go to Viet-Nam . . ." The stage is dark and when Shain begins to speak, a special comes up on him standing on USR Platform. As MANOLO speaks DSL a special comes up on him. They remain in specials.

SHAIN: Sgt. Garza! (*No answer.*) Sgt. Garza!

MANOLO: Yes, sir.

SHAIN: Do you think you're ready?

MANOLO: Yes, sir.

SHAIN: You've been here a long time.

MANOLO: Fourteen months . . . sir.

SHAIN: Adjustment will be a problem for you at first, but you will learn to adjust. You're strong, intelligent . . .

MANOLO: I'm a junkie.

SHAIN: You must learn to deal with that. What do you feel right now?

MANOLO: Lonely.

SHAIN: And?

MANOLO: Afraid.

SHAIN: What are you afraid of?

MANOLO: Adjusting. I've never ever really been scared of anything or anybody and now all of a sudden I even jump at my own shadow. Sounds dumb, doesn't it?

SHAIN: It isn't unusual, I get scared too.

MANOLO: Of what?

SHAIN: Giving the wrong advice. (*Pause.*)

MANOLO: So what happens now?

SHAIN: You have to learn how to deal with yourself and your addiction.

MANOLO: What about Nam?

SHAIN: What about it?

MANOLO: How do I forget?

SHAIN: You never will entirely.

MANOLO: Why did we stay in Nam?

SHAIN: Politics I guess.

MANOLO: It always seems to boil down to politics, doesn't it, doc?

SHAIN: We committed ourselves.

MANOLO: We committed the people, the poor slob in the streets who could give a damn about Viet Nam or Cambodia or any other fucking place but his own backyard.

SHAIN: War is like that sometimes.

MANOLO: Yeah it is, isn't it? (*Pause.*) How many ended up junkies like me?

SHAIN: It's hard to tell . . . there were many.

MANOLO: Stinking, fucking war! And what the hell was it all about? Whenever you ask anybody, nobody seems to have an answer. Defending Democracy! What the fuck from? People are starving in this country right now and what do we do about it?

SHAIN: What do you want to do about it?

MANOLO: That's the problem, doc. I hate myself.

SHAIN: Hate can destroy you. Don't live in the past!

MANOLO: Why not?

SHAIN: There are too may things to do right now and in the future. Unless of course you want to kill yourself slowly with self-pity.

MANOLO: No I don't.

SHAIN: Then forget about Nam and what it did to you.

MANOLO: I keep having dreams . . . nightmares. Sometimes I wake up screaming . . . shaking all over like a scared little boy. I'm a grown man, but the little boy in me wants to keep coming out. Do you ever cry? I do. I cry . . . covered in sweat . . . I cry. I feel lost. You ever see a man get blown to bits? Not very pretty. Brains, bone, blood . . . women and children running and screaming . . . trying to get away from the bombs. Trying to stay alive. My nightmares are real and even when I'm awake I can still see them. I want to hit something, to strike back . . . but who do I hit? And who gives a damn?

SHAIN: You're alive.

MANOLO: I'm a junkie.

SHAIN: And you always will be.

MANOLO: Then maybe I'm just half alive, huh doc?

SHAIN: Not everything is ugly.

MANOLO: I used to think so, now I'm not so sure.

SHAIN: If you want to exist then you have to look for the good things, not just the bad.

MANOLO: I've got to go now. It's time and my bus is coming.

SHAIN: Don't ever quit trying!

MANOLO: Sure doc. (*Pause.*) Maybe someday I'll write about all this and laugh about it.

SHAIN: I think you should write about it.

MANOLO: Yeah, I can see me now: "the new great American novelist."

SHAIN: Why not?

MANOLO: I don't think this country is ready for a Chicano Mark Twain. (*Pause.*) See you, Dr. Shain.

SHAIN: Goodbye, Manolo. Take care of yourself.

The lights fade out slowly. Three months have passed and Manolo has returned to drugs. As the lights come up Manolo is sleeping on USL platform. Domingo is standing DSR looking out a window. After a moment Manolo stirs.

MANOLO: (*Tries to get up; feels dizzy.*) O-o-o-h! I feel like I've been run over by a truck.

DOMINGO: Es temprano, get some rest.

MANOLO: You got a frajo?

DOMINGO: Simón. (*Crosses to him and lights it.*) Ten. How do you feel?

MANOLO: How long you been here?

DOMINGO: Toda la noche.

MANOLO: No me acuerdo. I don't remember.

DOMINGO: I found you last night in a gutter next to a phone booth. Estabas bien loco and you were crying.

MANOLO: ¡YA! No quiero saber. (*Pause.*) Why didn't you just leave me there?

DOMINGO: La chota was coming and I didn't want you to get arrested.

MANOLO: ¿Y qué? So I'd spend a night in jail.

DOMINGO: Más que una noche . . . you had this in your hand. (*Holds out nickel bag of junk.*)

MANOLO: (*Grabbing it.*) Give it here, ¡es mío! (*Pause.*) What do you care?

DOMINGO: ¿Por qué, Manolo?

MANOLO: Because. ¿Y qué?

DOMINGO: You're going to kill yourself with that shit!

MANOLO: It's my life and I can do any fucking thing I want with it.

DOMINGO: ¡Pendejo! Don't be stupid!

MANOLO: Fuck you!

DOMINGO: How long you been on this stuff?

MANOLO: I don't know. What difference does it make?

DOMINGO: It makes a lot of difference. You can see a doctor, get some help.

MANOLO: What do you know? Anyway I've been that route and it doesn't make a damn bit of difference. After Nam, estaba prendido and I was sent to a rehab center. I spent fourteen pinche meses in that fucking center.

DOMINGO: So what happened? ¿Qué té pasó?

MANOLO: I came back to this pinche barrio, that's what happened. It hasn't changed, in fact it's worse.

DOMINGO: Why don't you try to change it instead of feeling sorry for yourself?

MANOLO: How the fuck do you expect me to change it?

DOMINGO: Puedes comenzar by getting off your ass and getting rid of that shit going through your arms.

MANOLO: Is that going to bring back my jefita and my carnal? Is it?

DOMINGO: I'm sorry about your mother y tu carnal, but being an addict isn't going to do you or them any good. Do you think your jefita would want to see you like this? Don't disgrace her memory by turning to drogas as an escape. Carnal, listen to me!

MANOLO: Dios mío, I've tried y no puedo. I can't. Everytime I close my eyes I see my mamá looking at me saying, "hijo mío vaya con Dios." Those were the last words I heard her say before I left to that stinking war in Nam.

DOMINGO: Carnal, yo té ayudo . . . if you'll let me.

MANOLO: She died alone and I couldn't do anything to help her.

DOMINGO: She wasn't alone, her friends were with her.

MANOLO: BUT I WASN'T! (Silence.) I couldn't bring myself home to see her. When I was notified that she was dead I didn't cry . . . all I could do was stare. "Mi jefa is dead," I said. "But how can that be?" I flew home to the funeral and then back to Nam the next day. I wanted to go back . . . I wanted to die!

DOMINGO: You have to forget all that!

MANOLO: GODDAMNIT, EVERYBODY WANTS ME TO TRY AND FORGET! No puedo, I can't forget . . . I can't . . .

DOMINGO: I'm sorry.

MANOLO: How can I make it work, Mingo? I used to know how y ahora nada. I can't help remembering and living in the past, pero right now in the pinche present . . . that's hard. Can you tell me how?

DOMINGO: No. I don't have a magic formula . . . I just try to take the good with the bad.

MANOLO: What's good? Being a tecato is good? War is good? Hate is good? This pinche barrio is good?

DOMINGO: Do you hate the barrio?

MANOLO: Simón, I hate it! (Pause.) I don't know what I hate.

DOMINGO: You've got a lifetime in front of you.

MANOLO: I haven't got anything but shit in front of me.

DOMINGO: You really think that?

MANOLO: That's a fact.

DOMINGO: What about Teresa?

MANOLO: What about her?

DOMINGO: She loves you! She's loved you since we were niños.

MANOLO: That was before.

DOMINGO: ¿Antes de qué?

MANOLO: Before I became a junkie . . . a tecato.

DOMINGO: So you decided she doesn't love you anymore?

MANOLO: Simón, I decided.

DOMINGO: (Angry.) And who the fuck are you, God?

MANOLO: Don't hassle me, Mingo!

DOMINGO: O perdón, you know everything, nobody loves . . . nobody cares . . .

MANOLO: Shut up!

DOMINGO: Go see a doctor!

MANOLO: I DON'T WANT TO SEE ANY PINCHE DOCTOR!

DOMINGO: ¡TE PUEDE AYUDAR!

MANOLO: I DON'T WANT ANY HELP!

DOMINGO: (Exasperated.) Aw man, you don't know what you want! (Starts to exit.)

MANOLO: Mingo!

DOMINGO: (*Stopping.*) ¡Qué!

MANOLO: Tú eres mi mejor amigo . . . you're my best friend . . . you know that?

DOMINGO: (*Calming down.*) I'll be back later when you're not feeling so terco.

MANOLO: Orale, nos vemos.

DOMINGO: ¿Tienes hambre?

MANOLO: No, I'm not hungry.

DOMINGO: But you've got to eat.

MANOLO: Don't start, okay?

DOMINGO: Sure. Get some rest.

MANOLO: Simón, I will. (*El* LOUIE, the local pusher, pimp, appears. He is tall, slim, and mean looking. He dresses flashy but with a certain style and class. He is as shrewd as he is ruthless.)

LOUIE: ¿Pues qué pasa, esos batos?

DOMINGO: (*With hate.*) Well if it isn't the local pimp. What the hell do you want?

LOUIE: What kind of a way is that to say hello, Mingo?

DOMINGO: I'm not saying hello . . . I'm saying goodbye, stupid.

MANOLO: What do you want?

LOUIE: Estos batos. It's just a friendly social call. Oh, and Mingo, I ain't no pimp, dig? I'm a businessman.

DOMINGO: You're a third rate punk!

LOUIE: No me insultes, dig? Stay cool!

DOMINGO: I'll stay cool when I want to stay cool.

LOUIE: What did you eat for breakfast, alka-seltzer tablets?

MANOLO: Well, Louie?

LOUIE: Cálmala, ese. Give me a chansa.

MANOLO: Don't call me ese!

LOUIE: Orale, whatever you say . . . heavy dude. (*Enters and walks around.*)

DOMINGO: Let me throw him out, Manolo.

MANOLO: Not yet.

LOUIE: ¿Qué eres tú, his bodyguard or something?

DOMINGO: Or something.

LOUIE: Maybe I should have said watchdog, bow, wow! (*He chuckles.*)

DOMINGO: In that case you better watch your ass because I may decide to bite it off.

LOUIE: Este bato, ¡chuléate ya!

MANOLO: Louie!

LOUIE: Simón. (*Pause, he gives* MINGO *a dirty look.*) Can I talk in front of your dog? (*No reply.*) Orale, I will then. (*Crossing away.*) Punto number one: ¿cuánto is your habit costing?

MANOLO: Too much.

LOUIE: Simón, I can dig it. So how do you pay for it?

MANOLO: I make out.

LOUIE: How would you like to make some real heavy feria?

MANOLO: Doing what?

LOUIE: I need somebody who knows the barrio, somebody la gente respects. I figure that's you.

MANOLO: What makes you think I'd work for a punk like you?

LOUIE: You got a habit, you need money. I can help you, you can help me.

MANOLO: Chale. I won't help you. Even if I could, mejor me mato primero before I'd lift a finger to help you.

DOMINGO: Why don't you crawl back the way you came in, Louie?

LOUIE: (*Loud.*) Like I'm talking to the man, not you punk! (*Pause.*) You could make five hundred grandes a week and have all the horse you need.

MANOLO: No deal.

LOUIE: That's too bad, ese.

MANOLO: For you or for me?

LOUIE: For you. You see, Manolo, the streets are empty.

MANOLO: What do you mean?

LOUIE: No junk.

DOMINGO: He doesn't need it.

LOUIE: ¿Todavía estás aquí?

MANOLO: (*Fear in his voice.*) No junk?

LOUIE: Está seco. Dry baby, dry. Like it's no place to be found.

MANOLO: There's always junk.

LOUIE: No way, ese. There's nothing to be had. No more joy juice for your arm, ese.

DOMINGO: Bastard!

LOUIE: Up yours! (MINGO *attacks* LOUIE.)

MANOLO: (*Stopping* MINGO.) No Mingo!

LOUIE: Come on ese Mingo, be a hero.

MANOLO: That's enough, Louie!

LOUIE: Come on puto, try something!

MANOLO: Ya corta tu pedo, Louie!

DOMINGO: Someday, Louie, I promise you.

LOUIE: Simón, someday you're going to waste me. Bullshit!

MANOLO: You got anything else to say?

LOUIE: Chale. But you're a fool, Manolo.

MANOLO: Chansa, but I'll go cold turkey if I have to.

LOUIE: (*Laughs.*) You'll do what? You're crazy, ese.

MANOLO: Maybe. But I sure as hell don't need you.

LOUIE: You ever gone the cold turkey before? Have you ever seen anybody go that way? Your body screams with pain and you puke on yourself and you twist and turn and shit in your pants. Cold turkey, my ass. You're a tecato, ese. Your body doesn't just need junk it craves it!

MANOLO: I'll manage.

LOUIE: No you won't, ese. You're going to die like some pinche perro in the streets, real slow and painful.

DOMINGO: (*Knocks* LOUIE *to ground.*) ¡Pinche cabrón! ¡Te voy a matar! (MANOLO *grabs* DOMINGO *and shoves him away from* LOUIE.)

LOUIE: (*Gets up and pulls out switchblade.*) Come on, Sundance Kid, I'm going to carve you like a piece of carne!

DOMINGO: (*Trying to break loose from* MANOLO.) ¡Déjame, Manolo!

MANOLO: It's not worth it! Now, cálmate! (MINGO *relaxes a bit.*) Get out of here, Louie!

LOUIE: Sure. (*To* MINGO.) Next time you lay a finger on me you're the one who's going to be dead, dig?

DOMINGO: Stupid punk!

LOUIE: Simón! (*Pause.*) You're making a big mistake, Manolo. I could help you. But why don't you ask your nursemaid to help you?

MANOLO: Split, Louie, before I decide to kick your ass myself, dig?

LOUIE: Have it your way, ese. (*Starts to exit.*) One last thing, though. If you do get a hold of some stuff, make sure it's the right thing, otherwise it might kill you. (*He grins.*) And I wouldn't like to see that happen to you, dig?

MANOLO: Don't worry your ugly ass about it.

LOUIE: ¿Quién está worried? Well, alli los watcho. (*Turns.*) Be cool, dig! (*Exits laughing.*)

DOMINGO: You should have let me beat the hell out of the son-of-a-bitch.

MANOLO: Chale. Besides if you did he'd send his goons after you, and *that* I wouldn't want.

DOMINGO: No le tengo miedo.

MANOLO: Who's being stupid now, hothead?

DOMINGO: That bastard pisses me off!

MANOLO: El no vale nada, so don't worry about it.

DOMINGO: You're right, but I'd still like to rearrange his face. (*Pause.*) What are you going to do now?

MANOLO: No sé.

DOMINGO: Maybe you should see . . .

MANOLO: Don't say it!

DOMINGO: What?

MANOLO: About going to see a doctor or whatever, I don't want to hear it.

DOMINGO: ¿Por qué? You could get some help.

MANOLO: Chale. I don't care about that.

DOMINGO: But there are doctors and clinics . . .

MANOLO: ¡Ya! I said no!

DOMINGO: Then why don't you go along with el Louie?

MANOLO: Cut me some slack will you?

DOMINGO: You're scared aren't you? I can see you are scared.

MANOLO: ¿Y qué? So I'm scared, who gives a shit?

DOMINGO: I give a shit.

MANOLO: My time has run out Mingo, can't you see that?

DOMINGO: Only if you want it to.

MANOLO: ¿Sabes por qué soy tecato? Porque I couldn't handle Nam, and I couldn't handle losing my jefita and my carnal, because this barrio stinks . . .

DOMINGO: You've got to fight it!

MANOLO: I use drugs, remember? That's how I fight it.

DOMINGO: Give it time, you'll find another way!

MANOLO: ¡No tengo tiempo! No time, ese, just memories. (*Pause.*) Mingo, my life turned out to be rotten and I've got to live with it. I got no choices. I went to war, I had no choice. I came back to the barrio, because where else could I go? I went to drogas because I couldn't find any other choice. So let's just leave it at that. (*Pause.*) ¿Tiempo? What time have I got? My jefita's dead, my brother's dead and I'm dead too. In Nam there was death, in the barrio is death . . . I can't seem to get away from death. Everywhere I turn or go la muerte is waiting. Espérame, I will join you soon. The barrio seems to call out my name y me dice, "Manolo tu tiempo has come and you must die!" So why should I disappoint it? ¿Cuál tiempo tengo? ¿Cuál? (*The lights fade and in the distance the cry of voices.*)

As the lights fade up, one day has passed. MANOLO *is seated in his living/bedroom, staring off into space, when a knock is heard at the door. He ignores it. Knock again.* TERESA *speaks from behind the door.*

TERESA: Manolo!

MANOLO: (*Turning.*) ¿Quién es?

TERESA: Teresa.

MANOLO: Teresa? What are you doing here?

TERESA: I want to see you. Open the door.

MANOLO: (*Crossing to door and opening it.*) ¿Por qué?

TERESA: (*Standing at doorway.*) Quiero hablar contigo.

MANOLO: What about?

TERESA: You haven't come to see me since you got back, and I wanted to know how you were. (*Enters room.*)

MANOLO: Estoy bien. Please leave me alone!

TERESA: What's the matter with you? Why are you doing this?

MANOLO: I just want to be alone . . . I need to think, to work things out.

TERESA: I want to help you.

MANOLO: Help me how?

TERESA: What's happened to you, Manolo? I know you have problems but why have you stayed away from me? Have I done something to hurt or upset you?

MANOLO: No. (*Pause.*) I'm not the same anymore; can't you see that?

TERESA: I can see that you're in pain and you seem troubled, ¡pero déjame ayudarte, por favor!

MANOLO: Nadie puede ayudarme. Mi vida ya no es mía.

TERESA: That's not true; you mustn't think like that.

MANOLO: Soy tecato. (*No reply.*) Did you hear me? I said I'm a junkie, and a good for nothing junkie. Now please leave me alone!

TERESA: How can I leave you alone? Soy mujer y te quiero. Don't you understand that? I love you. (*He turns away.*) Please Manolo, don't ignore me like if you don't care, because I know you do.

MANOLO: Please Teresa, I can't even look at you without feeling ashamed. Leave me alone, please.

TERESA: You've never let anything beat you before; don't start now! I want to be with you and I want to help you.

MANOLO: There's nothing you can do.

TERESA: No one's condemning you.

MANOLO: I've condemned myself.

TERESA: You've got friends, people that care about you.

MANOLO: Why should anyone care?

TERESA: You did a lot of good things for people in this barrio and they don't forget, you know that.

MANOLO: I'm in the gutter, Teresa.

TERESA: No you're not.

MANOLO: Las drogas have me. They control me. I can't help myself . . . can't or won't, what difference does it make?

TERESA: You're alive, and as long as you're alive you can learn to fight it. You mustn't give up.

MANOLO: How can I look at my friends cuando tengo tanta vergüenza? I've created a prison for myself . . . pero you can't see the bars porque están en mi cabeza. I can't even feel my soul anymore.

TERESA: My dear, sweet Manolo, ¿qué te han hecho? What have they done to you?

MANOLO: I've done it to myself. (*Pause.*)

TERESA: (*Extends her hand.*) Aquí está mi mano, open to you as it always has been . . . please take it.

MANOLO: (*Manolo looks at her for a moment and starts to cross to her.*) Teresa, I . . . (*They embrace.*)

TERESA: Don't say anything. Just hold me and let me hold you. (*He holds her with a strong embrace as if he is clinging to his last chance.*) I'm going to help you. Everything is going to be alright, you'll see. (*A female voice is heard calling out the name of Teresa.*)

MANOLO: (*Pulling away.*) Who's that?

TERESA: Sounds like María. (*Cross to door, opens and shuts it.*) ¡Aquí estoy! ¿Qué pasa? (*To* MANOLO.) She looks worried. I hope nothing bad happened. (MARIA *enters. She is the same age as Teresa, attractive, with dark hair. She is Teresa's best friend.*)

MARIA: I'm sorry to interrupt, but I've been looking all over for you!

TERESA: What's the matter?

MARIA: You've got to come home right away!

TERESA: What's wrong? What's happened?

MARIA: It's your brother, Mingo.

TERESA: Mingo? Did he have an accident? Is he alright?

MARIA: He's been arrested.

TERESA: What? Why?

MARIA: Last night somebody killed Louie and . . .

MANOLO: Louie's dead?

MARIA: Yes and the police say Mingo shot him.

TERESA: Mingo would never kill anybody.

MARIA: They've arrested him anyway because somebody saw Mingo coming out of the place they found Louie's body.

MANOLO: Who arrested Mingo?

MARIA: Sgt. Jiménez.

MANOLO: But he's a narco, not homocide.

MARIA: I was there when they took him away.

MANOLO: You're sure it was Jiménez?

MARIA: Of course, I'm sure.

TERESA: What's the matter, Manolo?

MANOLO: I don't know, but I've got a feeling there was probably some drugs involved in this. Otherwise Jiménez wouldn't be around.

MARIA: Your mother wants you to come home Teresa.

TERESA: Tell her I'm on my way.

MARIA: But she said right away.

TERESA: Allí voy, don't worry!

MARIA: Bueno, whatever you say. (*She exits.*)

TERESA: You don't think Mingo shot Louie, do you Manolo?

MANOLO: Of course not. Mingo's no killer and besides he had nothing to do with Louie.

TERESA: Who would want to kill Louie anyway?

MANOLO: Louie was a punk and he had more enemies than it was wise to have. Ese bato was scum, the lowest kind. He used his own raza to push his junk on. I had reason enough to kill him.

TERESA: You didn't, did you?

MANOLO: Don't worry, no lo maté. (*Pause with hate.*) But I wish I had. (*Pause.*) You better go now, tu mama te está esperando.

TERESA: Do you think Mingo will be alright?

MANOLO: He's going to be alright. Besides, it was probably one of Louie's own goons that killed him and it will come out before long.

TERESA: Que Dios quiera.

MANOLO: ¡Tu mamá!

TERESA: Sí, I'm going. Hasta después. (*She starts to exit, stops.*) And you? Are you going to be alright?

MANOLO: Simón.

TERESA: Take care of yourself.

MANOLO: Ni modo, ¿verdad?

TERESA: I love you.

MANOLO: Thanks. (*She rushes up and kisses him. He holds her for a slight moment. She breaks away and exits quickly. MANOLO speaks to the now empty doorway.*) I love you, but what's the use? Soy tecato and what kind of a life is that for you? (*Slams door shut. He goes behind chair and takes out a spoon, a needle, and a nickel bag of junk. He prepares it, then sits center and ties off his arm and injects himself. The lights go into blues. MANOLO falls back and a dream begins to the sound of a storm and Chicano rock music mixed together. Images appear around him. USL a figure in black, face covered, beckons to him. The figure is death. USR are two figures, a man and a woman. They are waving Huelga flags. On USR platform stands the figure of* TERESA, *arms extended to him. Directly behind him the figure of a soldier, weapon in hand pointed at* MANOLO. *The figures are in specials that come on one at a time.* MANOLO *tosses and turns. The figures vanish one at a time. Then two men come out in front of him, one stage right the other stage left. A strobe comes on and the storm and music build. The men turn and face each other as if holding a knife in their hands. They go through a slow motion fight almost like a dance, slashing each other. Finally after about two minutes they both stab each other and freeze holding on to each other as the strobe goes out. A small special comes back up on* MANOLO.)

MANOLO: ¡Dios mío . . . dear God ayúdame! (*He collapses as the light fades out slowly and the music grows louder.*)

It is late night of the same day. CARMELA *and* JOEY BOY *are sitting CS.* CARMELA *is 16 years old and a pretty girl; she is* MARÍA'S *younger sister.* JOEY BOY *is 17 years old and* CARMELA *and* MARÍA'S *brother. He is small in size. We are somewhere in the barrio.*

JOEY: Did you hear about Manolo?
CARMELA: What about him?
JOEY: They say he's a tecato.
CARMELA: Who told you that?
JOEY: I heard María talking to Teresa.
CARMELA: Busy body.
JOEY: Well it's true, I heard them.
CARMELA: So it's true. It's none of your business anyway.
JOEY: Yeah, but just think about it: Manolo a tecato.
CARMELA: He was probably wounded in Viet Nam, it happens all the time.
JOEY: Sí, pero still . . .
CARMELA: I don't want to talk about it.
JOEY: Bueno, don't get so huffy.
CARMELA: Well, be quiet then.
JOEY: I can talk if I want to; it's a free country, remember?
CARMELA: Talk about something else then.
JOEY: Mingo's out of jail.
CARMELA: He never shot anybody anyway.
JOEY: Yeah, but whoever shot Louie did this whole barrio a favor.
CARMELA: (*Looking at the sky.*) Look! A shooting star!
JOEY: Where?
CARMELA: You missed it, it's gone now.
JOEY: So I missed it, big deal.
CARMELA: I like to look at shooting stars.
JOEY: Come one Carmela, let's go home.
CARMELA: You go if you want Joey Boy, I want to enjoy the night some more.
JOEY: Es tarde.
CARMELA: It's not that late.
JOEY: Well I'm going. (JOEY *starts to exit as* BIMBO *and* TANK, *two of Louie's goons come in.* BIMBO *is the smaller of the two but he does most of the talking.* TANK *is big and mean.* CARMELA *sees them and is frightened.*)
CARMELA: Joey Boy!
JOEY: What's the matter. (*Turning around, he sees the men.*) Come on Carmela, let's

get out of here. (BIMBO *and* TANK *are now only a few feet away.*)

BIMBO: ¡Oye, muchacho!

CARMELA: Who are they, Joey Boy?

BIMBO: No sé. You better go!

CARMELA: Not without you.

BIMBO: Hey, boy, I'm talking to you.

TANK: Uh.

JOEY: What do you want?

BIMBO: A little information.

JOEY: What kind?

BIMBO: You know a guy named Manolo? (*No answer.*) Sure you do; he lives around here.

JOEY: What about it?

BIMBO: You know where we can find him?

JOEY: No. (*Turns to* CARMELA.) Come on Carmela, let's go. Mamá y papá will be waiting for us.

BIMBO: (*Grabbing* CARMELA.) Not so fast, you haven't answered my question!

JOEY: Leave her alone!

TANK: (*Grabbing* JOEY *and pushing him away.*) Uh!

BIMBO: We're not going to hurt her, are we Tank?

TANK: Uh.

BIMBO: Now, why don't you be a good boy and tell me ¿dónde está Manolo?

JOEY: No sé. Now leave her alone!

CARMELA: Let go of me, you're hurting me!

BIMBO: Relax, chula, nobody's going to hurt you. Qué bonita, ¿verdad Tank?

TANK: Sí.

BIMBO: (*Running his hands over her shoulders.*) Nice body, ¿verdad Tank?

TANK: Sí, Bimbo.

CARMELA: What do you want?

BIMBO: Where's Manolo?

CARMELA: We don't know.

BIMBO: Tank! (*Indicates* JOEY BOY. TANK *grabs him.*)

JOEY: What are you doing? Let me go!

BIMBO: Shut up kid! Now, where can we find Manolo?

JOEY: No sé! (TANK *twists his arm.*) ¡Ay!

CARMELA: Por favor!

BIMBO: How old are you, little girl?

CARMELA: Sixteen.

BIMBO: She's a niña. Do you want her, Tank?

TANK: Sí! (*Starts to go for her.* JOEY *tries to grab* TANK.)

JOEY: NO! (TANK *turns and hits* JOEY *across the mouth sending him falling to the ground.* CARMELA *screams and* BIMBO *covers her mouth.*)

BIMBO: Are you a virgin, little girl? (*Releasing her mouth.*)

CARMELA: Please . . . dear God!

BIMBO: (*Laughs.*) ¡Así le gustan al Tank!

TANK: ¡Sí, Bimbo, sí! (JOEY BOY *gets up and tries again to get to* TANK. TANK *hits him in the gut and he falls out cold.*)

CARMELA: (*Struggling and breaking free.*) Joey Boy! (TANK *grabs her and picks her up. She screams as he sets her down on ground.*)

BIMBO: Now little girl we're going to have a little fun!

CARMELA: ¡Dios mío, por favor, don't!

BIMBO: Hold her down Tank!

TANK: ¡Simón . . . simón . . . simón! (TANK *holds her as* BIMBO *begins to undo his belt.*)

CARMELA: HELP ME!

BIMBO: It's no use to scream, señorita; it won't hurt a bit. (BIMBO *begins to pull up her dress.* JOEY BOY *has gotten up and runs to his sister, kicking* BIMBO, *and he topples over.* BIMBO *gets up as* TANK *grabs* JOEY *by the arms.* BIMBO *is about to hit him.*)

DOMINGO'S VOICE: María, Teresa! Where are you?

TERESA'S VOICE: Over here, Domingo!

BIMBO: (*To* TANK.) Hold the girl, somebody's coming!

TANK: Uh!

BIMBO: (*Grabs* JOEY BOY.) Keep your mouth shut, or we break the girl's arm!

MARIA'S VOICE: Joey Boy! Carmela!

BIMBO: ¡Vámonos! Let her go!

TANK: No!

BIMBO: Come on baboso, ¡déjala ir! (*He starts off.*) ¡Andale!

TANK: Shit! (*Letting her go and following* BIMBO. CARMELA *screams and* JOEY BOY *goes to her.*)

JOEY: Are you okay? (*She cries holding on to* JOEY.)

DOMINGO: (*Running in.*) What's wrong? (MARIA *and* TERESA *enter.*)

MARIA: Carmela, ¿qué té pasa?

CARMELA: They tried . . . to rape . . . me!

MARIA: Who, Carmela? Who?

DOMINGO: I'll go call the police!

CARMELA: No, please don't! María please!

TERESA: Maybe the police can help.

CARMELA: I don't want mamá y papá to find out, please!

DOMINGO: María?

MARIA: It's okay Carmela, we won't call them. But what happened?

JOEY: A couple of guys were looking for Manolo and we told them we didn't know where he was.

CARMELA: They hit Joey Boy.

DOMINGO: They hit you?

JOEY: I'm okay. It's Carmela I was worried about. Those guys were animals.

MARIA: Who were they?

JOEY: One guy was named Bimbo and I think the other was Tank.

DOMINGO: Bimbo and Tank, ¡pinches putos!

TERESA: Do you know them, Mingo?

DOMINGO: They were a couple of Louie's henchmen.

TERESA: Why would they want to hurt Carmela and Joey Boy?

DOMINGO: Because they're punks and they get their kicks by scaring people.

JOEY: What do they want with Manolo?

DOMINGO: Who knows? But I'd like to find out. Did you tell them anything?

JOEY: We told them we didn't know where he was, but I guess they didn't like the answer.

TERESA: What if they find him, Mingo?

DOMINGO: Don't worry, Manolo can take care of himself. But we better get out of here.

CARMELA: You won't tell papá, will you María?

MARIA: There's no need, as long as you're okay.

CARMELA: Gracias.

JOEY: I'd like to get my hands on those guys.

CARMELA: Sí, tonto. So they could hit you again?

JOEY: You're lucky I was around!

80

MARIA: Quit arguing and let's go home.

DOMINGO: Listen!

TERESA: What? (*They all stop.*)

DOMINGO: Do you hear anything?

TERESA: No.

DOMINGO: That's what I mean . . . not a sound, ni un perro. That's strange don't you think?

CARMELA: I want to go home.

JOEY: Yeah, let's get out of here. (*They exit. Blackout.*)

Scene 2

It is mid-afternoon of the following day, somewhere in the barrio. MANOLO enters looking tired and worn. He sits CS. CHANO enters with a guitar in his hands.

CHANO: (*Strumming guitar, notices MANOLO.*) Orale, Manolo! What is like happening, bro?

MANOLO: ¿Cómo está? Chano? What ya doing?

CHANO: Getting down, bro! Just like always, bro. What's doing by you?

MANOLO: Nada, just resting.

CHANO: Say bro, you alright? Anything wrong?

MANOLO: Chale, I'm okay.

CHANO: How about playing a little tune on my guitar, bro?

MANOLO: Chale, not now, Chano.

CHANO: Come on bro, I can see you is *down* and a little jam might help you to find what happened to *up*. What do you say, bro? Gimme a little tune, teach me a little song.

MANOLO: I wish I could Chano, but not now.

CHANO: Whatever you say bro.

MANOLO: Do you believe in ghosts, Chano?

CHANO: Say what?

MANOLO: Ghosts. Things from your past?

CHANO: Shit yes!

MANOLO: Ever see any?

CHANO: Shit no! Don't plan on it either, no way bro! I stay out of their way and they be cool about staying out of my way too! What's the matter, bro, you seen one?

MANOLO: Simón, sometimes.

CHANO: Uh, uh, uh! That is like heavy bro! Tell me about it bro!

MANOLO: I wish I could, Chano.

CHANO: Just you and me bro.

MANOLO: I know Chano, but I can't. You might think I'm nuts.

CHANO: Este bato, are you kidding, bro? They're ain't nobody as nuts as me, bro.

MANOLO: Where did you get the guitar?

CHANO: Some dude loaned it to me. Of course he don't know that yet.

MANOLO: Stole it! Aren't you afraid of getting caught?

CHANO: Chale! Why bro, I'm so fast when I steal a radio I leave the music behind!

MANOLO: (*Chuckles.*) I believe you, Chano.

CHANO: Here bro, check it out! (*Hands him guitar.*)

MANOLO: You've got good taste Chano. Here. (*Handing him back guitar.*)

CHANO: Keep it bro, it's a gift.

MANOLO: Some other time Chano, pero gracias.

CHANO: If you're worried about the turkey it belonged to, there's no need. He's got a bunch of others to keep each other company.

MANOLO: It's not that, Chano. It's just that I don't need it right now.

CHANO: Sure enough bro, whatever you say. (*Takes back guitar.*)

MANOLO: I better go. See you later, Chano.

CHANO: Going any place special, bro?

MANOLO: Chale, nowhere special, just walking along. ¿Por qué?

CHANO: Just thought I'd tag along, bro.

MANOLO: Thanks Chano, but I'd like to be alone, if it's just the same to you.

CHANO: No sweat bro, I understand.

MANOLO: Thanks, Chano. (*Starts to leave.*)

CHANO: Say, bro.

MANOLO: What?

CHANO: There are rumors in the street you might want to know about.

MANOLO: What kind of rumors?

CHANO: Remember Jiménez?

MANOLO: What about him?

CHANO: He pulls a lot of heat.

MANOLO: He's a son-of-a-bitch.

CHANO: Talk is you're hooked on junk.

MANOLO: What if I am?

CHANO: Jiménez is trying to make contact with all the junkies in the street.

MANOLO: Come on Chano, get to the point!

CHANO: You know they released Mingo, don't you?

MANOLO: No but I'm glad to hear it.

CHANO: Turned out he was somewhere else when Louie got blown away.

MANOLO: What's all this got to do with me?

CHANO: Well you see, bro. Jiménez thinks it might have been one of the junkies that blew away Louie.

MANOLO: He does, huh?

CHANO: Simón. And bro, you are prime suspect número uno.

MANOLO: Why me?

CHANO: It's no secret, bro, that you hated Louie and Louie hated you.

MANOLO: I hated him alright.

CHANO: Better stay low bro, till the heat is off.

MANOLO: I've nothing to hide, Chano. I didn't kill Louie even though I might have wanted to.

CHANO: Jiménez thinks you did.

MANOLO: Fuck Jiménez!

CHANO: Just thought I'd tell you bro.

MANOLO: Thanks Chano. (*Starts to leave.*)

CHANO: Where you going, bro?

MANOLO: Find Jiménez.

CHANO: Say what? You crazy, bro?

MANOLO: Like I said, I've got nothing to hide.

CHANO: Simón, but that dude is trouble.

MANOLO: Right. (*He exits.*)

CHANO: ¡Este bato! Heavy makings in this here barrio. I guess I'll go see what's happening somewhere else. (*He exits singing "La Bamba." Fade out.*)

Scene 3

It is about thirty minutes later, at MANOLO'S *apartment. The apartment is empty, and as the lights rise, there is knocking at the door.* DOMINGO'S *voice is heard.*

DOMINGO'S VOICE: Manolo! Manolo, are you in there?

MARIA'S VOICE: Open the door. Let's go in. (*The door opens and* MINGO, MARIA, TERESA *and* JOEY BOY *enter.*)

DOMINGO: Hey buddy, where are you? (*To* JOEY BOY.) Joey Boy, go look in the other room. (JOEY *goes into other room.*) I don't think he's here, Teresa.

TERESA: Where could he be, Mingo?

DOMINGO: With him there's no telling.

MARIA: Don't worry Teresa, he's probably just out doing something.

TERESA: I guess you're right.

JOEY: (*As he enters.*) He's not around, Mingo.

DOMINGO: Thanks for looking, Joey Boy.

JOEY: Sure. (*Seeing* JIMENEZ *approach.*) Oh, oh. We've got company. (JIMENEZ *appears in doorway. He is about 35 years old, medium height and build. They turn towards the door.*)

DOMINGO: What do you want, Jiménez?

JIMENEZ: Manolo. Is he home?

DOMINGO: No he's not home.

JIMENEZ: You expecting him soon?

TERESA: We don't know where he's at, Sgt. Jiménez, or when he's coming back.

JIMENEZ: (*Entering room, checking it out.*) Well that's too bad. I was looking forward to seeing him again.

DOMINGO: Sure you were?

JIMENEZ: It's true, Mingo, I was.

DOMINGO: Nobody really cares, Jiménez.

JIMENEZ: Still sore cause I ran you in, Mingo?

DOMINGO: No. I just don't like you, that's all.

TERESA: Mingo!

DOMINGO: He's a pig, Teresa.

TERESA: He's not doing anything to you.

DOMINGO: He doesn't have to.

JIMENEZ: It's a job, punk.

DOMINGO: Punk your ass!

JIMENEZ: Don't get me riled!

DOMINGO: What are you gonna do — beat on me?

TERESA: Stop it, Domingo! (*Pause.*) He's not here, Sgt. Jiménez.

MANOLO: (*As he enters.*) Somebody looking for me?

JIMENEZ: I was.

MANOLO: Well, the local fuzz. What can I do for you?

JIMENEZ: I wanted to ask you some preguntas.

MANOLO: Name, rank and serial number.

JIMENEZ: Cute.

MANOLO: So what's your beef this time?

JIMENEZ: Don't know if I have one yet.

MANOLO: I'm sure you'll think of one.

JIMENEZ: Where you been the last few days?

MANOLO: Around.

JIMENEZ: Anybody with you?

MANOLO: Sometimes.

JIMENEZ: Where were you two nights ago?

DOMINGO: He was with me.

TERESA: And me.

MARIA: I was there too.

JOEY: Y yo también.

before I looked.

TERESA: Are you sure? (CHANO *calls out.*)

CHANO: Manolo! Hey bro, are you there?

DOMINGO: In here, Chano! (CHANO *enters, a bit embarrassed, holding a gun in his hand.*)

MARIA: Did you fire that shot Chano?

CHANO: Simón . . . pero . . .

TERESA: ¡Tonto! You scared us half to death you dummy!

CHANO: I'm sorry bros and sisters I didn't know it was loaded.

MANOLO: Where did you get that thing anyway?

CHANO: Found it, bro.

DOMINGO: You found it?

CHANO: Simón bro, I found it.

TERESA: You mean stole it, don't you?

CHANO: Chale, this time I found it.

MANOLO: Well, put it away before you shoot your toe off!

CHANO: Sure, bro, sure. (*Starts to put it in his pants.*)

MANOLO: You better unload it before you shoot something else off!

CHANO: Oh, simón. (*Does so and then puts it in his belt.*)

MANOLO: Don't ever do that again, ¿entiende?

CHANO: Sure, bro.

DOMINGO: You don't even know how to shoot a gun, do you Chano?

CHANO: Chale, but I can learn.

TERESA: Not around here you won't!

MARIA: Amen on that.

CHANO: I get the hint sisters.

MANOLO: (*Sitting center stage and rubbing his arms. He is in need of a fix.*) Déjenme solo for a little while!

DOMINGO: Come over to my chante, Manolo.

MANOLO: Later. Now leave me alone, please.

TERESA: Will you come over?

MANOLO: Simón, I'll be there.

DOMINGO: (*Notices that MANOLO is getting edgy.*) Will you be alright?

MANOLO: Simón.

MARIA: Come on Joey Boy!

JOEY: But . . .

MARIA: ¡Que te vengas ya! (JOEY *crosses to leave.*)

DOMINGO: Be careful, Manolo. Come on Teresa, vámonos.

TERESA: Manolo.

MANOLO: ¿Qué?

TERESA: Nada. (*They all start to exit.*)

MANOLO: ¡Chano!

CHANO: Yeah, bro?

MANOLO: Come here a minute!

CHANO: What can I do for you bro? (*The others exit.*)

MANOLO: (*Beginning to hurt.*) Can you score for me?

CHANO: Aw bro . . .

MANOLO: I need it Chano!

CHANO: Yeah I can score.

MANOLO: Do it Chano y por favor hurry! (*Hands CHANO some money.*)

CHANO: No need bro, I got a couple of favors coming my way.

MANOLO: Gracias, Chano.

CHANO: I'll be back soon bro! (*Exits.*)

MANOLO: (*Sits holding his stomach, the pain growing inside him.*) Please hurry, Chano . . . please! (*The lights shift and* MANOLO *is flashed back in his past to* SHAIN'S *office.*)

SHAIN: The last time we spoke you mentioned politics.

MANOLO: So I did.

SHAIN: Do you want to go into politics?

MANOLO: Not much chance of that, is there doc? I mean being a junkie and all?

SHAIN: It's possible.

MANOLO: Forget it, I don't want to be a servant of the people anyway.

SHAIN: You wouldn't consider it?

MANOLO: No.

SHAIN: I see. What are some of the things you like to do Sgt. Garza?

MANOLO: Things I like to do?

SHAIN: Hobbies, sports, the like.

MANOLO: I like music.

SHAIN: What kind?

MANOLO: All kinds.

SHAIN: Do you play an instrument?

MANOLO: Guitar.

SHAIN: Does it help you relax?

MANOLO: Sometimes.

SHAIN: When you have a problem do you turn to music?

MANOLO: I used to.

SHAIN: Why don't you now?

MANOLO: I don't know!

SHAIN: Does being an addict have anything to do with it?

MANOLO: You're the doctor, you tell me!

SHAIN: Do my questions bother you?

MANOLO: What the hell do you think?

SHAIN: Do you know why I ask you these things?

MANOLO: I don't give a fuck, doc!

SHAIN: I'm trying to help you.

MANOLO: Do what?

SHAIN: Perhaps find an answer to your addiction.

MANOLO: You can help me by leaving me the fuck alone, doc! Or by giving me what I need: a fix. That's how you can help me.

SHAIN: Don't you want to rehabilitate yourself?

MANOLO: Being a junkie suits me just fine.

SHAIN: You like depending on drugs?

MANOLO: What difference does that make?

SHAIN: Do you or don't you?

MANOLO: To tell you the truth, Dr. Shain, it doesn't really matter any more.

SHAIN: Can you remember when you had your first fix?

MANOLO: No.

SHAIN: Do you want to remember?

MANOLO: Goddamnit, doc, quit asking me so many fucking questions!

SHAIN: How else can I help you if I don't ask questions? (*Pause.*) Now when did you have your first fix?

MANOLO: I don't remember!

SHAIN: Try!

MANOLO: (*Straining.*) I guess it was when I went back to Nam.

SHAIN: Were things different for you?

MANOLO: More people were dead.

SHAIN: Friends of yours?

MANOLO: My mother was dead! My brother was dead! You could say they were friends!

SHAIN: I'm sorry.

MANOLO: Well don't be!

SHAIN: You were very close to them?

MANOLO: Are you close to your mother?

SHAIN: Yes, I'm close to all my family.

MANOLO: Then you know how I felt?

SHAIN: Did you feel responsible for their deaths?

MANOLO: I wasn't there to help them, if that's what you mean.

SHAIN: You blame yourself for that?

MANOLO: I blame the war.

SHAIN: Is that why you turned to drugs?

MANOLO: I couldn't get them off my mind. My brother was stabbed to death in an alley and my mother died of pneumonia and I didn't even get a scratch in Nam.

SHAIN: No, but you got a habit.

MANOLO: Big fucking deal, so I got a habit! Why don't you get me a fix?

SHAIN: Would that make you feel any better?

MANOLO: For a doctor you ask some pretty stupid questions.

SHAIN: Will giving you a fix help your mother or brother? Will it make your guilt go away?

MANOLO: Son-of-bitch doc, you can be a pain in the ass!

SHAIN: Do you really want to depend on that little white powder to help you get rid of your problems? Or would you rather face up to them like the normal human being that you are?

MANOLO: GO TO HELL! (CHANO *enters and stares at* MANOLO *who is holding his hands over his ears. Light on* SHAIN *fades and he exits.*)

CHANO: Hey Bro! Manolo! (*Walks up to him and grabs his arm,* MANOLO *jumps.*) You okay, bro?

MANOLO: Chano! I didn't hear you come in.

CHANO: I know bro. You was mumbling something to yourself about a fix and your mother and some doctor.

MANOLO: Yeah . . . I guess I was just talking out loud. (*Pause.*)

CHANO: I got a score, bro.

MANOLO: What? Yeah, give it to me!

CHANO: Here you go bro! (*Hands him a bag of junk.*)

MANOLO: Leave me alone now, will you.

CHANO: I'm gone, bro. (*Pause.*) Can I get you anything else?

MANOLO: No, nothing.

CHANO: See you, bro. (*Starts to exit.*) You sure, bro?

MANOLO: ¡Nada! (CHANO *exits.* MANOLO *looks at the bag, crosses to the bed and pulls a small bundle out from under the mattress. He slowly unwraps his spoon and needle. Setting the paraphernalia down, he rubs the bag in his palm.*) I must've been dreaming. (*There is a knock at the door. He quickly hides the paraphernalia under the mattress and shoves the bag into his pocket. There is another knock and* SGT. JIMENEZ *speaks from behind the closed door.*)

JIMENEZ: ¡Manolo! I know you're in there. Open up!

MANOLO: It's not locked. (JIMENEZ *opens the door and enters.*) What the hell do you want now?

JIMENEZ: Cálmala, I'm not here to hassle you.

MANOLO: Just your presence hassles me. Now what do you want?

JIMENEZ: What are you so jumpy about?

MANOLO: I'm just jumpy ¿y qué? Is there a law against it?

JIMENEZ: No.

MANOLO: So ask your questions and get the fuck out of here!

JIMENEZ: I wanted to see you alone.

MANOLO: ¿Por qué? You got some deep dark secret?

JIMENEZ: I know you're a junkie. I know you been one since Nam.

MANOLO: So what of it?

JIMENEZ: I'm just surprised, that's all.

MANOLO: So you came to look at the junkie freak, is that it? Well get an eyefull ¡y déjame ya!

JIMENEZ: You're the last guy I thought would ever get hooked on that shit.

MANOLO: It wasn't hard at all, believe me.

JIMENEZ: Was Nam that bad?

MANOLO: Just another barrio, like this one.

JIMENEZ: You disappoint me, Manolo.

MANOLO: What is it with you? You getting soft in your old age? You're usually out to bust any pothead, pimp or punk kid in the streets and now you're here preaching at me?

JIMENEZ: I don't have to bust you, punk.

MANOLO: O sí, ¿por qué no?

JIMENEZ: You'll have to get rid of that shit sooner or later. That is if you're half the man you think you are.

MANOLO: Fuck off and leave me alone!

JIMENEZ: You dumb bastard! Using junk as an excuse for feeling guilty about the world. You don't need that shit!

MANOLO: How do you know what I need?

JIMENEZ: Look at you! You're a slob, you know that? This is the dude that people used to look up to? What a joke!

MANOLO: You're a son-of-a-bitch, Jiménez!

JIMENEZ: And I make no bones about it, ese. But you? Now that's something else. You don't know *what* you are! All you know is that you got to have that fix to keep you going, right? Just one more fix, is that it? And then you promise yourself that it will be the last one, right? Shit no! The next one you got to have even more, don't you? You keep shooting up until you run out of veins and the only thing left is your toes!

MANOLO: SHUT UP!

JIMENEZ: Sure punk, I'll shut up, but first you answer some questions!

MANOLO: I didn't kill Louie.

JIMENEZ: You don't have to convince me of that. All I have to do is take one look at you and I know you wouldn't have the guts to kill a fly.

MANOLO: Don't push me, Jiménez!

JIMENEZ: You don't know what push is punk! (*Pause.*) Did you know that Louie was carrying that stash?

MANOLO: No.

JIMENEZ: He talked to you, didn't he?

MANOLO: So?

JIMENEZ: He made you an offer, didn't he?

MANOLO: ¿Y qué?

JIMENEZ: You must of known he was expecting to get that junk.

MANOLO: He didn't tell me a damn thing.

JIMENEZ: I want that horse, Manolo.

MANOLO: I haven't got it, pig!

JIMENEZ: Of course if you knew where it was you would tell me, wouldn't you?

bang! (*He laughs.*) Fuckers.

TERESA: Por un minuto I thought you were going to shoot them.

JIMENEZ: So did I. How's Mingo? You okay?

DOMINGO: I never thought I'd be happy to see you.

JIMENEZ: That makes two of us. What did the goon squad want?

DOMINGO: They were looking for Manolo.

JIMENEZ: Sooner or later I figured they would. Where is he?

TERESA: He went for a walk. He had just left when those animals got here.

JIMENEZ: You want to press charges?

DOMINGO: ¿Para qué? They'll just get out again.

JIMENEZ: Cool 'em off for a bit. (MINGO *starts to get up.*) Can you walk, Mingo?

DOMINGO: I think so. My stomach feels like it's in my back.

JIMENEZ: It'll be sore for a while. Here sit down over here. (*Center.*)

TERESA: Why don't they leave Manolo alone? He doesn't have anything they want.

JIMENEZ: It's going to be hard to convince them of that.

DOMINGO: Why, Jiménez?

JIMENEZ: They know that Louie met with Manolo. So they figure that they made some kind of deal and that Manolo knows where Louie might have hidden the junk.

DOMINGO: Manolo told Louie to go to hell! I was there.

JIMENEZ: They don't know that. And until they find out where that horse is, they're not going to be happy. That's a half a million bucks floating around somewhere and they won't stop 'til they find it. (*Pause.*) There's something else.

DOMINGO: What?

JIMENEZ: They figure if anybody had a good reason to kill Louie it was Manolo.

TERESA: ¿Pero por qué?

JIMENEZ: You remember how Manolo's brother was killed? (*They nod yes.*) Well it was Louie who stabbed him.

TERESA: Louie?

JIMENEZ: Yeah, but unfortunately we could never prove it, so the fucker got away. Anyway, I think Manolo found this out somewhere along the way and he made some threats. I'm sure Bimbo and Tank were aware of this and so when Louie turned up dead they just naturally figured Manolo did it.

DOMINGO: Manolo would never kill anybody.

TERESA: You don't think Manolo did it, do you?

JIMENEZ: Let me let you in on a little secret. The body that we have in the morgue is not Louie.

DOMINGO: What?

JIMENEZ: It's not Louie but some guy who was dressed up to look like Louie.

TERESA: Then who's body is it?

JIMENEZ: Probably some poor slob that would be hard to trace. His face was blown away and he was carrying ID that said he was Louie.

DOMINGO: You think Louie arranged it?

JIMENEZ: For sure. What I don't know is if Bimbo and Tank are in on this.

DOMINGO: So Louie is still alive? That son-of-a-bitch!

TERESA: I want to go find Manolo.

DOMINGO: Sí, vamos.

JIMENEZ: When you find him, fill him in and then tell him to give me a call, okay?

DOMINGO: Simón, I'll do that.

TERESA: Gracias for helping us.

JIMENEZ: Sure.

DOMINGO: I still don't like you Jiménez.

JIMENEZ: Don't worry, I won't hold it against you. (TERESA *and* DOMINGO *exit.*

JIMENEZ *walks over to window, looks outside.*) Ay, qué barrio éste. (*A gunshot is heard and* JIMENEZ *falls.* LOUIE *steps into the room, crosses to* JIMENEZ'S body and kicks it.*)

LOUIE: That's right, pig, I ain't dead. You're the one that's dead. (*Points gun at the body.*) Next I get Manolo. (*He laughs as lights fade and music builds to blackout.*)

Act III, Scene 1 UN DIABLO

JOEY BOY *is sitting stage right reading a book.* CHANO *enters. It is the following day and it is cloudy with the wind blowing through the trees.*

CHANO: Bom, di bom di bom di bom bom bom! Yeah, yeah, yeah! Jiménez da pig is dead . . . uh, uh, uh! Trying to save a bro from self-destruction. Listen to my story! Amen bros and sisters . . . amen. (*Notices* JOEY) Say bro . . . Joey Boy.

JOEY: (*Looking up.*) What is it Chano?

CHANO: What ya doing?

JOEY: Reading.

CHANO: I didn't know you was a reader, little bro?

JOEY: I thought you knew everything, Chano.

CHANO: There are some things that do escape my eyes from time to time, but not much. Hey, did you hear about Jiménez?

JOEY: Simón I heard about it.

CHANO: Too bad isn't it? And I was beginning to like that dude.

JOEY: Do you think they'll blame Manolo?

CHANO: Are you kidding, why would they do that?

JOEY: Well he was killed in his house.

CHANO: Yeah, but Manolo wasn't even around and Mingo and Teresa had just left when it happened.

JOEY: The police were there last night, at Manolo's chante.

CHANO: Simón, but they just asked a bunch of questions and then split.

JOEY: Who'd be dumb enough to kill a cop like Jiménez?

CHANO: It would have to be some crazy dude, that's for sure.

JOEY: What about Bimbo and Tank?

CHANO: Sssh! Not so loud little bro, you don't want nobody to hear your saying that!

JOEY: Why not?

CHANO: Those batos are dangerous and they wouldn't like it.

JOEY: Son cabrones and I'm not afraid of them.

CHANO: Don't be saying you're not afraid of them dudes! Don't you know they'd cut you up like bacon just for the fun of it? Leave those batos the hell alone, ese!

JOEY: I bet you they killed Jiménez.

CHANO: You keep talking like that and I'm going to split, little bro. (CARMELA *enters and she is angry.*)

CARMELA: JOEY BOY!

JOEY: Oh, oh! (*Closes book and starts to run when* CHANO *stops him.*)

CHANO: What's the matter little bro?

JOEY: I have to run.

CARMELA: Come here you runt!

JOEY: (*Pointing at* CARMELA.) That's why. (*To* CHANO *who is holding his arm.*)¡Déjame ir!

CHANO: Calm down little bro, it's just Carmela.

CARMELA: (*Crossing to them.*) ¡Te voy a matar! (JOEY *gets behind* CHANO.)

CHANO: Orale, wait a minute, sis!

CARMELA: I'm not your sis! Now come here, Joey Boy!

JOEY: No way, Carmela.

CHANO: Calm down, woman! What you so all fired hot about?

CARMELA: Him! That's what!

CHANO: What'd you do, little bro?

JOEY: I didn't do nothing.

CARMELA: (*Attacking* JOEY *who circles around* CHANO.) I'M GOING TO SCRATCH YOUR EYES OUT!

CHANO: Come on esa, relax!

CARMELA: Get out of my way, Chano!

JOEY: No, Chano, don't!

CARMELA: You runt! You told mamá y papá about Bimbo and Tank!

JOEY: I couldn't help it!

CARMELA: You couldn't help it! ¡Cabrón! Wait till I get my hands on you.

CHANO: Wait a minute! Hold it! What about Bimbo and Tank?

CARMELA: None of your business! Joey Boy!

JOEY: Hell no, Carmela, I'm not getting near you.

CARMELA: Now papá won't let me go out at night, you runt! You and your big mouth!

JOEY: I'm sorry.

CARMELA: Sí, you're sorry, that's not going to help you now.

CHANO: Aw, come on sis, he said he was sorry. Why don't you forgive him and let bygones be bygones?

CARMELA: Not until I get him back for opening his big mouth.

JOEY: It's your fault! If you would have come with me when I told you, none of this would have happened.

CHANO: What happened? What happened?

JOEY: Bimbo and Tank tried . . .

CARMELA: Shut up Joey!

CHANO: Tried what?

JOEY:. . . to rape her.

CARMELA: Joey!

CHANO: Bimbo and Tank?

JOEY: Simón.

CARMELA: I'm warning you, Joey!

JOEY: They were looking for Manolo and found us instead and when we couldn't tell them where Manolo was they hit me and tried to rape Carmela.

CARMELA: You're going to get it now, Joey! (JOEY *runs out and* CARMELA *follows.*) When I catch you!

CHANO: Hey wait a minute! Shit, they didn't tell me what happened! Oh well? Nunca pero nunca is there a dull moment around this here barrio. Bom, di bom di bom di bom bom bom. Yeah, yeah, yeah! (*As he starts to exit* LOUIE *and boys enter.*)

CHANO: (*Hesitant.*) Like what's happening . . . bros? (LOUIE *appears as* BIMBO *and* TANK *move aside, revealing his presence.* CHANO *is awestruck.*)

LOUIE: Chano . . . Chano . . . Chano.

CHANO: ¡EL LOUIE! But . . . but . . . híjole ese . . . you a ghost? (TANK *and* BIMBO *laugh.*)

LOUIE: (*To* TANK *and* BIMBO.) Shut up! (*They stop.*) What do you think, ese?

CHANO: I don't never think, bro.

LOUIE: Simón. Well don't worry ese, I'm real.

CHANO: Pero I thought you were dead, bro?

LOUIE: That's what I wanted you to think ese. Pero aquí estoy, ¿no?

CHANO: Right on bro, you is right there. What I understand is like what's going on bro? I mean here you are bro? Right here?

LOUIE: And you know what else, Chano?

CHANO: Chale bro, what?

LOUIE: I'm going to stay here, dig?

CHANO: Whatever you say, bro.

LOUIE: You don't like me do you, Chano?

CHANO: I never said that bro?

LOUIE: Do you like me Chano?

CHANO: Well . . . bro . . . I . . .

LOUIE: Do you?

CHANO: I never gave it much thought, bro.

LOUIE: You know what, Chano? Now that Jiménez is dead I own this barrio, because there isn't anybody to get in my way.

CHANO: Like you say bro, nobody.

LOUIE: If I wanted to Chano, I could kill you.

CHANO: Scared? Kill me, bro? ¿Pero por qué? I ain't done anything.

LOUIE: But I could if I wanted to, dig?

CHANO: I don't guess I could stop you, bro?

LOUIE: Tank!

TANK: Simón, boss?

LOUIE: (*Indicates* CHANO.) What do you think, Chano? (TANK *takes out a knife and walks towards* CHANO.)

CHANO: Aw, come on . . . bro! ¡Por favor! I haven't done nothing to you, bro!

LOUIE: ¿Qué pasa ése, you scared?

CHANO: Sure I'm scared bro! I don't want to die . . . please bro!

LOUIE: Get on your knees, Chano.

CHANO: (*Dropping to his knees.*) Simón, bro . . . whatever you say.

LOUIE: Bimbo, did you ever see anything so funny in your life, ese? Chano on his knees.

BIMBO: Simón, boss he looks pretty funny.

LOUIE: ¿Qué crees tú, Chano? You think you look funny?

CHANO: (*Nervous.*) I guess I do, bro.

LOUIE: You're a bug, you know that, ese? And I ought to step on you!

CHANO: Why, bro?

LOUIE: ¡Porque me da la gana, that's why! (*Pause.*) But I'm not going to Chano, because I've got something I want you to do for me, dig?

CHANO: Anything, bro . . . anything.

LOUIE: I want you to go to Manolo and tell him that you talked to me. And I want you to tell him that I want that stash that he stole from me.

CHANO: What stash, bro?

LOUIE: He'll know what I'm talking about, ese. You tell him I'm coming after him and that he had better get smart and meet with me. You got that?

CHANO: Simón, I got it.

LOUIE: One other thing Chano, spread the word that I'm not dead.

CHANO: Spread the word, bro?

BIMBO: You heard the man.

TANK: Uh.

CHANO: You want me to start now, bro?

LOUIE: Simón. Now get outa here!

CHANO: I'm gone, bro! (*Gets up and runs out.*)

BIMBO: We gonna get Manolo, boss?

LOUIE: Simón.

TANK: We gonna kill him?

Photo Montage: José G. González

ollage of scenes from productions
the following teatros (in
habetical order): Alvarez-Castillo
n José), Artes Contemporáneas
icago), Campesino (San Juan
utista), Cuatro (New York),
ngaño del Pueblo (Gary), Gente
n José), Libertad (Tucson),
scarones (México), Mestizo (San
go), Niños (Pasadena), Nanyelli
éxico), Quetzalcoatl (Seattle),
cha (Chicago), Urbano (Los
geles).

LOUIE: Chansa que sí.

BIMBO: What about his camarada Mingo?

LOUIE: Simón, him we waste. But first we get the horse.

TANK: Uh.

LOUIE: I'm a genius, ¿Verdad, Bimbo?

BIMBO: You sure are boss. You worked everything out real good.

LOUIE: Everybody thought I was dead. (*Laughs and they laugh. He stops, they stop.*) Put my clothes on that wino and blew his face away. (*He laughs, they laugh, he stops, they stop.*) Soy un diablo ¿qué no? (*Laughs, they laugh, stops, they stop.*) The best part was wasting Jiménez. Y ahora nobody can stop me, nobody. (BIMBO *and* TANK *laugh.*) Shut up! ¡Vámonos! (*they exit and* CHANO *reenters.*)

CHANO: ¡Ah, chinelas! This is un poco bad and serious too. Simón que yes. That bastard is still kicking. I better go look for my bro, Manolo, and make him wise to el Louie. (*Exits and lights fade out.*)

Scene 2

Later that afternoon, just before dusk. It is cooler now, and the wind is still blowing. As the lights rise, MANOLO, TERESA, DOMINGO *and* MARIA *are seated, somewhere in the barrio.*

DOMINGO: Híjole I'm full, I think I ate too much.

TERESA: Como siempre.

MANOLO: Simón, I've been noticing lately that you're getting a bit gordo.

DOMINGO: That's muscle!

MANOLO: The only muscle you've got is in your head.

DOMINGO: At least I'm not sitting on it, like you are.

MARIA: I think I ate too much myself and a good nap would be nice right about now.

DOMINGO: Can I join you?

MARIA: Sure, we've got some spare beds.

DOMINGO: That's not exactly what I had in mind.

MARIA: That's too bad.

DOMINGO: Qué gacho you are mujer.

MANOLO: It's your breath Mingo, but I didn't have the heart to tell you.

DOMINGO: Simón, my breath.

TERESA: Parece que va a haber muchas estrellas hoy en la noche.

MARIA: Carmela loves to look at the stars.

DOMINGO: Simón, and it almost got her in trouble.

MARIA: It hasn't stopped her.

TERESA: It's a shame you have to be afraid to go out alone at night.

DOMINGO: Yo no tengo miedo.

MANOLO: That's because you don't know any better.

DOMINGO: Hey you guys, quit picking on me, will ya?

TERESA: Pobrecito, he's feeling paranoid. Don't worry Mingo, we still love you.

DOMINGO: Simón, you have a funny way of showing it. (*Siren is heard.*)

MARIA: Listen to that siren! I wonder who it's for.

DOMINGO: Hey Manolo, remember the first time we heard those new sirens cuando we were chavalos?

MANOLO: What about it?

DOMINGO: (*Laughing.*) El "Spider" thought we were being invaded by somebody from outer space.

MANOLO: Oh simón, and he ran and got under the car. ¡Qué loco! All you could see was those funny legs and arms trying to get under the car.

DOMINGO: Simón, I laughed myself to sleep esa noche. (*Laughing*.) "Orale Spider, it's just a siren!" Those were some times, ¿que no, Manolo?

MANOLO: They sure were. It took us fifteen minutes to get him out from under that carro.

TERESA: Who's Spider?

MANOLO: His real name era Juan pero we called him Spider because he had long arms and legs.

MARIA: ¿Juan Cortés?

MANOLO: Simón. He used to have a real foxy carnala that Mingo used to always chase around.

DOMINGO: Hey that's right! I wonder whatever happened to them?

MANOLO: No sé. They probably both got married by now.

DOMINGO: Janie Cortés, that was her name! Boy was she a fox! (JOEY BOY *and* CARMELA *come running in.*)

CARMELA: ¡María! ¡María!

MARIA: Slow down! ¿Qué te pasa?

JOEY: ¡El Louie!

DOMINGO: What about him?

MARIA: Está vivo.

MANOLO: You saw him?

JOEY: Simón. He was with Bimbo and that ape Tank.

MARIA: We thought he was dead.

DOMINGO: Jiménez was right. He's still alive, Manolo.

MANOLO: What a way to spoil my dinner, finding out Louie is alive.

TERESA: I told you he was alive.

MANOLO: You sure it was Louie and not somebody who looks like Louie?

JOEY: Nadie looks like Louie.

CARMELA: It was Louie, that's for sure.

DOMINGO: ¿Crees que te busca, Manolo?

TERESA: ¡Ay, Manolo!

MANOLO: He knows where to find me.

TERESA: But Manolo he's . . . (CHANO *comes in running.*)

CHANO: Manolo, my bro! I finally found you. And have I got a heavy one for you.

MANOLO: Louie's not dead.

CHANO: Now bro, how'd you know that?

MANOLO: It seems everybody knows about it, Chano.

CHANO: Shit, I must be getting old. I seem to be the last one to know what's coming down around here lately.

DOMINGO: Did you talk to him?

CHANO: Boy did I ever! He scared the fuck out of me, pinche cabrón.

MARIA: Did he hurt you?

CHANO: No, pero he threatened to kill me.

TERESA: Kill you?

CHANO: He made me get down on my knees while that slob Tank held a knife on me.

DOMINGO: That son-of-a-bitch!

MANOLO: ¿Por qué, Chano?

CHANO: He just wanted to lay this rap on me about being el control del barrio. I didn't argue with him, that's for sure. But I sure wish I would have had my cuete with me. I would have blown his balls off.

MANOLO: Chale, it was better that you didn't.

CHANO: He wants me to deliver a message to you, bro.

DOMINGO: Why doesn't he come in person, the bastard?

CHANO: He's planning to. Pero he told me bro to tell you that he wants his stash and that he wants you to wise up and meet with him.

DOMINGO: Then there is a stash missing?

CHANO: Simón, and Louie ain't stopping at nothing to get it back.

TERESA: See Manolo, what did I tell you?

MANOLO: Cálmala, he's full of shit.

CHANO: The bato is nothing but a giant nurd and you ought to get him Manolo, before he gets you!

DOMINGO: Simón, buddy let's get him?

CHANO: He especially wants you, Mingo, my bro.

DOMINGO: Well, let the puto come. I'll be waiting for him.

MANOLO: Chale, he wants me, not you.

DOMINGO: You heard what Chano said, he especially wants me?

CHANO: That's right, bro.

MANOLO: Pues ni modo, we'll wait for him together.

TERESA: What do you mean you'll wait for him?

MANOLO: Why not Teresa? We can end this thing once and for all.

DOMINGO: A todas madres, ass kicking time! Just like the old days.

MARIA: But they've got guns!

DOMINGO: So we'll get guns.

TERESA: Manolo!

CHANO: Say bro, if you need guns?

MANOLO: Chale, no guns.

CHANO: I could get some real cheap?

DOMINGO: ¿Por qué no, Manolo?

MANOLO: Porque I don't want anybody getting killed that's why.

CHANO: You sure, bro, no guns?

MANOLO: Simón. (*Pause.*) Mingo, Chano, you come with me. The rest of you go home.

JOEY: I want to go with you.

MARIA: No seas tonto. You're going para la casa!

JOEY: But María?

MANOLO: She's right, Joey Boy, you better go home.

JOEY: I'm not a kid.

CARMELA: Nobody's saying you are, dummy, but they don't want you to be in the way.

JOEY: Shut up, Carmela!

CARMELA: Don't tell me to shut up, you runt!

MARIA: Come on both of you, let's get home. Teresa?

TERESA: What do you expect us to do Manolo, just wait and see if you get killed?

MANOLO: Nadie's going to get killed! Don't worry, mujer! Now please go home with María.

TERESA: Be careful Manolo.

DOMINGO: Don't worry sis, we can handle Louie.

TERESA: I'll be with María. Please call me?

MANOLO: Simón, we will. (TERESA, MARIA, JOEY *and* CARMELA *exit.*)

CHANO: Hey bro, one other thing I didn't tell you while the ladies were here is that Louie killed Jiménez.

MANOLO: I figured it was one of them. Those bastards will stop at nothing to get what they want.

DOMINGO: They're nothing but scum, esos batos.

MANOLO: Por eso tenemos que tener cuidado.

DOMINGO: You got a plan, buddy?

102

MANOLO: We just wait for him and see what he wants.

CHANO: He bro, do you know where the stash is?

MANOLO: Simón.

DOMINGO: You do? ¿Pero cómo?

MANOLO: That's the funny part. I stumbled on it by accident.

CHANO: What do you mean, bro?

MANOLO: Well, when I heard Jiménez was looking for me I figured I had to have a place to hide my stash in case he was out to bust me for holding. I couldn't keep it at home so I tried to think of a place I could keep it and get to it when I needed it. That's when I remembered about the old shack by the river.

CHANO: The one where all the bums used to hang out at when we were kids?

MANOLO: That's the one.

DOMINGO: So what happened?

MANOLO: Well there used to be an old beat up stove in there and behind it was a secret compartment that Louie and I found when we were chavalos. We never told anybody about it, pero then I remembered and so I went over there. As I was getting there I saw Louie come out and head over to his car. I waited until he drove away y después I went in and I found his stash in the same place I was going to put mine.

CHANO: ¡Qué loco!

DOMINGO: Por eso he thinks you got it because you and him were the only ones that knew about it?

MANOLO: Simón. And if I would have told Jiménez maybe he'd still be alive.

DOMINGO: You can't blame yourself for that bato!

MANOLO: I should have killed Louie like I had planned on doing in the first place. While I was in that rehab center that's all I thought about . . . killing ese bato. El mató a mi carnal . . . stabbed him in the back of some fucking alley.

DOMINGO: Jiménez said they could never prove it.

MANOLO: Simón. Anyway when I found that stash I thought I had a better way to get back at him. La única cosa is that I didn't want anyone to get hurt. Y mira lo que pasó, Jiménez got killed, you and Joey Boy get beat up, Carmela almost got raped . . .

DOMINGO: You can't think about esas cosas now; they are over and done with! We have to get back at that bato for what he did.

CHANO: That's right, bro! I didn't take to it very good when he made me kneel down and I'm just itching to get the bato back for it.

MANOLO: We've got to be careful, those batos will be carrying cohetes and they won't hesitate to use them. As long as they think I've got the dope they'll play it cool, pero if they don't, pues no sé. You batos don't take any chances.

CHANO: No way, bro.

DOMINGO: ¿Ahora qué hacemos?

MANOLO: Chano, you go find el Louie and tell him I'll meet him here tonight.

CHANO: What time, bro?

MANOLO: Midnight. No, you better make it one o'clock.

CHANO: Orale, bro.

MANOLO: And Chano be back here at midnight.

CHANO: Can I bring my gun just in case, bro?

MANOLO: Chale, just bring yourself.

CHANO: Over the trees and over the fences I go. Juégala fría, bro. (*Exits.*)

DOMINGO: You gonna get the stuff, Manolo?

MANOLO: I don't have it anymore, Mingo.

DOMINGO: What the hell did you do with it?

MANOLO: I mailed it to Jiménez the morning after I went through cold turkey.

JOEY: I would, just to get away from you.

CARMELA: Nobody's stopping you.

MARIA: Por favor, stop arguing you two! Can't you ever stop bickering?

JOEY: She started it!

CARMELA: No I didn't!

MARIA: Ya! I don't care who started it. I just want you to stop.

CARMELA: Okay. (*There is a pause and everyone is looking at Teresa.*)

TERESA: I wish Manolo was here to enjoy this day with us.

DOMINGO: I know what you mean.

TERESA: When I was a little girl — just a niña — he used to pull my trensas.

DOMINGO: I remember. You used to complain to papá about it and he would tell you not to worry, that he wouldn't pull them if he didn't like you.

TERESA: Then I fell in love with him. I had a mad crush on him and he would just ignore me.

DOMINGO: We were just kids then.

TERESA: When we grew up I still loved him and he was so gentle conmigo . . . just like he was touching una rosa. I can still feel him.

DOMINGO: He's still with us, he'll always be with us.

CHANO: My bro, Manolo, was a heavy dude.

TERESA: ¿Por qué? Why . . . did he have to die?

MARIA: He's not dead, Teresa. It's like Mingo said: "siempre estará con nosotros."

DOMINGO: We all miss him, Teresa . . . pero as he would say, "ni modo." maybe it was better this way than dying from an overdose or something like that.

TERESA: But he was fighting that.

DOMINGO: Sí, I know, pero even the night he was shot he needed a fix. He couldn't help it.

TERESA: He would have won out, Mingo . . . I know he would've . . . I just know it.

DOMINGO: He once told me that he felt that his tiempo had come and that one way or another he would die. Maybe he really knew this and it was just a matter of how and when. Era un hombre bueno y sincero who found it hard to cope with la vida and no matter what, it was going to catch up with him. Pero he was happy at the end Teresa.

CHANO: Amen, bro.

TERESA: I want to do something for him, Mingo.

DOMINGO: ¿Qué, Teresa?

TERESA: I want to help others like Manolo that get caught up in their problems and can't always help themselves. People think drug addicts are freaks and instead of helping them they turn away. Pero just like anybody who's sick they can be helped. They more than anybody need love and understanding, isn't that true, Mingo?

DOMINGO: Sí, Teresa it's true. We should do something to help. Manolo would like that.

CHANO: At least we won't have to worry about that scum Louie anymore because he's going to be in jail for a long time.

JOEY: I hope he rots there.

CARMELA: And Bimbo and Tank, too.

CHANO: There has to be a way to keep las drogas out of the barrio and maybe someday there will be.

MARIA: ¿Nos vamos para mi casa?

DOMINGO: Sí, let's go. Teresa?

TERESA: I'd like to sit here por un rato.

DOMINGO: Sure. Come on you guys, let's go. You coming, Chano?

CHANO: Simón, bro, I'm coming. (*They exit. TERESA sits alone thinking of*

108

Manolo. MANOLO'S *spirit enters from back and walks over to Teresa. He looks at her and smiles as he walks to her side and kneels down. He reaches over and kisses her hand.*)

MANOLO: Te quiero con toda mi vida y con toda mi alma . . . I'll always be with you.
(TERESA *smiles and raises her hand with a knowing look that he is near by.*)

Jaime Carrero

THE FM SAFE

Jaime Carrero is one of the very few writers who has been able to bridge the gap from Island to Mainland by producing works in English for production in New York and works in Spanish for Puerto Rican theatres. Born in Mayagüez in 1931 and raised in Puerto Rico and New York, Carrero was nurtured in the cultural milieu of both locations and participated in important artistic movements on the Island as well as on the Mainland. Quiles, in Poesía nueva puertorriqueña, places Carrero among that first group of literary and political rebels at the University of Puerto Rico that included such poets as Hugo Margenat, Jaime Luis Rodríguez, Anagilda Garrastegui, and Quiles himself.[1] But Carrero was also one of the pioneers of a Nuyorican or Neo-Rican identity,[2] as he called it back in 1964.[3]

Despite the arduous creative task of writing in two different languages and serving two distinct audiences, Jaime Carrero has been recognized as a talented writer of both Spanish and English. He has received the Ateneo Puertorriqueño's highest awards for the novel, short story, and drama,[4] the Illinois Arts Council Award for poetry,[5] and seen a volume of his plays published,[6] as well as various works produced by such exciting companies as Puerto Rico's Teatro Anamú and New York's Puerto Rican Traveling Theatre. And recently the Spanish version of The FM Safe received the prestigious Premio Eugenio Fernández García awarded by the literary journal Sin Nombre.[7]

The FM Safe is the fourth Carrero play to have have been produced by the Puerto Rican Traveling Theatre, a professional bilingual company founded in 1967 by the distinguished actress-director, Miriam Colón — the others were Pipo Subway No Sabe Reír in 1972, and Noo Jall and Flag Inside both in 1973. Like Carrero, the Puerto Rican Traveling Theatre also brings the Island and Mainland together to underline the bicultural reality of Puerto Ricans. Thus the theatre has produced works by Nuyoricans like Piri Thomas and Pedro Pietri as well as by Islanders like René Marqués and Luis Rafael Sánchez. Among other plays produced in Spanish are works by the Spaniard Fernando Arrabal, the Argentine Osvaldo Dragún, the Chilean Jorge Díaz and even the classical French master, Moliere.

The FM Safe deals with the psychological and social effects of the internal colonization of Puerto Ricans in the New York Barrio. As such, if it were not for the triumph of the indomitable spirit of the protagonists, MARCE and VIDAL, the play would portray a very gloomy picture of dehumanization and alienation under the pressures of societal disintegration. Crime and violence seem to permeate the air as VIDAL, a liquor store proprietor, finds it necessary to assume a fortress mentality in order to survive in this ghetto that seems more reminiscent of a lawless, frontier town than a neighborhood in a crowded metropolis. The drama really centers on his development as a character, for he has internalized the "law of the jungle" survival code of the streets and a machismo that has been reenforced by both Anglo and Latin culture: the gung-ho U.S. Marines and the cocky, strutting masculinity of his pet rooster.

---

[1](Rio Piedras: Editorial Edil, 1971), p. 26.

[2]See: Robert F. Muckley, "Introduction," Notes on Neorican Seminar (San Germán: Inter American University, 1972), p. 2.

[3]Quiles, p. 30.

[4]Raquelo tiene un mensaje was awarded first prize in the Certamen de Novela del Festival de Navidad in 1967 and his short story, "El Album de Doña Lucía Tiene Una Página Vacía," was awarded the third prize for short stories. Los Nombres, his second novel, also won recognition from the Ateneo. In 1966, Flag Inside won the Ateneo's first prize for drama.

[5]For his poem, "My Graphological Yo," published in The Rican 1/4 (May, 1974), 63-66.

[6]Teatro (Río Piedras: Ediciones Puerto, 1973).

[7]The play was just published under the title "La caja de caudales" Sin Nombre 8/4 (Enero-Marzo, 1978), 63-99.

The FM Safe *joins* Olú Clemente *in this male-dominated anthology in presenting strong female characters.* MARCE, VIDAL'S *wife, is the positive force that refuses to just survive by allowing this disintegrating society to transform what is most emotionally and morally genuine in her human nature. She rebels, fights back, and not only brings* VIDAL *back to his senses, but turns the tables on the forces of evil represented by the robot-like* RADIOS 1, 2, 3 *and* FERNANDO, *a character very similar to that malevolent spirit,* EL LOUIE, *in Rubén Sierra's Manolo.*

The FM Safe

CHARACTERS:
VIDAL
MARCELINA
PROFESSOR
FERNANDO
RADIOS 1, 2, 3

ACT I
The inside of a liquor store. Dim light. VIDAL *comes out. It is cold and he is using a blanket to protect himself. It is a holiday: Columbus Day, but* VIDAL *is ready to open the store for business even if it is against the law. He thinks that in a Spanish neighborhood there is no other law but his own. He turns the lights on. Takes off the blanket and gets a turtleneck sweater from under the counter. Studies it. Puts it on. Gets a .38 revolver. Makes sure that it is loaded. Puts it inside his sweater and tries to "hide" its bulging presence. Turns the radio on. Salsa music. Folds the blanket and takes it inside. The Radio Announcer gives the correct time: "It's 6:30 a.m. and this is Ron W. with the early salsa."*

VIDAL: (*Looking at his watch,*) Ron, cabrón, you're wrong! Ron, you're a jamón! It's 6:45 a.m. (*The Announcer continues with the music. More salsa.*) No, no. Ron's right — Christ! I should've stayed some more time in bed. (*Hesitates, moves around.*) Jesus, am I getting nervous like a woman? (*Sings, following the lyrics from the record*) Six-thirty. Man! — this is too much. (*Yawns.*) Shit! (*Fixes his sweater around his neck*) Man. (*Moves rhythmically to the sound of salsa. Does some push ups. Gets up and fixes the bulging revolver again. Continues with the words of salsa. Looking at himself in the reflected image does a series of Charles Atlas exercises. Kicks the air like a karate fighter.*) Christ — I don't know what's the matter with me. (*Moves his head around.*) Christ — the Shadow is in the hospital. Why should I worry? Jesus, I know that. (*Hits his open hands — first his right hand, then his left hand.*) Don't tell me that you're getting scared. (*Pause.*) Shit, I shouldn't talk to myself. It's a bad sign. (*Looking around.*) What woulda happened if people saw me talking to myself? (*Moves his head again and rubs his neck.*) Maybe this is the first sign. (*Smiles.*) C'mon, man — you're not crazy. Just . . . just a little nervous. (*Stands firm in the center of the store and shouts.*) Awright, I'm not going to warn you again. Hey, you out there! (*Takes the revolver out.*) If anybody tries to get in I'll blow his head off, understand? (*Hides the revolver again.*) Not bad. Not bad. Shit, better than in the movies. (*Shouts and takes the revolver out again.*) Stay put! Don't move! Freeze! This is the Puerto

Rican Alan Ladd, you hear? (*Relaxes. Hides the revolver.*) Not bad, not bad at all. (*Pause.*) Jesus . . . ¿será verdad? No, it can't be true! The Shadow can't come around 'cause the Shadow is sick and sick men don't fool around with me. (*Gesturing at his own shadow on the wall.*) C'mon, you old bastard, get up! I'm gonna blow your brains up and then I'll eat them like fruit salad. (*Tense again. Suddenly a rooster is heard in the background. VIDAL goes in. Brings out a rooster that he keeps for cockfights somewhere in the neighborhood. To the animal:*) How're you Macho. And don't sing so loud, man. Don't you know that people are sleeping? And then — your sound is very queer in this city, you know. (*Pause. Plays around with the rooster.*) I know what I'll do — if the Shadow comes around I'll let Macho eat his pecker. (*Laughs.*) You're out of sight, baby. (*Kisses rooster. Takes a bottle and opens it. Takes some rum in his mouth and sprinkles the rooster giving it a bath like the old jibaros from the Island do before the fights.*) Yeah, Macho, you're very special. (*Somebody knocks at the door. VIDAL rushes inside with the animal.*) Shit. (*From inside.*) Who's there? (*Puts hand on bulging revolver.*) So early in the morning? — ¿quién es? (*Goes to the door but does not open it. Recognizes the PROFESSOR.*) So, it's you. (*Pause.*) What're you want?
PROFESSOR: Please, open the door.
VIDAL: Why should I?
PROFESSOR: Please, be nice and open the door.
VIDAL: It's too early, man.
PROFESSOR: I know that. Please. It's very cold outside.
VIDAL: C'mon, man, there's a law that prohibits opening a liquor store during a holiday.
PROFESSOR: I can't hear you. (*Pause.*) Why don't you turn that radio off so I can hear you.
VIDAL: Man, go home.
PROFESSOR: You know I don't have a home anymore. I don't have a real home . . . but . . . but the whole neighborhood is my home! You hear me?
VIDAL: It's a holiday.
PROFESSOR: You always open . . . holiday or no holiday . . .
VIDAL: (*Turns the radio off.*) Christ. (*Opens the door.*) Shit, come right in. I don't know why I do the things I do. (*Pause. Serious. Pointing his finger.*) But you better finish the cage . . . or . . . I think it is finished. (*Noticing that the old man is not moving.*) Come in, man.
PROFESSOR: Thank you very much. Thank you very . . .
VIDAL: (*Interrupting him.*) Shut up, man. Quit that polite shit.
PROFESSOR: (*Shaking, puts his hands in his pockets searching for some money.*) My God! I do have a hole in my pocket.
VIDAL: And you've lost your money, ah?
PROFESSOR: I swear by the purity of the Virgin Mary.
VIDAL: That hole in your pocket is part of your body. (*Laughs.*)
PROFESSOR: No. I am telling the truth. I had thirty-five cents in coins. (*Pause.*) At any rate, I want to express my deep and sincere thanks . . . for . . .
VIDAL: Cut it out man, you never had thirty-five cents and you had that hole in there thirty years ago, and the word you want to use is *thirsty* not thirty. My rooster in there got more brains than you! But to show you that I appreciate your talent I'm gonna pay you in advance for the cage. (*Goes in. Brings out a cage for the rooster. Apparently it is finished but unpainted.*)
PROFESSOR: It ain't finished.
VIDAL: It has a door, hinges, everything — what're you mean unfinished?
PROFESSOR: It's gotta be polished and painted. (*Examines some bottles.*) What color do you want. (*Pointing at some bottles. A red like this? Yellowish? Pinkish? Blue?

VIDAL: Wait, wait. Hold it, man. This is fine. I like it just the way it is. It's fine. I'm gonna pay you right now so you go home. Today's a holiday in case you forgot, man. (*Searching for money in his pockets.*)

PROFESSOR: No sir . . . I mean . . . You know, people are like ah . . . nails ah . . . you know, bending, unbending, bending, unbending, bending . . .

VIDAL: Hold it, hold it. Jesus, man! Are you saying you don't want to get paid?

PROFESSOR: Ah . . . Yes, that's what I said.

VIDAL: I don't get it. (*Suspicious.*) Or maybe I do understand. You don't wanna get paid 'cause you figured out that I'll be giving you booze everyday — is that so? Answer me. Everybody needs money these days, so don't give me that shit. (*Noticing two shopping bags that belong to the* PROFESSOR.) What're you carry in those shopping bags?

PROFESSOR: (*Defensively.*) Ah . . . Oh, nothing . . . I . . . I carry my . . . ah . . . equipment . . . my stuff . . . I'm a carpenter . . .

VIDAL: You look more like a bum to me . . . (*Examines his rags.*) Look at you! — you wear the same clothes all the time. And . . . Don't be offended, man but you stink.

PROFESSOR: (*Not paying attention.*) Once . . . Ah . . . I carry my stuff around 'cause once they robbed me — Yessir, they robbed me.

VIDAL: (*Walks back again behind the counter. Uninterested. Making conversation.*) Did you go the police?

PROFESSOR: Oh, no, no.

VIDAL: (*Annoyed.*) Why not?

PROFESSOR: Oh, no, no. I like to make friends. I make friends easily. Ah . . . Oh, no, no. Not the police.

VIDAL: You get fucked up and you don't try to get the law? Why?

PROFESSOR: I take life as it comes . . . Like the thirty cents I had . . .

VIDAL: Thirty-five, you said thirty-five cents.

PROFESSOR: Yes, yessir, thirty-five cents . . .

VIDAL: (*Getting a bottle from behind the counter, pours a big glass of whiskey. Gives it to the* PROFESSOR. *He drinks it fast and slowly stops shaking. Then relaxes.*) All right, I've given you a little gratitude with Macho's blessings. How's this for a friend? How about it?

PROFESSOR: I'm very grateful for your kindness.

VIDAL: That's one thing I like about you — you always find the exact words. But you better use less words around here. I appreciate you but there are other people that don't.

PROFESSOR: The words?

VIDAL: Yeah, less words.

PROFESSOR: Oh, no. I do it because you like it. And it's a habit with me.

VIDAL: Is your hole in your pocket another habit? And if you ask me, a shopping bag is no place to keep important things. (*Smiling.*) Of course, unless you're a bum and you live under a bridge. (*Calming the* PROFESSOR *down.*) Don't get me wrong — I know you are a carpenter.

PROFESSOR: I must admit that I have to lie now and then . . .

VIDAL: I'm beginning to think that you lie all the time.

PROFESSOR: (*To impress* VIDAL *he continues with his pompous vocabulary.*) Well, don't put it in such harsh terms. Say that circumstances beyond my control force me to step out of my habitual pattern.

VIDAL: (*Mixture of surprise and admiration for the* PROFESSOR.) Awright, awright! (*Turns the radio on but very low.*) You like it this low, Professor?

PROFESSOR: That's the civilized way.

VIDAL: (*Tense again but not knowing why.*) Why don't you get a steady job and stop wasting yourself?

PROFESSOR: (*Takes a cigarette butt and lights it.*) Are you my friend?

VIDAL: I'm your friend but you irritate me when you don't listen.

PROFESSOR: Yessir, but . . .

VIDAL: There's nothing that irritates me more than somebody that don't listen to good advice.

PROFESSOR: (*Pause.*) Would you please stop interrupting me so I can answer your question?

VIDAL: I didn't ask you a question.

PROFESSOR: Yessir, you did.

VIDAL: (*With curiosity mixed with more irritation.*) Oh, yes. It was about that thing: wasting yourself. Awright, why don't you get a job like a decent man?

PROFESSOR: I had a job. (*Smokes.*) But I don't care anymore for a job. (*Smokes again.*) Jobs are like jail sentences; you carry your chain twenty-four hours a day around your neck. (*Smokes again and burns his lips. Throws the butt away and spits on the floor.*)

VIDAL: (*Annoyed.*) Hey, don't do that! Don't you know that if you spit on the floor in any public building you go to jail? There's a law against that.

PROFESSOR: I am very sorry. (*On his knees, tries to clean the floor with a dirty handkerchief.*) Now. That's that. (*Gets up.*) I had a job. But what's the use of having a job when you have no real home of your own.

VIDAL: I don't understand you.

PROFESSOR: We are friends and friends are not supposed to understand each other. Friends are for helping other friends. *Understanding* is a religious word. And since God is the only one that *UNDERSTANDS* people, we will never know the meaning of the word.

VIDAL: When you speak like that you're weird, man. I don't understand you.

PROFESSOR: That's why I like you. You don't try to understand me.

VIDAL: To tell you the truth — I don't have to compete with a dude like you, man. I already own a good business.

PROFESSOR: Well, it gives me pleasure to know that you don't have to compete with me. (*Studies the bottle of expensive whiskey.*) That's why I like you.

VIDAL: That's why you're a bum — that's what you should say, man.

PROFESSOR: Bum? Well, ah, ah, ah . . . — that's not a civilized word — not a civilized word. I'm a carpenter — not a steady job — but just the same a carpenter.

VIDAL: (*Irritated.*) You white people criticize Puerto Ricans because you say that we live like pigs. But look at yourself: you're more of a pig than any of us. Look at yourself. (*Pause.*) I learned how to be a man in the Marines and I am very proud of that. I'll never walk around dirty — just, just like you. Have you seen yourself in the mirror?

PROFESSOR: (*Smiles.*) I . . . I must admit that there's some truth in what you're saying.

VIDAL: (*Wondering.*) Jesus, if you only had a good job! If you can make a nice cage for Macho you can be useful, man. (*Pause. Nervous.*) But I like you because you don't harm people. You're good in your own way. (*Pause to look at the door.*) Not like our own people and the Blacks out there. We hate each other and want the other dead. (*Pause.*) And the worst is your own people. Like take my father-in-law . . . My EX father-in-law I should say . . . The son-of-a-bitch lends me some money to pay for a license and some back taxes and now he claims that this business is his. Can you imagine that? This business his own! (*Pause. Walks around talking to himself.*) Either I pay him OR ELSE! Hey, are you listening? (*Pause. Smiles.*) Oh, forget it. Why am I telling you these things anyway? You're just a bum, anyway. (*The rooster is heard two or three times.*)

PROFESSOR: Oh, I'm sorry.

VIDAL: (*Inviting her again.*) Marce.

MARCELINA: (*Turns the radio off.*) You always want everything your own way.

VIDAL: Right. And if I told you to swing with the Professor you swing with the Professor. And if I say: give me your ass, you got to give me your ass. (*Walks back and forth from the front door to the counter.*) Yessir, that's how it should be. I say: open legs — you open your legs. Adio', man! (*Loud.*) You hear me? (*Louder.*) You hear me? (*The rooster is heard again.*)

MARCELINA: I hear you and I hope that the goddamned rooster dies. It makes me sick. Phew! — what a smell!

VIDAL: (*Walks around like an animal in a cage.*) ¡Carajo! Coño. If I risk my life in this fucking place I expect you to give me some respect now and then. Adio'. (*Pause. Facing her.*) You hear me? (*Pause.*) Everything I've done in my life I've done it with pure heart and guts.

MARCELINA: (*Ignoring his remarks.*) I smell liquor here.

VIDAL: When I bought this place I knew it was going to be a tough situation. In fact, since I came to New York when I was a kid of eleven I said: "I'll never go back again to the shack where I lived with my family. In Puerto Rico." (*Takes a bottle and makes it spin on the counter.*) Just as clear as you see this bottle spin like a merry-go-round that's as clear as I saw this place. (*Pause to continue playing with the bottle.*) My ex-father-in-law said: "It's a tough neighborhood." And I said: "Mira, Sombra, I'm just the match for it." Like I said, óyelo, man! I looked right in his eyes and told 'im: "Man, once a tough marine, you remain tough." They don't take sissies in the service. (*Keeps on playing.*) Give me the name of one *Spic* in this city that don't push himself up showing his guts with his own click and you're giving me a yellow brand of Puerto Rican. I've learned to fight hard and I do the hardest fighting that I can. That's why I'm here. That's why you take the money to the bank 'cause baby, I'm the boss. (*As soon as he finishes a strong statement like that he spins the bottle faster and faster.*) I've got this Spanish blood in me, see? I intend to keep that blood.

MARCELINA: Stop that. (*Tries to take the bottle away from him and drops it. It breaks.*) Shit.

VIDAL: Now, look what you've done!

MARCELINA: You're to blame — why don't you quit that childish nonsense of OH ONCE A MARINE ALWAYS A MARINE. I'm TOUGHER than YOU, TOUGHER than the DEVIL, TOUGHER THAN (*Makes faces and ridicules him.*) GOD!

VIDAL: (*Takes a broom and begins to clean the broken glass.*) Yeah, right, I'm tougher than GOD, 'cause HE made me!

MARCELINA: God taught us to be intelligent so we could see when a dump like this wasn't producing . . . (VIDAL *gets a mop and begins to clean the liquid on the floor.*) It's up to us to use our intelligence. God gave many, many lessons but you were late, right, Vidal? (VIDAL *is finishing with the mop.*) You missed the whole batch, ah Vidal?

VIDAL: (*Taking the mop inside. From the other room.*) GOD even taught us how to be horny!

MARCELINA: (*Sudden burst of laughter.*) What? What . . .'re you saying? (*Can't control her laughter.*) What???

VIDAL: (*Emerging, very serious.*) As I said: GOD taught us how to be horny — you know, how to carry the big antennas . . . (*Uses his fingers to show two horns.*) I don't think it's funny. (*Pause.*) To wear shiny horns on our foreheads is plenty ridiculous, you know that? (*Takes the broom again. Keeps cleaning smaller pieces of glass.*) And He approved of it. Then if He didn't — then, how come He decided to be the father of Jesus Christ rather than let poor Joseph do his thing with the

Virgin. (*Watches* MARCELINA *laugh.*) That's not funny!

MARCELINA: GOD . . . (*Cannot control her laughter.*)

VIDAL: Sure, Joseph was the real father, you know that.

MARCELINA: That's . . . that's supposed to be . . . a miracle. Boy oh boy!

VIDAL: (*Takes the trash to the trash can and hides the broom.*) I make my own miracles!

MARCELINA: You say that because your ex-flame gave you two shiny horns — Am I right, baby?

VIDAL: (*Menacing.*) Just what d' you mean by that?

MARCELINA: Nothing, baby.

VIDAL: You better begin shaping up or else! You damn well know that I left the son-of-a-bitch before she could double cross me.

MARCELINA: That's not the way I remember it. Don't you remember how you kicked your brother-in-law's ass right in the office when the Shadow wasn't there? The boy took some cash from the Laundry's register. (VIDAL *doesn't say anything, but takes another bottle and begins the same game again.*) The boy was in Junior High. He was tall but skinny. Shoulda seen him now. Anyway, your ex-flame was in Atlantic City with a copy. (VIDAL *is not paying attention or tries to show a superficial concern with some bottles behind him.*) (MARCELINA *smiling.*) Mighty interesting bottles, ah Vidal? (VIDAL *takes the bottle again and plays with it.*) Hey, stop that. That's very expensive liquor.

VIDAL: You're beginning to repeat yourself.

MARCELINA: Viidaaallll . . . I'm Fernaaannnnddooooo . . . You kicked myassss . . . when I was a boy . . . But nowwww I'm a mannn . . . Ammmm coming to get youuuuuu . . . now. (*Takes a tablecloth from near the counter and puts it over her head.*) Now I'm the Shadow . . . and I'm sending my sonnnnn to kick yourrr asssss . . . Viiiddaaaallllll . . .

VIDAL: (*Stops playing.*) This Vidal is getting fed up with your jokes.

MARCELINA: I'm not joking. (*Takes off the tablecloth and throws it away.*)

VIDAL: There's a Spanish saying that everyday a pendejo leaves the house and I bet that today you're the pendeja that left the house. (*Laughs loudly.*)

MARCELINA: It smells here of whiskey and it ain't from the bottle you broke . . . and it ain't from the rooster's shit!

VIDAL: Forget what I said a while ago about not opening. I wanna make some extra dough today. Today I'm Vidal Columbus if you know what I mean.

MARCELINA: The Professor's been here?

VIDAL: Don't you change the subject, you hear?

MARCELINA: I'm not changing no subject and I don't care to change the subject and you don't scare me.

VIDAL: Since when you care about the Professor?

MARCELINA: I don't care about the Professor. I just want to know if he came here today.

VIDAL: I told the Professor that you hate his guts.

MARCELINA: So he was here, ah?

VIDAL: I didn't say that he was here. I just said that I told him that you hate his guts.

MARCELINA: Did you give him booze?

VIDAL: I didn't say that the Professor was here.

MARCELINA: He was here all right. You can't destroy or evaporate the so-called built-in-power of whiskey. When I came in the stench was a built-in experience in the whole place. And the poor man is sick, you know.

VIDAL: All right, he was here. So what?

MARCELINA: And you gave him booze again.

VIDAL: I gave him booze.

VIDAL: I'm not scared.

MARCELINA: Well, I am!

VIDAL: The beard is a sign of strength and it scares people.

MARCELINA: You wanna make use of my money before I die.

VIDAL: Too bad that you can't grow a beard. I'm not scared.

MARCELINA: If you're not scared, how come you carry a gun and don't let me use it to go home with the money? Or to the bank. For twelve days in a row I've been around with a lot of money. You know how dangerous that is? (*Waiting for* VIDAL'S *reaction. None.*) Even the guard at the bank noticed that you don't go there anymore. Oh, he said to remind you of a larger or logger or lugger — you know, some kind of a gun he said you've got. He wants to buy it.

VIDAL: It's a German LUGER — a good gun. But I don't sell it.

MARCELINA: I didn't know you had a German gun.

VIDAL: Baby, there are plenty of things that you don't know about me.

MARCELINA: You should tell me.

VIDAL: You must ask!

MARCELINA: Why do you keep so many secrets from me?

VIDAL: There are things that must be secret — like what we do here.

MARCELINA: Don't kid yourself about that.

VIDAL: I know my people and they'll never suspect of what we do here.

MARCELINA: Don't kid yourself about that.

VIDAL: I know my people and they'll never suspect of what we do here.

MARCELINA: They suspect, Vidal. You've been here for too long.

VIDAL: They don't have enough brains to discover what we do.

MARCELINA: Like the Spanish proverb: eyes that don't see, heart that don't feel???

VIDAL: Yeah, just like that. If people don't see what we do, they don't have no feeling for it.

MARCELINA: (*Goes to her coat. Takes the plastic bottle with pills. Takes one. Before putting it under her tongue.*) I'm tired of serving as guinea pig. Christ, I don't want to get killed. (*Takes the pill.*)

VIDAL: All right, stay here and I give you the gun.

MARCELINA: (*Fans her mouth.*) Man, this is hot!

VIDAL: Hey, you're the one that's not listening now.

MARCELINA: You don't understand. What I'm saying all the time is that we've got to sell this dump.

VIDAL: Those few punks from around here are going to be put away very soon.

MARCELINA: Few punks? (*Pause.*) I never forget a face. I'm sure that that punk with the radio is here because of your father-in-law. He's around. I smell it. They'll be here today! When are they going to be put away, Vidal? When? Tomorrow? Next month? Next year? When, Vidal, when? (*The rooster is heard again*)

VIDAL: (*Exits. From inside.*) Soon! Soon!

MARCELINA: Not soon enough for my nerves.

VIDAL: (*Coming in.*) Just hold it for a while.

MARCELINA: It's dangerous, Vidal.

VIDAL: You make it worse. Like what you did to that punk with the radio.

MARCELINA: Well, they better learn how to behave. Especially the Shadow's son!

VIDAL: That's no way to be cool.

MARCELINA: I don't know how to be cool anymore.

VIDAL: You don't know how to be nothing anymore.

MARCELINA: What d' you mean?

VIDAL: You've got a short memory. (*Trying to touch her again.*)

MARCELINA: And you're a sex maniac. Besides, I'm not a magician. No woman in these circumstances would open her legs just like that for the hell of it.

VIDAL: You're supposed to be my wife.

MARCELINA: And we're supposed to make love home, not in a liquor store or under a table.

VIDAL: You've got to use your imagination.

MARCELINA: Apply that advice to yourself: go to the toilet and masturbate.

VIDAL: One of these days you'll regret it — and . . . everything you're saying. (*Takes the coat off the chair.*)

MARCELINA: (*Rushing to get her coat.*) Hey, don't touch that coat. (*Takes it from his hands.*)

VIDAL: Is it made out of gold?

MARCELINA: Just don't fool around with it! Your hands are dirty.

VIDAL: What're you hiding?

MARCELINA: Nothing.

VIDAL: Keeping secrets from me?

MARCELINA: Of course not! But I'm tired of this place.

VIDAL: With the exception of two or three punks we're surrounded by good people — our own good people.

MARCELINA: Two or three punks? Two multiplied by a thousand and divided by zero-zero in such a way that 90 percent are surrounding this place.

VIDAL: What are you saying?

MARCELINA: That they stink . . . those punks stink. And our people don't learn, never learn. We hate each other so much that we kill what's good in each one of us. You're a very good example. You could do a lot of good if you had some little love in yourself for the others . . . and for me! (*Imitating the typical individual that goes along with nationalistic slogans for his own sake, the typical demagogue.*) Viva Puerto Rico, man! Yeah, man, we're gonna make it! Right on! Dig it man! I love you! Power to the people! And baby you're exactly like that. (*To* VIDAL — *pointing at him.*) You're exactly like that. You see an old Puerto Rican lady in the subway asking for Soundview Avenue in the Bronx and you're the first one to say: Jesus, these hicks should go back to Puerto Rico! And I say to you: Vidal, fuck you. You also stink! (*Pause to get some air.*) Everybody in this neighborhood hates your guts because you're just for yourself like everybody in this place. You say: Hey, charge that guy another quarter. And one quarter here and another quarter there makes up a lot of hate, Vidal, HATE! Jesus, why can't we be more civilized? Tell me man — just a little help here and there — that's what I ask. Is that too much to ask? Everybody around here acts like a poverty pimp. And baby, you're not different. This business is hate; your gun is hate; Fernando is hate; la Sombra is hate . . . (*Sits down heavily.*)

VIDAL: You don't know how to relax. That's your problem.

MARCELINA: (*Visibly tired.*) How about you? How about you. You don't even spend money for a good time.

VIDAL: Sure, I do.

MARCELINA: Vidal, when was the last time that we had a real good time? And I don't mean the beach or the country side. I don't even mean the movies . . . and we used to see every movie that came to the RKO! Of course, that's when I was a kid.

VIDAL: Was it a long time ago . . . (*Sarcastic.*) LADY?

MARCELINA: Of course not! (*Smiling.*) Hey, buddy, there's a subject that you hate to touch. Don't let me remind you of it!

VIDAL: Go ahead.

MARCELINA: (*Getting up.*) You better stop that AGE-STUFF baby, 'cause you damn well know that you're already past the nostalgia break for the twenties! In fact, your whole life is the history of nostalgia.

VIDAL: You didn't have a dime when you were a kid.

from me?

PROFESSOR: May I say something?

VIDAL: What?

PROFESSOR: May I say something?

VIDAL: Now, Professor — I don't think you can change this or do you?

PROFESSOR: I can make a suggestion.

VIDAL: Go ahead.

PROFESSOR: Do you have an alarm?

MARCELINA: Yes, we have an alarm. A very expensive alarm.

VIDAL: (*Shows the revolver.*) And I've got this alarm. (*Hides the revolver again.*)

PROFESSOR: Why don't you both go to the bank together — or take the money home together?

VIDAL: Because somebody must stay here. If two or three punks can lift a few bottles from under somebody's nose, imagine what can happen if I get out of here.

PROFESSOR: But then, what's the use of having an expensive alarm if you cannot simply go home and relax?

VIDAL: That's to show you, man, that you are a bum and bums have no responsibility. (*The rooster is heard again.*) It takes brains to do what we do — you know that?

PROFESSOR: But . . . but, don't you have a safe?

VIDAL: (*Suddenly takes the* PROFESSOR'S *hand and almost carries him over to where* MARCELINA *is standing.*) Come here, you bum. (*Holds his wife and pushes the* PROFESSOR'S *hand under* MARCELINA'S *skirt. First she tries to get away but* VIDAL *is holding her with a strong grip.*) Now, feel that! (*The* PROFESSOR *tries to bring his hand back.* VIDAL *holds his hand firmly.* MARCELINA *tries to cover herself but he continues to push the* PROFESSOR'S *hand under her skirt.*) You like that, you like that?

MARCELINA: (*Suddenly she raises her skirt.*) This is what you want? (*Her panty hose is full of money.*)

VIDAL: (*Still holding the* PROFESSOR'S *hand.*) What a piece of ass, ah Professor? And look what's surrounding it. What d'you know — it's the dirty money! The green vegetable! The magic paper! (*Pushes the* PROFESSOR *and he falls to the floor.*) That's my safe, Professor! But you're a bum. You can't understand this. That's my responsibility! (*Silence.*)

MARCELINA: You are very stupid, you know that? (*Pauses.*) Why did you have to do that? Now he knows.

VIDAL: (*Laughing.*) So what, he's just a lousy bum, a dumb-jerk!

MARCELINA: He lives in the streets. (*The* PROFESSOR *is getting up.*)

VIDAL: (*Holding the* PROFESSOR *by his rags.*) Now, listen you bum, what I've shown you stays in your fucking mind, you hear? (*Pushes him around.*) And it will stay inside your head now, tomorrow and forever. (*Hits his face with his open hands.*) And don't you dare open you big mouth. Understand?

PROFESSOR: I'm not going to say anything . . . (*Tries to cover his face.*) I . . . don't want . . . any trouble . . . I like you very much . . . and . . . and . . . very grateful to you . . . You've given me warmth . . . and I appreciate that . . .

MARCELINA: All right, leave the old man alone.

VIDAL: I'm not gonna do nothing to him. (*Keeps slapping the* PROFESSOR'S *face.*) I just wanna teach 'im a lesson that he'll never forget. (*Pushes the* PROFESSOR *around mercilessly.*) You said something about the sky, right, right? Did you? C'mon speak up! The law of good manners show that you gotta answer me! Answer me!

MARCELINA: (*Tries to free the old man. To* VIDAL.) Don't be stupid! He's just an old man!

VIDAL: (*Still holding the* PROFESSOR.) Did you come here to spy? Answer me? Do I scare you?

PROFESSOR: Yes . . . yessir . . . yessir . . .

MARCELINA: Let him go! You're hurting him. He's just an old man. Vidal, please.

VIDAL: He's saying yessir to everything I say. It means that he's a spy! Are you? (*Takes the old man by the neck.*) I'll let you go as soon as you tell me something about the sky and something about things that are perfect and something about facts, facts, facts . . . (MARCELINA *struggles now with him. But he continues to hold the old man by the neck.*) C'mon, speak up. Are you scared of me?

MARCELINA: Stop it, Vidal. Stop it!

VIDAL: ¡Coño! I wanna make sure that he keeps his mouth shut. (*To the old man.*) You're gonna keep your mouth shut, right? Do you have a name? Yeah, you've got a name. I know your name. Your name is pidgeon, stool-pidgeon! And you came here to spy on us!

MARCELINA: That's enough, Vidal!

VIDAL: (*Holds the old man by the rags now.*) You're too old to be part of a gang, but they have ways to get your mouth open. You keep your mouth shut, you hear? It's for your own good.

PROFESSOR: (*Coughing.*) Yessir . . . yessir . . .

VIDAL: All right. (*Pushes him out of the store.*) Get the hell out of here you stinking bum! (*The* PROFESSOR *exits. To* MARCELINA.) And you, how dare you question me in front of that dumb jerk. (*Suddenly he holds his waist where the revolver is and looks at her furiously. Blackout.*)

ACT II

VIDAL *comes in from back door. Shaved. Clean.* MARCELINA *is looking out in silence. Sounds of street coming alive. The sound can stay in the background from time to time. The rooster is heard several times.*

VIDAL: (*Tries the lights. He wants everything under a strong light. Tries again.*) Marce, about this light? (MARCELINA *does not answer.*) Marce, you prefer all the lights? All right, I'll keep all the lights on. (*Turns on a switch and the light is very bright.*) Marce, look I shaved. Yep, a clean shave is like a good cup of coffee, real coffee. (*Looking at* MARCELINA.) A cup of real good coffee — homemade. (*Turns the lights down a little and leaves them like that.*) Yeah, that's better. How d'you like this light?

MARCELINA: (*Sad.*) You're changing, Vidal.

VIDAL: (*Still playing with the switches.*) What?

MARCELINA: (*Without looking at him.*) You're getting harsh and mean.

VIDAL: What? Hey, if you wanna talk to me look this way. I've got a face, you know.

MARCELINA: When you react the way you did with that poor old man, you're not better than the Shadow or his son.

VIDAL: Why don't you go home and cook something good to cele brate Columbus Day?

MARCELINA: And you're breaking the law.

VIDAL: (*Leaving the regular lights on. Reacting fast.*) Breaking the law — what law?

MARCELINA: Many laws. Some written. Some not written.

VIDAL: Would . . . please, explain yourself?

MARCELINA: You served liquor in here. You keep an animal in here. You're opening today.

VIDAL: We pay the police.

MARCELINA: Suppose some rookie or somebody else comes around? How you explain these things?

VIDAL: Listen, if you wanna talk to me come closer and look in my face. You're getting too serious and I don't like that.

MARCELINA: (*Coming to him.*) Why don't we close up and take the day off? We can go someplace and eat and then see a show downtown.

VIDAL: Are you out of your mind? Why do you think I've stayed here all these long days and nights? You think we can just get out of here and forget everything? (*Laughing.*) If Columbus risked his ass in the ocean I can risk mine right here.

MARCELINA: Then you'll have to risk your ass alone, baby because I'm walking out. (*Takes the coat.*)

VIDAL: Please, understand. If we go downtown, by the time we come back there'll be nothing here. (*Pause.*) It's not that I'm against having a good time. Sure, I'd like to blow some money, too . . . now and then.

MARCELINA: (*Finishes getting her coat on.*) For the last twelve days I've been to the bank every morning, except this morning . . . And every night . . . I'll go home now and I'll take the little money I've got — but that's the end. From today on you solve your own problems. Count me out.

VIDAL: (*Stopping her at the door. Embraces her.*) Wait, baby, wait. You're not going to leave me here today, are you?

MARCELINA: I'm saying that today you risk your goddammed life and you do it alone! (*Pause.*) Get Macho to help you.

VIDAL: I need you.

MARCELINA: Would you promise something?

VIDAL: What?

MARCELINA: To close for the day.

VIDAL: I can't.

MARCELINA: (*Opens the door to go.*) Know something, Vidal, I'm tired of asking the guard at the bank to open the toilet to get the money out of the panty hose. (*Closes the door and gets in.*) Listen to this before I leave. The guard is a very courteous man, but, goddamnit, he may think by now that my diarrhea is like an avalanche 'cause it don't stop. They may think at the bank that I'm dying of some intestinal cancer or something. Last week I couldn't face the guard. He said: "Don't bother to explain: here's the key, open it yourself." And he went away laughing. Shit! Vidal, I'm tired. Dead tired. (*She opens the door.*)

VIDAL: (*Holding her.*) Hold it. Okay.

MARCELINA: Okay what?

VIDAL: We'll close the store.

MARCELINA: (*With relief.*) Okay, get your coat.

VIDAL: No, wait. Come on. We'll decide what to do. (MARCELINA *does not move.*) Let's have a little drink before we leave.

MARCELINA: (*She comes in.*) All right, just a little wine.

VIDAL: Sure. (*They both go in but they do not close the door. He goes in to look for a bottle and two paper cups. He comes in.* MARCELINA *takes off her coat.*) Just one drink. (*Pours two drinks. He stands behind the counter and she sits near the door.*) Come closer woman. (*She moves slowly.*) Closer. I don't bite. (*She comes near the counter.*) C'mon, smile woman. (*She smiles faintly.*)

MARCELINA: Salud. (*She drinks in silence.*)

VIDAL: What's eating you?

MARCELINA: You treated me like a whore.

VIDAL: What?

MARCELINA: I'll never forget it.

VIDAL: (*Trying to kiss her.*) Oh, man, that was just a joke. Jesus Christ, I was joking.

MARCELINA: (*Drinks slowly.*) I'll never forget it. You treated me like trash. I may not be a lady that you find in the movies but I have feelings. (*Serious face.*) You forced that dirty hand on me. That stinking bum touched me.

VIDAL: Wait a minute. Don't get me wrong. I . . .

MARCELINA: I'm sorry for the old man but . . .

VIDAL: Wait, wait a minute. You're all wrong! I just wanted to show him my bank. To touch you? MAN! That wasn't my intention. I swear. I just wanted to tell the man: Mira, stupid, I've got brain: I designed this safe, it's my safe.

MARCELINA: (*With indignation.*) What? Again you're wrong because I was the one that suggested the idea of the panty hose.

VIDAL: Oh, no.

MARCELINA: Oh, yes. You know something, the trouble with you is that you have no imagination. You're too goddamned down to earth. There's no romance in you!

VIDAL: (*Laughs. Then a straight face.*) Well, let me tell you something; don't force the issue too much. You can walk out on me anytime you like baby. There's no paper that binds us together. (*Laughs.*) If your old man only knew.

MARCELINA: (*Furious.*) Keep my father out of this filthy con . . .

VIDAL: An imaginary ceremony. An imaginary honeymoon. (*Keeps on laughing*) Go, Marce. Go ahead. (*Takes the coat. She takes it from his hands and throws it on the chair.*) Ooooopppppsss — excuse me, lady.

MARCELINA: (*Drinks her wine and asks for another one. Then drinks slowly, looking at VIDAL curiously and smiling at him.*) You just gave me an idea, Vidal. I wanted to leave just a while ago. But now, I'll stay here with you and we will face everything together since this wine has some magic power that's giving life to me. I feel it. (*Pause.*) Just don't forget that half of this store is mine and twenty percent belongs to the Shadow. The rest, baby, is yours. (*Smiling and looking at him curiously.*)

VIDAL: What're you doing?

MARCELINA: What?

VIDAL: Why do you smile like that?

MARCELINA: I always smile like that, especially when I've had two drinks in a row.

VIDAL: No, you look strange.

MARCELINA: (*Goes to him and kisses his forehead.*) Now, baby. You see how I love you — and how I take care of you.

VIDAL: I don't know what's eating you up. (*Pause.*) Hey, and why'd you say I don't have no imagination? I know damn well that I have imagination.

MARCELINA: (*Matter of factly.*) I suggested the panty hose.

VIDAL: Well, in a way.

MARCELINA: In ALL ways. I cooked up the idea. (*Smiles.*) You wanted to take the money out of this place in a hat and hats don't work here. You know that. Nobody uses hats anymore. It was plainly too obvious. (*Pause. Asks for more wine. VIDAL serves it.*) Then, what about the idea of the battery box? (*Laughs.*) Shit! Everybody knows that I can't carry a battery around. That was stupid!

VIDAL: All right, all right, so it was your idea.

MARCELINA: Like when the dog began scratching its ears. I suggested the soxs for the four legs and you said that it was your idea.

VIDAL: Well, I said: "Cover the dog's legs."

MARCELINA: You didn't even say that.

VIDAL: I said: "The fucking bitch is making a bloody mess of his ears." (*Laughs.*)

MARCELINA: That's what you said. That's the way you react. (*Looking at him and smiling.*) You have no imagination, darling.

VIDAL: (*Hits his chest, laughs.*) No imagination, ah? When my daughter got married two years ago . . .

MARCELINA: A year ago.

VIDAL: Two years ago.

MARCELINA: One. I remember because around that time we began our thing together.

VIDAL: Anyhow, when my daughter married that . . . (*Searching for the word.*)

MARCELINA: Fag?

VIDAL: (*Laughing.*) Yeah, right — that fag. When she married that fag I cooked up some ideas too. (*Goes inside. Comes out with a top hat on and an old marine jacket that barely fits.*) You see this? (MARCELINA *begins to laugh.*) Go ahead and laugh. But let me tell you that I looked en . . . en . . . dignified that day.

MARCELINA: (*Goes to a corner, gets an umbrella, opens it and gives it to* VIDAL.) Now you're ready for the circus act! (*Laughs loudly.*)

VIDAL: The day I made corporal in the Marines I drank twenty four cans of beer — in a row — one — (*Gestures as if drinking, throws away one 'can.*) bang! — two — bang! — three . . . I had a bet with this redheaded Irish guy and I won . . . A small bet — $10.00.

MARCELINA: And you drank twenty-four gallons of whiskey the night your daughter married that fag!

VIDAL: (*Acts as if going up the church aisle.*) I was sweating . . . I barely touched the baby's hand . . . (*Imitates a trumpet with the beginning of the "Wedding March." He ends with a very loud shrieking sound. They both laugh for a while.*) And just to think . . . (*Can't stop laughing.*) To think . . . that I paid that guy $30.00 for that: three fucking seconds of trumpet music. Ten dollars a second, and you say that I'm stingy?

MARCELINA: (*Surprised.*) You paid what, $30.00 for that? Play it again!

VIDAL: (*Stands at attention and imitates the sound again — this time as if he were playing reveille or taps.*) Just for that.

MARCELINA: Oh, you dumb idiot!

VIDAL: Hey, hey, watch your words.

MARCELINA: Are you out of your mind? $30.00 for that?

VIDAL: Oh, but you gotta understand — that guy was a friend of mine and he was trying to kick the drug, you know.

MARCELINA: You're still an out-of-this-world-blind-fucking stupid-ass idiot!

VIDAL: (*Begins to dance around.*) Aha, aha, the wine is getting to you!

MARCELINA: I didn't know about those $30.00. (*Pause. Gives the glass to* VIDAL.) Just a little more. (VIDAL *pours some wine. Hands the glass back to her.*) Well, you're not to blame. That ex-flame of yours was the one that made the plans for the wedding. A no good, pompous hick, that's what she is! $5000 for the hall. Can you beat that? $300 for a Rolls Royce! Jesus, rented just for half an hour! $700 for a Fifth Avenue wedding gown. Man! $700 for rugs, for the whole house for a girl and a boy that don't even know how to do it without a sex manual!

VIDAL: You think that's expensive? You know, the whole wedding and all . . . ?

MARCELINA: That's not expensive; it's criminal! No wonder she gives you two shiny horns!

VIDAL: (*Not paying attention to her.*) Marce, now that you're high, c'mon, let's do it under the table or under the counter.

MARCELINA: That bitch of yours danced all night with the cop. Or maybe you don't remember? Oh, yes, you were busy talking about cockfights!

VIDAL: C'mon, Marce, let's do it here.

MARCELINA: (*Facing him.*) You know, Vidal, you need me, you need me. You're like a child. You need protection.

VIDAL: C'mon, Marce . . .

MARCELINA: Your ex-flame made all the plans and the Shadow made sure you paid twice as much. That's when I began to help you. (*To herself.*) I know, I kept his books. But now the old bastard is in the hospital dying of cancer. Good for him! (*To him. Loud.*) Take off that ridiculous hat, damn it! And that goddamned jacket! You're not in the marines anymore.

VIDAL: (*Not paying any attention to her. Sings and dances for her.*)
Mira como bailo, nena.
To' esto pa' ti.
To' esto pa' ti.
Mira como bailo, nena.

MARCELINA: Stop that, you old, ridiculous man!

VIDAL: (*Keeps on singing.*) *Mira como bailo, nena.* You take pills, baby.

MARCELINA: So what!

VIDAL: *Mira como bailo, nena. To' esto es pa' ti.* Old people take pills!

MARCELINA: Sick people take pills. (*Suddenly a man with a radio enters, obviously a member of a gang. He is dressed in a jacket similar to* FERNANDO'S. *His radio is on very loud. He faces* VIDAL. VIDAL *stops his clowning around. Puts the hat on the counter but keeps the marine jacket on.*)

VIDAL: (*To* MARCELINA.) Shit, you didn't close the door.

RADIO 1: (*Lowering volume of radio but not much.*) Are you open today?

VIDAL: It depends.

RADIO 1: What d'you mean?

VIDAL: Don't know, it's a holiday.

RADIO 1: Are you the owner? (*Pauses to look curiously at* MARCELINA *and give a glance at the walls.*) Either you know or you don't know. (*Pause. Volume of radio up.*) Man, I don't dig your indecision. You must know that I don't get your message.

VIDAL: (*Loud to compensate for the volume of the radio.*) I'm giving you no message.

RADIO 1: Yessir, you're giving me a message.

VIDAL: Then learn how to read.

RADIO 1: Don't get smart.

VIDAL: Look, mister, I'm not open now.

RADIO 1: You're open during other holidays, why not today?

VIDAL: Because today I'm doing some exercises, as you can see.

RADIO 1: Are you making fun of me, hermano?

VIDAL: No.

RADIO 1: Then why'd you insist on twisting my words around? (*Closer.*) I don't like your wisecracks.

VIDAL: (*Tries to push the man out.*) Look, I'm not open today!

RADIO 1: (*Resists.*) That's not what you said. You said that you were not sure. I'm helping you: now you've got to make up your mind. (*Suddenly* MARCELINA *turns* VIDAL'S *radio on very loud.*) Hey, shut that radio off! (*Walking towards her.*) Hey, shut that radio off.

VIDAL: (*To* MARCELINA.) Are you out of your mind?

RADIO 1: (*To* VIDAL.) Tell your wife to shut that radio off.

MARCELINA: (*Loud.*) Why don't you tell me yourself?

RADIO 1: All right, turn that radio off!

MARCELINA: As soon as you turn yours off!

RADIO 1: What?

MARCELINA: (*Loud.*) Turn that goddamned radio off!

RADIO 1: (*Turns his radio off.* MARCELINA *turns her radio off. Pause. Turns his head in all directions.*) Man! I can't concentrate. (*Holding his head.*) Shit, I can't concentrate! (*Walks out of the store.*)

VIDAL: (*With relief.*) For a moment I thought I would use the gun. (*Pause.*) How'd you do it? (*Closes door.*)

MARCELINA: Do what?

VIDAL: Force him to shut the radio off.

MARCELINA: I don't know.

VIDAL: But you knew that he'd go out of here.

MARCELINA: I didn't know.

VIDAL: But he left and he left fast. (*Pause.*) I'm surprised.

MARCELINA: You're too easy to surprise.

VIDAL: He left fast. That cat's not coming back.

MARCELINA: You're wrong: he went out to get some help.

VIDAL: This is the second time you do it. That's a record. That guy's not bothering us no more.

MARCELINA: Don't kid yourself, that's Fernando's friend and I bet that they'll come back. And I'll bet that Fernando wants to get even with you; probably the Shadow wants his twenty percent in cash.

VIDAL: Why is it always you do something right and then you turn around and do something wrong?

MARCELINA: I'm learning from you. You like to joke around and I'm learning very fast. (VIDAL *takes off the jacket and throws it inside.*) Don't get angry, baby.

VIDAL: 'Am not angry.

MARCELINA: Tell me, why'd you decide to imitate Alan Ladd?

VIDAL: What the hell's that supposed to mean?

MARCELINA: You said that you liked to imitate Alan Ladd, didn't you?

VIDAL: Yeah.

MARCELINA: Why?

VIDAL: 'Cause he was short like a spik. You know, like me.

MARCELINA: Why do you need a gun, then?

VIDAL: What're you driving at? 'Cause if you ask me, I don't know.

MARCELINA: Let me be very clear to you, man. The next time you humiliate me like you did with the Professor touching me, I'll see to it that you pay dearly!

VIDAL: Oh, baby, I was fooling around. C'mon, ah.

MARCELINA: Don't fool around with me, Vidal.

VIDAL: Hey, you want some more wine?

MARCELINA: Why not? (*Gives him a paper cup.*)

VIDAL: (*Pours wine into her paper cup.*) No, shit, Marce, I wanna give you a birthday present.

MARCELINA: You'll give me a birthday present the day you behave and be good to me.

VIDAL: (*Looking into her eyes.*) I like your dark eyes. (*She laughs and pushes away.*) I'm serious. But I look at my eyes and aggghhh . . . (*Makes all kinds of faces against the side of a bottle.*) Phew! Jesus, what an ugly face!

MARCELINA: (*Laughing.*) Hey, stupid, you're getting a distorted reflection. (VIDAL *continues his clowning around.*) Hey, dummy, you' not that ugly. In fact, if I may say so, sometimes, sometimes you really look good . . .

VIDAL: C'mon, Marce, you know I'm ugly.

MARCELINA: No, I'm serious. When you stop acting like a grouchy old man . . . (*Takes his face in her hands.*) Yeah, you really look good.

VIDAL: (*Not believing her.*) You really think so?

MARCELINA: Chico, you know I love you.

VIDAL: You boost my morale up. I'm serious. (*Takes her face and kisses her gently.*) Boy, woman! You are my temptation. (*They kiss.*)

MARCELINA: God bless your temptations. (*Drinks.*)

VIDAL: (*Remembering.*) You know, I don't like to be soft . . . but . . . (*Pause suddenly.*) I . . . I love you. Might as well say it: yeah, I do. I'm tempted to close shop and get the hell out of here.

MARCELINA: (*Giving him the paper cup.*) I'll drink to that. C'mon, keep up your temptation. (VIDAL *pours wine into her paper cup and she drinks it at once and offers her empty cup again.*) For your temptations, Vidal. (*Drinks again.*) Wow.

VIDAL: (*While pouring the wine.*) Hey, Marce, you ever had a dream? You know, a deep down dream?

MARCELINA: Sure, everybody has a secret dream. What's yours, Vidal?

VIDAL: Tell me yours first.

MARCELINA: No, you tell me yours first.

VIDAL: Vidal, you bring this here. Vidal, you stay here. Vidal do this, Vidal do that. Why me?

MARCELINA: Okay, I'll tell you mine first. (*Drinks.*) I wanted to be a movie star like Deanna Durbin or Rita Hayworth. (*Does some singing and dancing around.*) How's that? (VIDAL *applauds.*) Now you tell me your secret dream.

VIDAL: Not bad, woman, not bad. (*She sits waiting for him.*)

MARCELINA: Well?

VIDAL: Sorry, but today's a holiday and I can't think straight during holidays.

MARCELINA: Oh, you crook, you damn crook.

VIDAL: No, wait, I'll tell you my secret dream. But you gotta promise me something. (*She nods.*) Promise me that you're not gonna laugh even if what I say sounds silly. (*Waits for her answer.*)

MARCELINA: Awright, go ahead. (*Raises her right hand.*)

VIDAL: Okay. Here we go. I was born in a wooden shack in a place called El Fanguito in San Juan. It was right over the swamp, Jesus, I still can remember the smell. Do you know that three years ago I went to Puerto Rico and there's no more Fanguito?

MARCELINA: Get to the point: your dream, your dream.

VIDAL: Would you hold your horses! Jesus, let me finish. It was a three-room shack and the last room was our storage: my father collected old boxes, newspapers, all kinds of cardboards and then sold them to a factory that made more paper. That room also had a hole in the middle of the floor; it was our latrine. I remember now, it was during WW II and I used to believe I was a bombardier from one of those bombers. (*Imitates sounds of airplanes and squatting. Moves his behind around.*) I looked around for floating leaves or pieces of wood or tin cans — you name it — and then, BANG! I would fire my bombs right over the floating thing that for me was a submarine or a destroyer. (MARCELINA *is smiling.*) Sometimes I said, "Shit, I wasted my ammunition and look at that beautiful air carrier that's coming."

MARCELINA: To the point.

VIDAL: Anyhow, it was in that very room where I had my dream. (*Tries to remember.*) I don't know if it was in Life Magazine or Colliers, you know, where I saw my dream. I was eleven. And one day I see this photograph of Times Square: a sailor sight-seeing with a gorgeous blonde-piece-of-ass. And well dressed people walking back and forth. (*Silence.*) That became my dream right there. And you know that I still keep that photograph somewhere in some suitcase home.

MARCELINA: Times Square was your dream?

VIDAL: (*Strong laughter.*) No, that gorgeous blonde-piece-of-ass! (*Calming down.*) No. It was Times Square. And I said to myself, "You gotta quit this business of bombing leaves and pieces of wood: go to Times Square." My dad came to New York, but died young. Then my uncle paid my way and brought us. I was fourteen. (*Silence.*) And when I was seventeen I joined the marines and said: "Fanguito, NEVER AGAIN!" I joined the toughest outfit! I had to show everybody that I can take anything and everything! Yeah. I fought every guy that

to feel down and pity myself. So I give up. But baby I know you up and down. You're transparent; I can see through you. (*Pause.*) It's your twisted way of saying that you're scared!

VIDAL: Me, scared? (*Laughs nervously.*)

MARCELINA: Vidal, today's a very important day for you and me. There's something in the air. I have taught myself to feel the air and get from it my life. I feel that today we will change. You and me. Like, there's something that must be said or something that must be broken. Like a magic something. (*Pause.*) You know, like taking a stand, like a soldier. They push me that far or you so far and that's as far as we will go. *A stand.* Like running all the time and then you decide to stop running. Like you say to yourself: *No more backing off.* (*Pause.*) You feel it in the air. The air is different and the sun shines differently. And when you get to that point there's nothing in the world that will force you to continue running. (*Pause.*) The whole pattern of life is new. You remember yourself walking very close to the walls, like protecting yourself. And then you say SHIT! No more of that; THIS IS MY STAND. I'll walk right through the middle of the sidewalk and I'll let everybody know that I'm through with running.

VIDAL: (*Applauds very hard.*) Bravo. Bravo. Bravo to the power of wine! More wine, lady? (MARCELINA *walks slowly to the counter. Pours some water and drinks it. She finds a piece of paper and pencil and writes. Shows it to* VIDAL. *He reads it out loud.*) Help, I AM A COWARD. Ha, ha. (*She writes again. Shows it to him.*) THE SHADOW IS BEHIND YOU. Big deal! (*She continues to write but keeps the paper to herself.*) Marce, listen to me. Hey, stop that! Let's think about the money. Hey stop that, ah! And c'mon speak up. (*Shows him the paper. Reads.*) I WILL NEVER SPEAK AGAIN. C'mon, who're you kidding! Marce, stop that, say something.

MARCELINA: Shut up. You talk too much. Suppose one day I decide not to talk no more. What would you do?

VIDAL: That'll be the day! SILENCE DON'T COME NATURAL TO YOU. Suppose I decide NOT TO CARRY THIS GUN NO MORE. WHAT WOULD YOU DO?

MARCELINA: Not a thing, baby. Not a thing. To carry a gun is natural with you.

VIDAL: You don't believe me, ah?

MARCELINA: NO.

VIDAL: (*Takes the revolver and places it on the counter near the money.*) Now, what d'you say?

MARCELINA: Nothing.

VIDAL: Suppose I walk to the door, far from the gun?

MARCELINA: (*Keeps writing on the piece of paper.*) Go ahead.

VIDAL: (*Walking towards the door. Slow then faster.*) I can see that you're nervous.

MARCELINA: Not me. (VIDAL *turns his back to the door. Then she screams.*) WATCH OUT!

VIDAL: (*Jumping forward and rushing for the gun.*) WHERE, WHERE??

MARCELINA: (*Laughing. Tears come to her eyes.*) VIDAL . . . What . . . WHAT . . . A . . . JUMP!

VIDAL: All right, all right, I'm jumpy. So what? (*Touches the gun but leaves it there.*)

MARCELINA: (*Still laughing.*) WOW! WHAT AN ATHLETE! WHAT A JUMP! (*Sits down again.*) I never saw anybody jump as high as you did. (*Laughing.*) You should've seen yourself! (*She slowly returns to a gloomy feeling of depression.*)

VIDAL: You had your laugh. Now, please take the money and hide it. Please?

MARCELINA: No.

VIDAL: Then, baby, have it your own way.

MARCELINA: (*Studying* VIDAL. *Getting up.*) You're getting pale.

VIDAL: You don't cook well.

MARCELINA: Now that I'm free and can move around I'll cook better. (*Walks to the*

142

door and back again.)

VIDAL: How come you stay here? Why don't you go out like you wanted to. Go out, see a movie and buy yourself a *paella.*

MARCELINA: I've got plans. I never like to eat by myself. I need company. (*She walks back and forth studying the distance between the door and the counter.*) I tell you what, why don't you go to Times Square and study it to see if you're missing something.

VIDAL: I'm not moving out of here. (*Nervous.*) Are you quitting now? 'Cause you said something about taking a stand . . .

MARCELINA: Taking a stand doesn't mean that you're quitting.

VIDAL: I don't get you.

MARCELINA: That's the story of your life: TAKING A STAND MEANS THAT YOU'RE WILLING TO FIGHT BACK! PUT THAT IDEA THROUGH YOUR THICK BRAIN, MAN! YOU READ ME NOW!

VIDAL: Awright, awright, you don't have to scream!

MARCELINA: It means that you're not backing off ever. Fight. FIGHT. FIGHT. FIGHT WITH F — FFFFFFFFFFFFFF — IGHT!

VIDAL: Isn't fighting what we're doing?

MARCELINA: NO. We're hiding ourselves. We're running away from the fight. We're choosing the wrong enemy.

VIDAL: Are you waiting for the Professor?

MARCELINA: Maybe.

VIDAL: Are you serious?

MARCELINA: I'm always serious. (*Pause.*) Vidal, have you seen a crab fight another crab? (*He is not very clear — gives some vague gestures.*) A crab goes like this — (*Opens her fingers to imitate the crabs' claws.*) — he goes back — (*She backs up.*) — but turns around and fffff-fight — FORWARD and attacks. (*Repeats the movement.*) And when you think that it is going away, MAN, WATCH OUT! BECAUSE, THAT'S WHEN IT BECOMES VERY, VERY DANGEROUS! So it turns back to go forward. The crab is a very smart animal. And when one of his claws holds one of your fingers and it never lets go. Sometimes you've got to kill the animal or break it in pieces and STILL they keep the old . . .

VIDAL: How d'you know that?

MARCELINA: I've studied crabs ON LOCATION BABY, in Puerto Rico. And the SOUTH BRONX IS FULL OF PUERTO RICAN CRABS.

VIDAL: (*Worried.*) Are we doing something wrong?

MARCELINA: (*Not paying attention.*) Today I'm beginning to have a plan in my mind. 'Cause I've got to have a plan, you know. It's the rule of life: you've got to have a plan. I've been your brain, your cook, your bank, your safe, your slave, your . . . YOU NAME IT AND I'VE BEEN IT! Today I'm going to free myself. Today I will gain my true independence. And the funny thing is that you helped me arrive at that decision. I think the Professor said something interesting when he mentioned something about people swallowing your name and your pride. And then he said something about peace of mind. I WANT PEACE OF MIND. I'M GONNA TEACH YOU A LESSON THAT YOU'LL NEVER FORGET.

VIDAL: What're we doing wrong?

MARCELINA: (*Faces him squarely.*) WE'RE DOING EVERYTHING WRONG.

VIDAL: Jesus, is it wrong to try to be decent?

MARCELINA: NO.

VIDAL: Is it wrong to try to be a hard working man?

MARCELINA: NO. Of course not.

VIDAL: Then?

MARCELINA: Did it ever hit you that we're in the wrong business?

VIDAL: What's wrong with a liquor store?

MARCELINA: What's wrong with a beauty parlor?

VIDAL: You answer me first: what's wrong with a liquor store?

MARCELINA: I would rather have a beauty parlor; it's a lot safer.

VIDAL: That don't answer my question.

MARCELINA: Want me to tell you what's wrong with you, baby? YOU ARE ON *AM* WHEN YOU SHOULDA BEEN ON *FM*. (*Imitates sound that to her mind makes the difference between an AM and an FM sound.*) Got it?

VIDAL: What's that supposed to mean?

MARCELINA: THE RADIO. AM and FM! As simple as that.

VIDAL: (*Takes him a long time to understand it.*) Ah, yes, yeah — yeah I like AM music . . . What's wrong with that?

MARCELINA: Your head's wrong. VARIATION, MAN, VARIATION!

VIDAL: What?

MARCELINA: Your head is full of *cucarachas* and you need variation. Variety is the *salsa* of life. You pretend that your nose is equal to your ears and that your ears are equal to your ASS. (*Laughing.*) Change to FM, honey. You need variety. VARIETY! (*Imitates the FM sounds.*)

VIDAL: Okay, I had enough! CHANGE YOUR TUNE 'CAUSE BABY you're getting monotonous.

MARCELINA: Are you scared to change to FM?

VIDAL: What?

MARCELINA: (*Laughing and dancing.*) LIKE TAKE A TANGO OR A POLKA: WHICH ONE YOU PREFER?

VIDAL: What?

MARCELINA: I LIKE A TANGO BEST BECAUSE IT'S ROMANTIC.

VIDAL: Stop it, stop it. Oh stop the bullshit, ah?

MARCELINA: How much you want to bet that you're not ready for an emergency.

VIDAL: Man! Everytime I want a straight answer from you all I get is a wisecrack!

MARCELINA: I bet I can reach the gun faster than you can in an emergency.

VIDAL: (*For the first time in a long while he feels capable and sure of himself.*) Sure — you wanna play around — count me in. (*Pause.*) Let's have the count down. Count to ten. Do it backwards like in the space program.

MARCELINA: (*Gets ready like a runner.*) Get ready! TEN, NINE, EIGHT, SEVEN, SIX, FIVE, FOUR YA! (*She runs and takes the revolver.*)

VIDAL: (*Getting up.*) Wait a minute, you've tricked me. I said to start from ten and count down . . .

MARCELINA: (*Points to him.*) I spoke about an emergency.

VIDAL: (*Cautious.*) Be careful, honey — that gun is loaded.

MARCELINA: In an emergency you have no preparation. You've got to be ready. (*Pointing at him with the revolver and seeing that he is nervous.*) How do you feel to be at the other end of the gun?

VIDAL: Marce, Marce be careful . . . You were drinking and drinking don't keep a steady hand . . . (*Makes a sudden move.*)

MARCELINA: Hold it there, baby. I may pull the trigger. 'Am nervous, you know. (*He stops. Then looks at the door. The* PROFESSOR *is looking in.*)

VIDAL: The Professor is at the door.

MARCELINA: (*Looks at the door.*) Tell the Professor to come in.

VIDAL: The door is closed.

MARCELINA: Then open it.

VIDAL: (*Opens the door and the* PROFESSOR *comes in. But the* PROFESSOR *does not lock the door.*) Hi, Professor.

PROFESSOR: (*Noticing that she has the revolver.*) Oh, I'm very sorry. Maybe I should come back later.

MARCELINA: No, no, Professor, come right in.

144

VIDAL: (*Nervous.*) Marce, watch out, you don't know how to handle a gun . . .

MARCELINA: Try me baby. (*She makes a sudden gesture as if ready to fire and* VIDAL *jumps backwards.*)

VIDAL: (*Sits down.*) Oh, I'm very tired.

MARCELINA: Get up. (*To the* PROFESSOR) You, sit down. (*The* PROFESSOR *sits down.*) That's very nice. (*To* VIDAL.) Now, you, come over here. (VIDAL *hesitates.*) C'MON, BABY — RIGHT HERE!

VIDAL: Marce. You're not funny.

MARCELINA: I'M NOT. (*She puts the revolver against his right temple.*) How'd you like this? (*To the* PROFESSOR.) Open your legs. (*The* PROFESSOR *hesitates.*) C'MON, OPEN YOUR LEGS. (*The* PROFESSOR *opens his legs.*) Very good. (*To* VIDAL.) Now, you, put your two hands in there.

VIDAL: What? Are you out of your mind?

MARCELINA: Do as I say. And remember that I'm very nervous and I may pull the trigger without even knowing . . . (*Pause.*) Put your two hands in between the Professor's legs. Touch him the way you forced me to touch him.

VIDAL: (*Furious but nervous.*) You'll regret this. (*Places his left hand in between the* PROFESSOR'S *legs.*) That's very good. Now, we're even. (*Laughs.*) Fantastic. (VIDAL *tries to grab the revolver but she steps back.*) YOU WANT TO GET HURT? (*Again, the revolver against his right temple.*) Now, Professor, come over here. (*The* PROFESSOR *gets up slowly. She moves away from* VIDAL.) C'MON PROFESSOR, WE DON'T HAVE ALL DAY! (*The* PROFESSOR *comes closer to her.*) Now, listen carefully: put your two hands around my waist and very slowly pull down my panty hose. (*The* PROFESSOR *puts his hands around her body.*) Careful. Just the panty hose. Go ahead. (*The* PROFESSOR *does it: first, one leg, then the other.*) That's very nice, Professor. Now give it to Vidal. (*To* VIDAL.) Take off your pants and put the panty hose on.

VIDAL: What?

MARCELINA: (*Menacing.*) Do as I say.

VIDAL: You're taking the joke too far.

MARCELINA: This is no joke, Buster.

VIDAL: The Professor knows how to dance. Why don't you ask 'im to dance?

MARCELINA: 'CAUSE, BABY, YOU'RE THE STAR OF THE SHOW. YOU KNOW, THE MAIN EVENT!

VIDAL: I bet that when an emergency comes, you're gonna know how to shoot straight.

MARCELINA: TAKE OFF YOUR PANTS. Do as I say or the emergency you're talking about will pop out before your eyes this minute. (*Hard.*) TAKE OFF YOUR PANTS!

VIDAL: Jesus, Marce, you must be drunk. Quit it, eh?

MARCELINA: This is fun! C'MON.

VIDAL: All right, let me go behind the counter.

MARCELINA: Why keep it a secret? Do it right here. We may need some burlesque music though. (*The rooster is heard.*) What d'you know, speaking about the devil . . . (*Laughs.* VIDAL *turns his back and takes off his pants.*) Now, put this on. (*Gives him the panty hose.*)

VIDAL: (*Nervous because of the way* MARCELINA *moves the revolver.*) Marce, be careful. You don't have a steady hand. (*Puts the panty hose on.*)

MARCELINA: Now, Professor, bring all that money. (*The* PROFESSOR *brings the money.*) Help him. Put it inside the panty hose. (*The* PROFESSOR *begins to put the money inside the panty hose. After he finishes, she laughs.*) Now, put your pants on. (VIDAL *puts his pants on.*) Baby, now you're ready for the bank. As you can see and feel, your anatomy is not ready to become a safe. Right? You feel that you can't hold a pack of green ones in front. I can do it. I did it beautifully.

For twelve days. I was an FM safe for twelve days. Now, you're an FM safe. (*Pause.*) You see, honey, we women are made in such a way that we can hold anything together right here, in front and in the back. We can hold it tight, very tight. (*Shows him by pressing her legs together and walking.*) You try to do that. C'mon, try. (VIDAL *tries to walk but the bundle around his waist bulges and slips down.*) TRY, BABY, TRY. DON'T MATTER, THE ONLY DECENT THING THAT YOU CAN DO IS CARRY HORNS. BIG HORNS! (*Laughs.*) God knew that we were to become a solid safe. THAT'S WHY HE GAVE US WIDE ASSES. TRY, BABY, TRY. (*Snaps fingers.*) We snap in front and we snap our back. (*Sings and dances around.*)

WE SNAP IN FRONT
WE SNAP IN BACK
THE WORD IS CUNT
THE WORD IS ASS.
WE WALK, WALK, WALK
SNAP THE BACK
SNAP THE FRONT.

(*Walks around as if she had the panty hose full of money. Then stops. Revolver down. Her two hands down. Visibly tired. Slowly she returns the revolver to its original place.*) Here's your gun. You can keep it. Jesus, I'm tired. (*Returns to her seat.*) How I hate this place. (VIDAL *looks at her and at the gun, but does not move. The* PROFESSOR *moves towards the door.*)

VIDAL: Wait, Professor, don't go. You don't want to miss the playoff. (*Feeling his waist.*) It doesn't feel bad at all. It's quite a SAFE. Don't you agree, Professor?

PROFESSOR: Yessir.

VIDAL: You want to play games, too, Professor? Why don't you go and get the gun, too?

PROFESSOR: I've given up all kinds of games.

VIDAL: Except booze.

PROFESSOR: Yessir, except that.

VIDAL: But you want free booze, right, Professor? (*The rooster is heard again. Points at other room.*) I paid $300 for that animal but I won't give not even five cents for you, Professor.

MARCELINA: Don't get mad at the Professor. If you want to get even you're looking at the wrong person. (*The music from a radio is heard at the door.*)

VIDAL: Oh, no! Marce, quick, close the door. (*She does not move.*) Professor, quick, the door!

PROFESSOR: I . . . I think it is . . . closed . . . I . . . ah . . .

VIDAL: NO, NO. IT'S OPEN.

MARCELINA: Why don't you close it yourself? Are you afraid to show your face? Are you afraid that somebody may read money in your eyes? (*Points at the revolver.*) C'mon, be brave. Take the gun and close the door.

VIDAL: (*Tries to walk but he notices that in order to move he must keep his legs very tight.*) Christ, I can't make it with this shit on! (RADIO 1 *comes in. The radio is on but not too loud.*)

MARCELINA: Here's the joker again.

RADIO 1: (*To the* PROFESSOR.) Well, look who's here. You're like a bad dream. You're everywheres . . . (*To* VIDAL.) You don't know me, but I know you.

VIDAL: (*Trying to be casual.*) I've seen you around — you came here a while ago.

RADIO 1: But you don't know my name.

VIDAL: You must be a group leader.

RADIO 1: You mean a GANG LEADER. Is that what you mean?

VIDAL: No. I said a *group leader.*

MARCELINA: I know who you are: YOU'RE A NO GOOD STUPID ASS LOOK-

ING FOR TROUBLE.

VIDAL: Marce! SHUT UP!

RADIO 1: (*To* MARCELINA.) Lady, you're small, but you've got a big mouth.

MARCELINA: You don't scare me.

RADIO 1: (*To* VIDAL.) You tell your wife to stay out of our business and everything will be all right. (RADIO 1 *turns the radio off and* FERNANDO *and two other men come in. Everybody carries a portable radio except* FERNANDO.)

MARCELINA: (*Getting up fast.*) Vidal, I knew it. I told you. But you don't listen. (*To* FERNANDO.) You're Fernando.

FERNANDO: I'm Fernando. (MARCELINA *tries to get closer but* RADIO 2, 3 *hold her back and she is pushed to a corner.* RADIO 2, 3 *remain with her.*) And Dad sends his regards. (*Shows a radio.*) This is a weapon whether you dig it or not. It gives me an alternative: either do business or don't do business. When I talk to people, I like to have music in the background. (RADIO 1 *puts his on, and* 2 *and* 3's *radios on but not too loud and all on the same radio station.*) Nice and cozy. (*To* VIDAL.) We have an old debt that must be settled right now. But before that there's a lesson for that I must teach you. We cannot conceal from you our intentions. (*To his men.*) Do we, brothers? (*They nod.*)

MARCELINA: That's a lot of shit!

FERNANDO: Marcelina, you better shut up.

MARCELINA: We're decent folks and we wanna be left alone.

VIDAL: Shut up, Marce.

MARCELINA: COÑO, VIDAL, DO SOMETHING! (*She looks at the revolver.* FERNANDO *notices the revolver and walks towards it.* MARCELINA *tries to free herself but cannot.*) Vidal, you yellow bastard! YELLOW! YELLOW! (*Cries a little.*)

FERNANDO: (*Takes the revolver and empties it, throwing the bullets around. Then returns the revolver to its place.*) A gun is as complicated as a sentence, (*Shows a long and pointed knife.*) but a knife is as clean as a simple word. (MARCELINA *bites* RADIO 3's *hand and tries to free herself. For a moment, she looks around for the bullets and finds two.*) Goddam, HOLD THAT WOMAN! (RADIO 1 *rushes for her.*)

MARCELINA: (*To* VIDAL.) GET THE GUN. GET THE GUN. RADIO 2, 3, *and* 4 hold her. RADIO 1 *takes the bullets from her hand and throws them back to the floor. They hold her and remain in a corner.*) VIDAL, YOU YELLOW BASTARD, DO SOMEthing . . . (*She cries openly and remains quiet.*)

FERNANDO: (*Places his knife on* VIDAL'S *ribs.*) You stay put. (*To his men.*) I didn't want to do this, but I think we will have a lot of fun. (*To* RADIO 1.) Hey, man, let's taste the merchandise. (RADIO 1 *takes the bottle and opens it.*) Taste it, man. (RADIO 1 *tastes it and passes it to* RADIO 2.)

RADIO 2: It's no good. (*empties it on the floor.*)

RADIO 1: (*Opens another one.*) This one tastes better. (*Passes it to* RADIO 2)

RADIO 2: No good. (*Empties it on the floor.*)

VIDAL: Hey, man, you're wasting good booze.

FERNANDO: (*Enjoying the show.*) SHUT UP, MAN. (RADIO 1 *and* RADIO 2 keep discarding them on the counter. Saying all the time that the liquor is "NO GOOD, MAN." RADIO 1 *gives a bottle to* RADIO 3 *and one to* FERNANDO. FERNANDO *takes two or three fast gulps and returns near* VIDAL. *The* PROFESSOR *is obviously opening his eyes to the waste going around.*)

FERNANDO: HEY, PET, COME 'ERE. (*The* PROFESSOR *moves towards* FERNANDO.) YOU'RE MY PET, ARE YOU?

PROFESSOR: Yessir . . .

FERNANDO: (*To* VIDAL.) I know you have an alarm for the police, I also know that you have a SAFE. (*To* PROFESSOR.) Am I right, Pet?

PROFESSOR: Yessir . . .

FERNANDO: All of these ingredients add up to one conclusion: *the law of diminishing returns.* Of course, that's according to my father, who's an expert in these things. (*To the* PROFESSOR.) The Professor knows what I mean. Go ahead, PET, tell (*Pause.*) Oh, come on, PET, we don't have the whole day.

PROFESSOR: The idea comes from economics. Basically . . .

FERNANDO: (*Noticing that the* PROFESSOR *is facing him rather than* VIDAL.) Don't look at me, don't tell it to me. I KNOW WHAT IT MEANS! (*Pointing at* VIDAL.) TELL IT TO HIM!

PROFESSOR: Basically that . . . (*Turning slowly to face* VIDAL.) your liquor store gave you as much as she could and that from today on you'll get less and less from it.

FERNANDO: VERY GOOD, PET!

VIDAL: What? This store is giving us our bread every day . . .

FERNANDO: And it's about time that you gave it up or pass it on TO THE REAL OWNER, ME!

VIDAL: Why, you . . . (FERNANDO *presses his knife against* VIDAL.)

MARCELINA: Vidal, be careful . . .

FERNANDO: I'm not the little punk that you used to hit, buster! Now I'm big and I have company and — (*Points at the* PROFESSOR.) I keep a pet. Just relax and everything will be all right. We have a message for you and as soon as we make it clear we will go. So, don't spoil the good conversation by doing some stupid thing. After all, we're all brothers, (*To his men.*) RIGHT FRIENDS? (*They answer:* "RIGHT!" *To* VIDAL.) We're actually doing you a favor. A liquor store is an anti-people weapon. (*Laughs.*) Right, BROTHERS? (*They answer:* "RIGHT BROTHER!") Liquor degrades human beings. (*Points at the* PROFESSOR.) Look at him. Let me show what I mean. (*Takes a bottle from the counter and shows it to the* PROFESSOR. *Opens the bottle.*) HEY, PET, you wanna drink, don't you? (*The* PROFESSOR *does not answer but walks towards* FERNANDO.) Go ahead, pet, tell us who you really are. (*The* PROFESSOR *hesitates.*) Then you don't really wanna drink.

PROFESSOR: (*Nervous.*) I'm a dogooder.

FERNANDO: Meaning?

PROFESSOR: That I have learned to converse skillfully and act just like a *geisha.* My job is to please everyone.

FERNANDO: Awright, Pet, show me the safe.

PROFESSOR: (*Pointing at* VIDAL.) Him.

FERNANDO: (*Pushing around the* PROFESSOR.) Pet, my dear Pet, what're you say-ing? (*Slaps his face.*) Tell me again. (*The* PROFESSOR *points at* MARCELINA *and covers his face.*) That's better. (*Pours some liquor on the floor.*) Now, come here, Pet. Do your job. (*The* PROFESSOR *falls on the floor and licks the liquid.*) You see how liquor degrades men? (*To the* PROFESSOR *again.*) My pet, be a dog. (*The* PROFESSOR *barks like a dog.*) Pet, be a cat. (*Does it.* FERNANDO *is laughing.*)

MARCELINA: Fernando, you're a mean son of a bitch!

FERNANDO: Shut your trap! (*Signaling his men to keep her quiet. They hold* MARCELINA *tighter.*) Awright, let's look for the money. (RADIO 1, 2, *and* 3 *begin to search* MARCELINA. FERNANDO *gives a bottle to the* PROFESSOR. *The* PROFESSOR *sits on the floor and drinks from the bottle.*)

RADIO 1: She's not the safe.

FERNANDO: What? (*To* MARCELINA.) Where's the money, woman? (*She does not answer.*) Hey, pet, come over here. (*The* PROFESSOR *barely makes it to his feet and stumbles toward* FERNANDO.) Where's the safe?

MARCELINA: Don't tell him, Professor! (*The* PROFESSOR *hesitates.*)

148

FERNANDO: Pet! Pet! (*The* PROFESSOR *points at* VIDAL.) Are you making fun of me? What're you, a smartaleck? (*Looking at* VIDAL *carefully*.) You know, my pet is right. This guy is too fat in the middle. (*Signals his men to move closer. Makes fun by using an effeminate sound.*) Oh, Oh, I can't concentrate! (*They all laugh. They all move around imitating the way* FERNANDO *moves, which is the way that both* FERNANDO *and* RADIO 1 *reacted when* MARCELINA *played around with the radio earlier in the play.*) Oh, oh, oh — (*His own voice now.*) You damn well know that we can concentrate. (*To* VIDAL.) Put your pants down.

MARCELINA: Don't let them do that to you, Vidal. Kick his ass!

FERNANDO: (*Signals* RADIO 2, 3 *to get closer. To* MARCELINA.) If you don't behave, I'll tie you down and I'll close your mouth and you'll suffocate. Remember, I know your problem. (*To* RADIO 2.) You hold her tight. (*To* RADIO 1, 3.) Open the safe. (*They hold* VIDAL *and put his pants down. They look and find the money around the panty hose. They laugh at the spectacle. They touch* VIDAL *all over, obviously trying to get a reaction from him.*) Vidal, you're not a man! You're a fag! FAG. (*He takes the money. To* RADIO 3.) See if you find more money.

RADIO 3: (*Finds the marine jacket and puts it on.*) Attention! (*Salutes, clowning around.*) By the left flank, mawrch. By the right flank, march! (*They laugh.*)

FERNANDO: (*Laughing at* VIDAL.) When your sergeant comes around you gotta stand at attention. (*Forces* VIDAL *to stand erect and his pants fall and he tries to keep them in place. All of this brings more abuse from the group.* RADIO 1 *gets the money from the cash register and finds the top hat. Puts it on, begins to clown around with* RADIO 3.) Bring the money here. (RADIO 1, *walking like Charlie Chaplin, brings the money. They are having a lot of fun. To* RADIO 3.) Hey you, get me that coat. Maybe there's more money there. (MARCELINA *reacts violently.*)

MARCELINA: Don't touch my coat, you bastard. Leave that coat alone. (FERNANDO *takes the coat and begins to search the pockets.*) Vidal, please do something. (*To the* PROFESSOR *who by now is drunk and sitting in a corner against the wall.*) Help him, Professor, help him! (RADIO 1 *and* 3 *echo the idea and repeat:* "HELP 'IM, HELP 'IM.")

FERNANDO: (*Finds a pair of women's gloves. He throws them in the middle of the floor which is now a collection of discarded bottles, paper, etc. Even* RADIO 3 *takes off the marine jacket and throws it in the middle.*) Let's see what's here. (*Finds the plastic bottle with the pills. Throws it on the floor.*) Junk! Simply junk! (*Finds an envelope. Opens it and there is an airline ticket to Puerto Rico.*) Oh, oh, the lady like to travel. Flight 347 to Puerto Rico. And dig this. (*To* VIDAL.) Your old lady wants to leave you Vidal. Look at the date of this ticket. It's for tonight. (VIDAL *opens his eyes and looks at* MARCELINA. *His eyes search for an answer.)*

VIDAL: (*To* MARCELINA.) You wanted to leave — WHY?

MARCELINA: (*Noticing that* FERNANDO *is enjoying the scene.*) Don't let them break you, Vidal. I was going to explain it to you. I swear. I swear. (FERNANDO *puts the radio on. Then the rooster is heard several times.* FERNANDO *looks at his men and they look back at him.*)

FERNANDO: You hear that, men? What is this, a zoo or something? (*He goes in and speaks from within.*) It's a cock, a very nice animal for arroz con pollo! Chicken in the basket, you know! (*The noise of the rooster moving around is heard.*)

VIDAL: Fernando, hijueputa! Leave the animal alone!

MARCELINA: Vidal, don't let him kill the animal. (*She wrestles.*)

FERNANDO: (*Coming in with a bundle in his hands. He comes closer to* VIDAL. *Holds his bundle over* VIDAL'S *head and blood begins to drip on his head.*) Here you are, shit-head.

MARCELINA: (*Suddenly she falls.* RADIO 2 *still trying to hold her.*) PLEASE, ANYONE, GET ME A PILL . . . A PILL! PLEASE!

PROFESSOR: (*Getting up but unable to understand what is happening, tries to move around.* RADIO 3 *pushes him and he falls. He searches for the bottle of* MARCELINA'S *pills. Finds it, but* RADIO 3 *takes it from his hands, opens it and lets its contents fall on the floor. He laughs.*) Give . . . me . . . Give me . . . (*The* PROFESSOR *gets up and holds* RADIO 3. RADIO 3 *takes his knife and stabs the old man several times.*)

FERNANDO: (*Taken by surprise, he calls* RADIO 3.) You stupid idiot, don't, don't! (*But it is too late. The old man falls to the floor.*)

VIDAL: (*Who was trying to hold his pants up and still see what was happening through the blood on his face, suddenly finds the moment he needed, and surrounds* FERNANDO'S *head with his powerful hand.*) YOU SON OF A BITCH! (FERNANDO *opens his mouth trying to find air.* RADIO 3, 2, *and* 1 *come to his rescue. They begin to wrestle* VIDAL *who falls to the floor.* MARCELINA *searches for the bullets on the floor.* RADIO 3 *sees that and tries to stop her. She kicks him in the groin.* RADIO 3 *falls to the floor with tremendous pains.* MARCELINA *finds one bullet and runs for the revolver.*)

MARCELINA: (*Finding the revolver but unable to put the bullet in it, begins to yell at* VIDAL, *almost out of her mind.*) DON'T LET 'IM GO. KILL'IM, KILL'IM. (RADIO 2 *and* 1 *kick* VIDAL *and finally they get* FERNANDO *off the hook, and* FERNANDO *is coughing all the way to the door.* RADIO 1 *and* 2 *carry him.* RADIO 3 *follows, still in pain. She runs towards* VIDAL. *Tries to clean the blood from his face.*)

VIDAL: (*Giving her the bottle with some pills in it.*) Take . . . take them . . . here . . .

MARCELINA: (*Tenderly.*) You did it, Vidal . . . You did it . . . (*She kisses him on the head.*) Are you all right?

VIDAL: (*Getting up.*) Yeah, I'm all right . . .

MARCELINA: You did it, Vidal. And you didn't need the alarm. You did it with your own hands. Oh, Vidal, you did it!

VIDAL: (*Still holding his pants.*) They killed Macho. Fernando . . .

MARCELINA: Yeah, but he made a mistake.

VIDAL: (*Coughing.*) What?

MARCELINA: He made the mistake to give you Macho's blood.

VIDAL: (*Smiles.*) Yeah. It was Macho's blood. But you helped a lot. (*Coughs.*) You helped a lot. I'm serious. (*Looking at the* PROFESSOR *on the floor.*) See if he is dead.

MARCELINA: (*Walks to where the* PROFESSOR *is.*) Poor old man — he tried to help, too. (*Touches his head.*) He's dead.

VIDAL: (*Still coughing.*) He was a good old man. A damn good old man. (*Pause.*) And we didn't even know his name.

MARCELINA: Yeah. We don't know his name. I mean, his real name.

VIDAL: Take your pill woman. (*Tries to smile.*)

MARCELINA: I don't really need it.

VIDAL: Then . . . (*He coughs and laughs.*) I know, you forced your *stand* on me . . . you know . . . what you said about *taking* a *stand*.

MARCELINA: Baby, you did it beautifully.

VIDAL: You helped a lot. I took my stand. (*Curious.*) You think Fernando will ever come back?

MARCELINA: Never!

VIDAL: (*To her. Tired voice.*) Turn that radio off. It's too loud!

MARCELINA: Yessir. (*Rushes to turn the radio off. Blackout.*)

Miguel Algarín and Tato Laviera

OLU CLEMENTE

Miguel Algarín and Tato Laviera combined their poetic and musical talents to create a ritualistic eulogy to Roberto Clemente, the heroic baseball player who met a tragic death while bringing relief to the earthquake victims in Nicaragua. Produced by Joseph Papp's New York Public Theatre, the play opened in the Summer of 1973 on the stage for King Lear *at the New York Shakespeare Festival's Delacourt Theatre in Central Park and then toured parks, schools, community centers and theatres around the city for over forty performances during the next two years.* Olú Clemente *was directed by Miguel Algarín and casted with equity actors by both playwrights. The music that was composed by Laviera was choreographed by Rudy Pérez and played by Los Pleneros de Loíza.*

Olú Clemente *emerges directly from the tradition of Afro-Caribbean literature as cultivated and popularized by such poets as the Cuban, Nicolás Guillén, and the Puerto Rican, Luis Palés Matos. In writing* Olú Clemente, *the playwrights sought to emphasize Clemente's African heritage and his upbringing in Piñones, where African roots are still very strong today. In particular, Algarín and Laviera were, in their own words, "striving for a piety of faith which is not Christian." Clemente is thus transformed into an African deity in the play and accorded a position among the other Siete Potencias Africanas that are still worshipped today in parts of the Caribbean and mainland barrios.*

But the overriding framework of this musical, spiritual celebration is borrowed from the performance format that is basic to Afro-Carribbean music, especially Puerto Rico's plena and Cuba's son. Essentially, performance of these traditional genres involves the production of Afro rhythms through such instruments as the conga, bongo, timbales and maracas and a poetic structure that allows for a solo vocalist/poetic improvisor, often called a sonero, *who alternates with or responds to and embellishes a refrain sung by a chorus (*coro*). This performance pattern has been basic to all Caribbean music of African influence and, in fact, has been the backbone of most popular Latin forms, from* rumba *to* guaguancó. *Algarín and Laviera have innovated by allowing the coro to also function in the manner of the chorus in classical Greek drama. In addition, the individual members of the chorus also assume separate dramatic roles: the women who represent the strengths of the tribe by attacking the negativity that destroys the Puerto Rican in the northern barrios.*

Olú Clemente *captures the spirit and the tone of the current evocation of African roots that has so dominated the fine arts and popular culture of Puerto Ricans and Cubans. Tato Laviera's music, even today being recorded by name salsa artists, continues this cultural exploration that has been so important since the 1930's. It is easy to see how a piece like* Olú Clemente, *with its celebration of a culture hero and its wonderful music and dance enchanted its audiences, even while addressing some of the more profound and controversial issues concerning Puerto Rican identity in New York.*

Olú Clemente

CHARACTERS:
A POET
SONERO
SIETE POTENCIAS (*also serve as Coro*):
    MARIA SOCORRO, *madre*
    RUTH MARIA, *hija*
    IRMA ANTONIA, *hija*
    VERA CRISTINA, *hija*
    JESUS ABRAHAM, *hijo*
    MIGUEL, *hijo*
    TITO, *hijo*
    MUSICIANS: *piano, trumpet, trombone, tenor sax, percussion (congas, timbales, panderetas, claves)*

SCENE ONE: *The stage is a ball park diamond. The first scene takes place in Piñones, Puerto Rico. The traditional "parrandas" are being celebrated. The news of Roberto Clemente's death reaches the people of Loíza. The parranda transforms into a frantic urgent musical evocation of the spirit of Clemente known as Olú, teacher and saviour.*

POETA: It is 12 o'clock, las doce, in a new year. It is 12 o'clock, las doce. By strange circumstances there's an urgency in my soul.

POTENCIAS: Urgency! Urgency! Urgencia! Urgencia!

POETA: Clemente died inside the waters of Piñones. He died when I touched land in Puerto Rico.

POTENCIAS: Urgency! Urgencia! El agua se menea. Se ahoga.

POETA: The first time I touched your land, after living 30 years in New York.

POTENCIAS: El agua . . . Se hunde . . . Se muere . . . Clemente.

POETA: What are these voices? I hear the soul of street women crying, diving, into the waters . . . I saw the plane fall, about an hour ago, I saw the plane fall . . . ¿Qué pasa? . . . Don't push me . . . ¿Qué me pasa? I feel like I'm being transformed. What's wrong? Clemente, tell me. Am I cursed? What kind of dream is this? Shall I come to celebrate the New Year, to find myself alone among so many mourners. Can't speak to anyone . . . There's no one I know. It is 12 o'clock.

POTENCIAS: Urgency . . . Urgency . . . Urgency, Urgencia . . . Rápido . . . Rápido . . . Se ahoga . . . Un rito . . . Nuevo Año . . . Penoso . . . El avión se cae . . . se cae . . . se cae . . . se cae.

POETA: I saw people in circles, they were praying, they were saying. .

POTENCIAS: Promesas. Promesas.

POETA: This old lady saying . . .

POTENCIAS: EL ESPIRITU DE CLEMENTE.

POETA: I knelt down, and I prayed. Coño, it had to be Clemente. I wish it were me. Damn it.

POTENCIAS: Clemente . . . Clemente . . . Regresa . . . Regresa . . . Clemente. ¡No! ¡No! ¡No! No puede ser, Clemente, Clemente.

POETA: I prayed hard, and I screamed, and the people gathered round me, and they prayed to Clemente. Una oración by the sea, by the sea, Clemente, vente inside of me, give me your beauty, help me transform. I want to sing my negroid verses. What is this? ¿Qué . . . me . . . vie . . . ne . . . por . . . den . . . tro . . . I feel something coming out of me, shaking me, moving me, as swiftly as the waves. I feel a second voice coming out of me.

SONERO: Soy.

POETA: Coming out of me . . .
SONERO: Soy el . . .
POETA: Coming out of me, coming from inside of me.
SONERO: Soy el espíritu . . .
POETA: I feel a spirit, a great spirit.
SONERO:

> Soy el espíritu del poeta,
> Mi nombre es Martín Elegua.
> Soy su guía, soy su cuerpo.
> Estaba yo encarcelado
> Adentro del lenguaje del sajón.
>
> Soy el espíritu del poeta,
> Mi nombre es Martín Elegua.
> Le enseñaré su español
> Porque hoy Clemente murió, me liberó. (*Begins the first song: "Al   Boricua y al Amor".*)
> *Mi Señor, Mi Gran Clemente, Señor,*
> *Usted hoy murió,*
> *Con los Dioses por delante,*
> *Lo llevaron a la gloria.*
> *Se sentó con el Señor. (Repeat Twice.)*

CORO: *Usted nos busca aquí, nos busca aquí, al boricua y al amor. (Repeat.)*

Instrumental interlude: First Song, "Al Boricua y al Amor"
SONERO: *Nos busca aquí, al boricua y al amor.*
CORO: *Nos busca aquí, al boricua y al amor.*
SONERO: *Con un vaso de diamantes, Clemente nos despidió.*
CORO: *Nos busca aquí, al boricua, y al amor.*
SONERO: *Lo llevaron a la gloria. Se sentó con el Señor.*
CORO: *Nos busca aquí, al boricua, y al amor.*
SONERO: *Con los brazos por delante, nos mandó su bendición.*
CORO: *Nos busca aquí, al boricua, y al amor.*
SONERO: *Todo el mundo se arrodilla, pide aquí la bendición.*
Instrumental interlude: First Song, "Al Boricua y al Amor"
CORO: *Al boricua y al amor.*
SONERO: *Con un vaso de diamantes.*
CORO: *Al boricua y al amor.*
SONERO: *Clemente nos despidió.*
CORO: *Al boricua y al amor.*
SONERO: *Con los brazos por delante.*
CORO: *Al boricua y al amor.*
SONERO: *Nos mandó su bendición.*
Instrumental Interlude: First Song, "Al Boricua y al Amor"
POETA: I see this spirit coming out of me, coming out of me. I am enthralled. My spirit
    sings. People can not see my spirit. They applaud me. But I can't sing. Estoy loco,
    estoy loco. It is as if I lived here.
CORO: Lo que tengo nunca se me fue.
        Lo que tengo nunca se me fue.
POETA: I feel tradition in my veins.
Instrumental Interlude: Second song, "Nunca se me Fue"
CORO: *Lo que tengo nunca se me fue, se me fue*
            Lo que tengo nunca se me fue, se me fue

SONERO:	*Hacia el pozo voy, y después para el Ancón.*
CORO:	*Caen más gotas que estrellas.*
SONERO:	*Olú allí me espera, mi dolor, mi dolor, mi pena.*
CORO:	*Caen más gotas que estrellas.*
SONERO:	*Más gotas que estrellas, más gotas que estrellas.*
CORO:	*Caen más gotas, caen más gotas, caen más gotas,*
	Caen más gotas que estrellas.

Instrumental Interlude: Sixth Song, "Más Gotas que Estrellas"

SONERO:	*Me caí por lo que vi allí . . . Caen más gotas que estrellas.*
	(Repeat once.)
CORO:	*Hacia el pozo voy, a visitar la Diosa de la Aldea.*
	Mil ruidos me acompañan,
	entrando todos en mis entrañas. (Repeat twice.)
SONERO:	*Estoy libre, estoy fuerte, Puerto Rico, mi sola protección.*
	(Repeat twice.)
SONERO y CORO:	*Y le canto a Puerto Rico en Piñones.*
	Y le canto a Puerto Rico en Piñones.
	Y obsequio mis inquietudes a Piñones.
	Diciendo alegremente, lo que tengo nunca se me fue.
	Lo que tengo nunca se me fue.
CORO:	*QUE CANTE EL POETA, QUE NO TENGA MIEDO,*
	QUE CANTE EL POETA, QUE NO TENGA MIEDO.
	ESTAS CON TU GENTE, NO TE VAMOS A ENGAÑAR
	QUE CANTE, QUE CANTE, AQUI CON SU GENTE.
POETA:	*Lo que tengo nunca se me fue.*
	Lo que tengo nunca se me fue, se me fue.
	Nunca, nunca, nunca, nunca, nunca se me fue.
	Lo que tengo nunca se me fue.
EVERYONE:	*Lo que tengo nunca se me fue, se me fue.*
	Lo que tengo nunca se me fue, se me fue.
	Nunca, nunca, nunca, nunca, nunca se me fue.
	Lo que tengo nunca se me fue, que otra vez.
	Lo que tengo nunca se me fue, se me fue.
	Lo que tengo nunca se me fue, se me fue.
	Nunca, nunca, nunca, nunca, nunca se me fue.
	Lo que tengo nunca se me fue. (Slow.)

SCENE TWO: *New York*

MARIA SOCORRO: Le tenemos que rogar:
"oremos por nuestra Potencia,"
Olú we want to celebrate
our spirits, we want to
frame our presence in
New York. We want
to sing the stunning life
of our talents,
we want to bleed from
the stage the sweat
of our tortured days
in el barrio frío,
in the helpless
caminar de esta
máquina de intereses

158

which shares its goodies
in a circuit of interests
that Puerto Ricans
never see:
"oremos por nuestra Potencia,"
Olú, give us energy
with which we can fight.

TITO: Can you keep the energy clean?
JESUS ABRAHAM: Congas
necesitamos congas
las congas para crear.
TITO: Sí, praise me with tambores.
JESUS ABRAHAM: Puerto Rico needs to have its people respected.
MIGUEL AND
JESUS ABRAHAM: Sí, sí, sí, sí, sí, sí, sí, sí, sí,
The city needs to have you
spread your beauty to
Staten Island, Queens, Brooklyn,
the Bronx. You need to lead
the people of New York
to spirtual cleanliness.
IRMA ANTONIA: *May all Puerto Ricans*
praise the
spirit of a hero-man
Clemente-man
Roberto-baseball-player-man

The SIETE POTENCIAS *tremble and shake to the conga music.*
RUTH MARIA: *Las llaves*
las claves,
el poder son
las llaves,
las que abren las
puertas, las que
te dejan entrar
sin que te llamen
PILLO,
las llaves son
la revolución
la rebeldia,
las llaves,
las claves,
las llaves are the key
to entrance and to power:
the key to not breaking into
600 Park Avenue
Son LAS LLAVES
porque sin las llaves
te llevan preso.
MIGUEL AND
JESUS ABRAHAM: *Las llaves*
son el miedo,
son el miedo,
las llaves de

159

	metal son el
	miedo. Cójanlas
	todas cójanlas.
	No esperen,
	inicien su acción.
JESUS ABRAHAM:	*The people we*

JESUS ABRAHAM: *The people we*
want to create
a religion for
can not arrive
till they get out
of factorías,
WE MUST WORK AT NIGHT
we can't spend the day
exploring the ritual
presentation of the tribe
back to itself,
we first pay dues
FACTORIAS, FACTORIAS, FACTORIAS, FACTORIAS,
FACTORIAS
Pay Dues,
Then Look,
Pay Dues,
Then Look,
Pay Dues,
Then
LOOK. (Congas go crazy playing.)

MIGUEL AND
JESUS ABRAHAM: sí, sí, sí, sí, sí, sí, sí, sí, sí, sí, sí.
MARIA SOCORRO:

Clemente's family,
la familia
Clemente is present
to the myth,
to the creation,
to the spirit
of Roberto's
force, to the spirit
that we beat our
drums for, la familia,
is here to gather energy,
to withstand its loss in
our celebration of Roberto.

TITO: You must
exhibit your
pasion for Roberto.

MIGUEL: We need a major
prayer to a major
god — Olú.

TITO: A rhythm from my drum
will release it for you.

MIGUEL: Let us give thanks
to Olú Clemente
for our daily knowledge:

160

Olú teach us to
dance on high pitch
fear, teach us to fight
sleep, to want more wakedness.
All will be done in
Heaven as it is in el barrio.
Olú, Olú
teach us to dance
on high pitch fear
Olú, Olú,
teach us to fight
on high pitch fear for
All will be done in
Heaven as it is in el barrio.

MARIA SOCORRO:
We, I, you, us,
we cannot help
the standing System of Justice
keep its course in declaring
us criminals,
beasts of loathing,
we cannot raise
the flag of contempt
against ourselves.

RUTH MARIA:
My children are not
CRIMINALS,
mis hijos no son
CRIMINALES.

IRMA ANTONIA:
Mi esposo no es
un pillo,
my husband is not a thief,
do not accuse me,
I am not the mother
of criminals.

VERA CRISTINA:
I am the mother
of beautiful
children born of a
beautiful Puerto Rican union.

MARIA SOCORRO:
A marriage bearing children
was not to be a curse
on society,
it was to be an offering,
IT IS AN OFFERING,
NO!
We reject all
Standing Systems of Justice.

IRMA ANTONIA:
We are the mothers of
What is called
DEFIANCE.
Here I sit watching
Roberto run
around the diamond,
a black Spanish

<pre>
                         speaking stallion:
                         running more than he
                         walks,
                         being free in
                         his knowledge of always ex-
                         pressing himself:
                         tirando para afuera.
MARIA SOCORRO: NO! to all external justice!
RUTH MARIA: We are at war
                         and our children are
                         the warriors of our nation:
                         A NATION OF BEAUTIFUL
                         WARRIORS.
VERA CRISTINA: We are the mothers
                         of salvation
                         for our
                         children have the
                         muscles of resistance,
                         they are the blood
                         of the promise,
                         they are not criminals
                         they are los dioses
                         of tomorrow.
MARIA SOCORRO: We, I, You, Us,
                         We are the mothers of the NEWNESS
                         We are the mothers of DEFIANCE.
</pre>

TITO: Y para continuar nuestro respeto al querido Roberto Clemente queremos hacer homenaje a todas las madres que sufren por sus hijos, los cuales están sometidos al peligro. Y lo hacemos así porque sabemos que tú, Roberto, desde allá donde estás sentado a la derecha de nuestros creadores, desde allá como Olú, el maestro, nos ayudarás para que estos niños puedan ser el futuro de nuestra patria. Sabemos que donde moras eres el ejemplo del hombre santo y bueno.

SOCORRO *and* IRMA *embrace. The two women walk towards shortstop.* RUTH *is touching* VERA'S *hair. As* SOCORRO *and* IRMA *arrive,* IRMA *looks towards the fence around home plate, and the other women follow. They move slowly, pointing towards the plate in an upward position.* MIGUEL *is on Third Base, as he looks at the women. There is spiritual cleanliness, a concentrated simplicity.*

<pre>
MIGUEL: There they are, the mother,
                         hablando del dolor,
                         pena que también Roberto
                         sufrió en su vida. Viviendo
                         entre dos razas.
                         They are
                         las madres de la tierra.
                         In Short — between two worlds
                         the calmness of trees
                         colliding with a jungle of buildings
                         las madres,
                         In . . . between . . . they are the wired
                         fences that protect us.
</pre>

VERA CRISTINA: Roberto tenía una mirada que me tumbaba los ojos.

RUTH MARIA: Tenía mucho poder. Roberto hacía todo lo que él quería.

MARIA SOCORRO: Las cosas son como Dios las dispone. Tú sabes que Roberto no murió. (*Looking at* JESUS ABRAHAM.) ¡No! El está aquí en el mundo haciendo milagros. (*Looking at* MIGUEL.) Roberto, yo quiero que tú lo sepas. Vera, Roberto va a ser el próximo San Martín de Porres.

VERA CRISTINA: El supo hacer todo lo posible con sus manos. Y también sufrió. Siempre trató de traer a nuestro pueblo a su punto de máxima fuerza. (*A little child,* ROBERTO ENRIQUEZ, *passes by playing a campana. He is always moving about the mothers as they talk.*)

IRMA ANTONIA: El fue un gran padre. Te has dado cuenta como es que el nene está interesado. El nene sabe que se habla de Roberto. El sabe que se habla de su papá.

RUTH MARIA: (*To* ROBERTO) Ven acá.

VERA CRISTINA: Sí, ése es Roberto Enríquez. Los de más edad ya saben o mejor conocen lo que ha pasado. Pero el más pequeño, como que lo espera por las noches. ¡El era su pasión!

RUTH MARIA: Qué lindo cuando son nenes y qué mucho peligro les queda en este mundo. Y en Nueva York olvídate. Ahí, no se salva ni uno. Todos llegan a lo mismo. Todos se pierden en el peligro.

VERA CRISTINA: Roberto siempre sufrió mucho por la juventud puertorriqueña.

RUTH MARIA: Raymond el hermano de la esposa de Jesús Abraham murió abandonado. Solo, sin nadie.

MARIA SOCORRO: ¿Por qué murió Raymond tan abandonado? Yo como que lo veo (*Holds her forehead.*) con gente, con muchos amigos.

RUTH MARIA: El tuvo que morir solo, sin que nadie lo ayudara.

VERA CRISTINA: ¿Por qué?

RUTH MARIA: ¿Por qué murió buscando sueños? Murió buscando el futuro en el humo de la perdición. No le culpo. El buscaba lo que lo balanceara.

VERA CRISTINA: Es que mueren tantos por ese gusto. Y es un gusto tan lejos de la familia. Es un gusto que nos amenaza.

MARIA SOCORRO: Pero, ¿quién dice que la amenaza la producimos nosotros? ¿Quién le vende a nuestros hijos este falso sueño de un balance químico que cada ocho horas necesita más fuego?

RUTH MARIA: Las calles están llenas de vicio. La destrucción es tan fácil de comprar como la aspirina.

MARIA SOCORRO: No, mi pregunta es ¿quién les vende el asunto ése que necesitan para lograr su "High"?

RUTH MARIA: En las calles, en todos lados, en todas las esquinas, en todas las bodegas del barrio.

VERA CRISTINA: Somos nuestros mismos destructores. Si son puertorriqueños los que la venden, somos nosotros los que nos matamos uno al otro.

RUTH MARIA: ¿De qué parte del mundo es que sale la pestilencia esa?

IRMA ANTONIA: Sale de la China, Turkey, India, Sud América. Come on! It comes from all around the world. De todas partes del mundo.

RUTH MARIA: ¿ Y qué puertorriqueño tiene el poder de negociar la venta a un nivel, tú sabes, un nivel internacional?

VERA CRISTINA: Hay mucho que nosotros no controlamos que nos destruye. Hay mucho que nos quiere tumbar pero que está fuera de nuestro alcance.

MARIA SOCORRO: ¡Miren ustedes! ¿Qué es un puertorriqueño para un chino, un indio, un africano? Para esa gente el puertorriqueño es un alfiler en el panorama americano.

RUTH MARIA: Así que en cosas de negocios el puertorriqueño es una paja en el horizonte.

IRMA ANTONIA: Ellos venden pero no son los que la traen. Yo tengo una hermana que le dieron cinco años por venderla. Pero ella no era la fuente, la fuente es la mafia, el gobierno, la policía.

VERA CRISTINA: Me dicen que se usa en las cárceles.

MARIA SOCORRO: Sí, ¡así es! ¡así es!

RUTH MARIA: ¿Y qué entonces? Somos todas madres, somos todas mujeres de hijos, somos todas la fuente de la sangre puertorriqueña. Somos la sangre.

VERA CRISTINA: Bien dicho. Pero se nos mueren los hijos en los pasillos de edificios fríos y estranjeros. Se nos mueren solos, sin ayuda, desesperados, se nos mueren sin MADRES, se nos mueren sin apoyo.

RUTH MARIA: ¿Y qué hacemos?

MARIA SOCORRO: No dejemos que eso pase. Yo no deseo ver a mi hijo destruido; yo no quiero ayudarlo en su vicio. Pero, Señor Mío, Dios querido, cuando me dicen que se nos mueren los hijos en pasillos sin amigos, eso no lo tolero yo.

IRMA ANTONIA: ¡Ni yo tampoco!

RUTH MARIA: ¿Y qué hacemos?

VERA CRISTINA: ¡A la meta! Tenemos que ir a nuestra respon sabilidad, a nuestros sagrados hijos que están en peligro.

IRMA ANTONIA: Look! We are not free to set our own laws.

MARIA SOCORRO: ¿Y si no tenemos el poder de defender los nuestros, qué tenemos?

IRMA ANTONIA: La ayuda del progreso.

MARIA SOCORRO: No lo creas. Nada es nuestro y el progreso es un embuste. Todos mienten.

RUTH MARIA: Sí, nuestra responsabilidad es ayudarnos.

IRMA ANTONIA: Bueno, tú sabes que a mí nadie sacaría un hijo de mi hogar.

RUTH MARIA: ¿Y si está en el vicio?

IRMA ANTONIA: No, a mí no, a mí no me lo llevarían.

MARIA SOCORRO: ¿Cómo que no? Ya tú, ella y yo sabemos que es la ley, que es la ley. Y con la ley no hay negocios.

IRMA ANTONIA: ¡A mí no! A mí no me lo llevarían.

MARIA SOCORRO: Con la policía a la puerta y el F. B. I. en la cocina ¿cómo te quedarías con tu nene en la casa?

IRMA ANTONIA: Con mis manos, con mis uñas, con mis dientes mordiría.

RUTH MARIA: Y yo te ayudaría.

MARIA SOCORRO: ¡Cálmense! Porque no he oído una proposición de acción. Ésta puede gritar su bravura pero cuando llegue la policía ellos se lo llevarán.

RUTH MARIA: Pero el punto es que no los dejaríamos llevárselo.

MARIA SOCORRO: ¿Qué proponen? . . . que todas nos unamos, que todas nosotras gritemos: "no dejen que se los lleven lejos de su hogar?"

VERA CRISTINA: Que idea tan simple y bella.

RUTH MARIA: No podemos tirarle al que está sufriendo. Nuestros hijos sufren bajo fuerzas que los odian.

MARIA SOCORRO: Los curamos nosotras, nosotras mismas, la madre cura, la madre de un hogar es la hoja verde tropical. Nosotras las madres tenemos que proteger a los hijos. Ellos bien lo saben. Desde ahora en adelante aquí no hay policía alguno que se me lleve a un hijo mío.

RUTH MARIA: ¡Que Dios que está en los cielos nos bendiga el momento!

IRMA ANTONIA: Que nos dé la fuerza del mañana de nuestra promesa.

MARIA SOCORRO: Mi casa es el humilde respaldo de mis hijos y en nuestras casas serán protegidos. Roberto, tú, Clemente lleno de Clemencia, sálvanos, reza por nosotros. Protégenos. Ayúdanos a salvar a nuestros hijos.

RUTH MARIA: Tú has de hacer muchos milagros. (RUTH MARIA and IRMA ANTONIA are alone. Center stage.) Yo como que necesito un aliento, un abrazo en el pecho.

IRMA ANTONIA: ¿Qué te pasa? ¿Tú buscas y no encuentras? ¿Ya el calentón abrazo se te olvidó?

RUTH MARIA: Eso lo manda Dios. Pero la seguridad, mi seguridad la creo yo.

IRMA ANTONIA: Yo he dejado mucha "oportunidad" perderse por verme cerca de mis hijos.

RUTH MARIA: Verdad es. Es malo estar sola. Con los hijos pero sola sin un hombre que me traiga felicidad.

IRMA ANTONIA: A mí me acaba de llegar.

RUTH MARIA: Y a mí me llegará.

IRMA ANTONIA: Ruth, ¿qué es un hombre puertorriqueño?

RUTH MARIA: Roberto Clemente, Don Pedro, Emeterio Betances, mi padre, mi hermano.

IRMA ANTONIA: Nuestros hombres viven con mucho dolor.

RUTH MARIA: En Nueva York lavan platos.

IRMA ANTONIA: No es eso, es otra cosa.

RUTH MARIA: ¿Cómo? ¿Qué?

IRMA ANTONIA: No tienen seguridad.

RUTH MARIA: ¿Cómo? ¿Qué?

IRMA ANTONIA: ¿Qué le pasa al check de cada semana?

RUTH MARIA: Se gasta.

IRMA ANTONIA: Y ¿cómo se van a levantar si se nos ahogan con cada paso?

RUTH MARIA: Ellos viven nadando.

IRMA ANTONIA: Los tenemos que respaldar en su lucha.

RUTH MARIE: Tenemos que darle orgullo que respetar a su lucha.

IRMA ANTONIA: Pero qué dolor, qué dolor, qué dolor el que trabaja tanto y le pagan tan poco. Qué dolor, la humillación de ganarse una miseria cuando se necesita mucho más.

RUTH MARIA: No podemos resignarnos.

IRMA ANTONIA: Pa' trás con el que me humilla al esposo. Pa' trás con el que me humilla al hijo. Pa' trás con el que me ultraje la hija — pa' trás, pa' trás.

RUTH MARIA: Basta ya con la humillación, está bien, ¡basta! Pero lo que cuenta es resistir la humillación. Lo que importa es que nos respeten (MARIA SOCORRO *enters.*)

MARIA SOCORRO: Nuestros hombres nos han dado respaldo, cariño, y sobre todo nos han dado orgullo.

IRMA ANTONIA: Pero nosotras siempre hemos luchado con nuestros hombres: Lola Rodríguez de Tió, Mariana Boracetti, a la que llamaban brazo de oro durante el grito de Lares, Lolita Lebrón que vive aún y no hablemos de la gran Vera Clemente.

RUTH MARIA: A Lolita la están matando por su dignidad.

MARIA SOCORRO: Esa dignidad y esa hombría nutrimos nosotras y le damos aliento.

IRMA ANTONIA: ¿Es que ustedes no ven que nosotras somos el futuro de nuestros hombres.

RUTH MARIA: ¡Eso es! Los hay, los tenemos. Mi hermano, mi Jesús Abraham es bravo. Tito es bravo. Miguel es fuerte.

MARIA SOCORRO: (*All the women join her.*) Tenemos poder. Nosotras vamos hacia adelante, pero necesitamos unirnos para darle respaldo a nuestros hombres.

TITO: (*The men at homeplate.*) That's Piñones. That's where the plane crashed. They looked for him for hours.

MIGUEL: ¿Dónde está Piñones? Over there?

TITO: That's Piñones!

MIGUEL: Tito, Piñones is directly in front view of the house. Roberto died within sight of his family.

of his struggle, his attaining fame without selling out his honor.

IRMA ANTONIA: Inside your home there is the spirit of love and contemplation.

TITO: La obra de Clemente fue la obra más grande de Puerto Rico: él, Roberto, supo darle su presencia a los niños, a los muchachitos peloteros de la isla. El no se olvidaba de el que lo necesitaba; su grandeza era su bondad y eso lo hizo inolvidable. El mundo lo quería porque él supo querer.

VERA CRISTINA (*To* IRMA ANTONIA.): Sometimes his fame would scare those he wanted closest to him.

RUTH MARIA: Roberto was insulted by the lack of attention paid to efforts; his team-mates looked on in awe. He stood at home-plate, sure of his footing; the only one that came through in a clutch. His team-mates marvelled.

MARIA SOCORRO: America made him into a smooth bronze thrill for its people. He wasn't black, but that's America's holdback. It deceives itself.

RUTH MARIA: America lies to itself: Clemente was black, not bronze. You hear that? He was not a new skin color. Black, not bronze!

VERA CRISTINA: Roberto was proud to be a Puerto Rican man close to his people.

TITO: Imagine when at first he couldn't understand el inglés del coach, an English-speaking disciplinarian talking about the action of the game.

VERA CRISTINA: The press reported his ailments as Roberto's psychosomatic ritual.

MIGUEL: He complained that his body hurt in all the vital parts, but he played in Pittsburgh. He played sin parar, pana sin parar, sin dejar de empujar hasta el extremo de su poder.

TITO: For years and years he played and heard multitudes cheer and feel proud in his presence, orgullosos de su presencia.

JESUS ABRAHAM (*To* VERA.) Roberto emerged as a brilliant symbol in the sun, a leader, a model for our struggling youth.

RUTH MARIA: He started every world series he played by looking forward to playing ball back in Puerto Rico.

MIGUEL: The cancerous problem is that America saw him as bronze; it was easier to see you as exotic ROBERTO! (*A pantomime baseball game starts.*)

TITO: While America saw him as a bronze, colored man batting balls, no matter what the curve. He was a lump of muscular earth that hit any ball.

VERA CRISTINA: Qué agilidad tenía Roberto, qué disposición.

TITO: You never really knew where the bat came from.

JESUS ABRAHAM: He just hit all the pitches.

MIGUEL: All the challenges that came at him.

VERA CRISTINA: He hit the balls that came at him.

MIGUEL: Balls coming at him.

TITO: Balls pitched at him.

RUTH MARIA: Balls flying towards him.

MARIA SOCORRO: All the balls they pitched at him were curve balls.

MIGUEL: (*Aggressive, angry.*) Balls at him.

MARIA SOCORRO: (*Confident at Roberto's capacity for batting them all.*) Balls at him.

RUTH MARIA: (*Clear statement to the audience.*) Curve balls at him.

TITO: (*Shields himself with his arms.*) At him, balls at him.

VERA CRISTINA: Balls at him.

ALL OF THE POTENCIAS TOGETHER (*Repeat four times*): Balls at him.

MARIA SOCORRO: I hear him say (*She grabs her forehead.*) "I die alone, no one knowing cómo me dolía la espalda, cómo me arropaba para calentar el cuerpo, para que el calor me llegara hasta la espina dorsal donde se reciben tantas penas, tantos accidentes de hueso penetrando hueso. (*Deep silence, then* MIGUEL *continues.*)

MIGUEL: He always had reserved energy for his public. Each time he played he knew each game was a judgment on his people.

JESUS ABRAHAM: He timed every move at the plate; it was a matter of looking at the ball and being ready.

TITO: He is not our only hero.

MARIA SOCORRO: No! There are more; let them through. Let them come all the way through. (*All of the* THROUGH *is said in unison by* LAS SIETE POTENCIAS.) THROUGH, THROUGH, THROUGH, THROUGH, THROUGH, THROUGH.

RUTH MARIA: (*Moving towards third base.*) Roberto committed his body to a discipline: to the daily torture of his muscles batting curves, to the daily pouring of his sweat, to the daily bending of his body energy into catching balls, balls of fire worth hundreds, hundreds, hundreds of thousands of dollars and millions of faces.

MARIA SOCORRO: Había muchos puertorriqueños among those faces who worshipped his form. But then el Caribe te tragó en buche.

MIGUEL: Te tragó en buche.

RUTH MARIA: Te tragó en buche.

IRMA ANTONIA: Te tragó en buche.

TITO: The blacks of Loíza played all night. Their congas searched while all the people waited, the poets described the happening, the searching for him, the over-all look leading to tears because we couldn't find him, we couldn't liberate him from the water, we couldn't get more time for the hombre-adult Clemente to stay on the planet. The waters claimed him. The poets talked of him in the duet of a controversia. Every one sought him; we had not yet realized death would teach us that dying is the next stage toward the fullest realization of where we are. What bothered Roberto, and what bothers me, is a hopeless Rican, the type that doesn't see outside of el barrio apartment that's got him trapped. The Rican who gets created por lo de afuera, by the outside, and forgets to fight.

MIGUEL: Yes, the one who ignores confrontations that would release anger, who struggles for restriction rather than release.

TITO: Few people manage to penetrate to the loco part of their mind, where a point of view can be changed.

MIGUEL: I hate hermanos who educate themselves into docility.

TITO: What is docility? (*A high pitched guaguancó begins. The rhythms become sharper, more intense. Each definition is accurate. Nothing is thrown away.*)

MIGUEL: Docility is acting on what has been learned rather than fighting back for having to pay 10ᶜ for a lavatory in the subway.

TITO: Docility es una situación donde las necesidades se tratan como si no existieran.

MIGUEL: Docility is too many people tucking their energies deep into their spines.

TITO: Don't let the Ph.D. behavioral psychologist put your children to sleep in New York schools and everywhere else.

MIGUEL: Docility is passive peace.

TITO: Docility drums pain.

MIGUEL: Docility is sleeping with despair.

TITO: Docility fears action.

JESUS ABRAHAM: Docility is paying 50ᶜ bus fare (LAS POTENCIAS *begin to walk towards third base.*)

MIGUEL: Docility empties out lungs.

JESUS ABRAHAM: Docility is believing Nixon.

TITO: Docility devours our minds.

MIGUEL: Docility is believing in standards.

RUTH MARIA: Docility bites at your muscles.

IRMA ANTONIA: Docility is eating your tongue.

MIGUEL: Docility atrophies hearing.

MARIA SOCORRO: Docility is depression.

MIGUEL: Docility shapes you.

MARIA SOCORRO: Docility is letting it happen to you.

RUTH MARIA: Docility stimulates withering.

MARIA SOCORRO: Docility puts sleep into our cells.

TITO: Docility fights our energies.

MARIA SOCORRO: Docility attacked by us is docility defeated by us.

MIGUEL AND POTENCIAS: When we become the tongue, eyes, nose, touch of all action that awakens our minds, then docility will be defeated by our being, a fighting, talking center of consciousness.

JESUS ABRAHAM: Clemente was the people. He put everything into his baseball. He beat rhythms with his fingers on the bat and made the ball sound like a conga.

TITO: Roberto aimed his hits into the Gods' dining room where he woke the witch that concocted his death.

VERA CRISTINA: His batting average was political. In baseball he had the straightest ball, right into the center of the diamond of our being.

MARIA SOCORRO: Poeta, Poeta, Poeta, much charged the space between Roberto's adulthood and his son's childhood was filled by his intense manifestation, by his being a field of electricity.

RUTH MARIA: He was a field of action on the diamond, on the sparkling sun-filled diamond that working people pack with their bodies. Roberto, they came to see your spiritual hits, your metaphysical handling of a bat and ball, your striking out twice, waiting 'til the very moment of need.

MIGUEL: The moment of the hit, tiene que salir el hit, the hit. Your metaphysical batting is the pitch of truth.

TITO: (*To* JESUS ABRAHAM.) Fuera del béisbol, Olú Roberto, el maestro, era un hombre humilde del pueblo.

JESUS ABRAHAM: Pero nunca, nunca olvidó que lo queríamos, que lo protegíamos, que sería respetado por el mundo. Y nunca buscó nada más que su respeto por medio de sacrificios, por medio de ese don de ser disciplinado, de adquirir la gracia que lo elevó al nivel del amor puro.

VERA CRISTINA:	Olú maestro,
	Roberto tú eres
	el filósofo del béisbol,
	tú, Roberto, tú eres,
	la filosofía realizada,
	tú, Roberto, tú serás la gracia del futuro
	del ahora puertorriqueño.
MIGUEL:	Roberto Olú, help us.
	Lead us.
	Teach us
	the future wisdom
	of death.
JESUS ABRAHAM:	We are the body,
	we are the head,
	we have to fight on one front,
	one fist,
	one people.
MIGUEL:	Roberto Olú maestro
	teaches we are one.
	Clemente's sangre

170

```
                        changed the Caribbean
                        waters into crimson
                        rage, the Caribbean
                        burned in anger,
                        the Caribbean sea
                        hate swallowing Roberto's energy,
                        there was a revolution
                        in the waters
                        of a sea made
                        of blood that fed
                        our teacher's mind.
JESUS ABRAHAM:          The Caribbean was
                        in convulsions of despair
                        as Roberto live hero:
                        our best pelotero humanist
                        tragaba el agua que arrancaba el fuego
                        para llevarlo al cielo:
                        fire from above,
                        el fuego del cielo, Clemente,
                        el sol Roberto
                        shines on las calles
                        de Nueva York,
                        el sol caribe,
                        pelotero sol,
                        Roberto, tú ardes,
                        tú eres la llama del mañana,
                        tú, Roberto, el mañana
                        del ahora y del pasado:
                        tú fuego eres:
                        tú agua quemas:
                        tú luna y sol
                        alumbras con tu ser.
```

LAS POTENCIAS *bow to* VERA. *She takes their hands. A circle of hands above the heads.* MIGUEL *goes out left center field.* JESUS ABRAHAM *goes out front stage right.* IRMA ANTONIA *goes out right center field.* MARIA SOCORRO *walks out from the pitcher's mound to the back of center field.* RUTH MARIA *leaves from front stage left.* TITO *stands with* VERA *out in left field. Lights out. Los Pleneros de Loíza play. The musicians play.*

Miguel Piñero

THE SUN ALWAYS SHINES FOR THE COOL

Miguel Piñero is probably the most successful Latino playwright, with nine of his plays already produced to raving revues everywhere from New York City to Los Angeles, his Short Eyes *made into a movie, and his talents in demand for film and television writing. Piñero first won national acclaim with* Short Eyes, *the hard hitting and rough-talking prison drama that took the theatre world by storm and garnered its highest awards (Obie and New York Drama Critics Circle Award for best American play of the 1973-1974 season). But Piñero has proven that this theatrical milestone, a play written by an ex-con "copping" the most respected prizes, was no fluke. It does not represent an outlaw's only moment in the lime-light of established society and its cultural institutions. The value of* Short Eyes *does not lie within the realm of sociology nor the Runyonesque, but in exposing that establishment society to a new view that is as much fantasy and artistic imagination, of course, as are the worlds created by Tennessee Williams or William Faulkner.*

Piñero's theatre is a milestone for its introduction to the stage of characters who previously appeared only as stereotypes, but now assume real lives of their own: the immigrant, the convict, the numbers runner, the pimp, the prostitute, the john. Their characteristic language, dress and underworld hardness all go to convincing us that we are truly eavesdropping on the backroom conversations, saloon talk and macho accounts of illicit sexual or criminal adventures that, without the convention of theatre, would otherwise be denied us. Piñero is a craftsman and a magician who casts his spell so well that the audience often has a hard time separating reality from the fantastic and powerful visions the playwright has conjured. His plays are not documentaries nor naturalistic exposés. They are romantic visions of the outlaw and his code of honor.

The Sun Always Shines for the Cool, *after an earlier version was produced by the Public Theatre in New York, opened on June 3, 1977, at Washington, D.C.'s Back Alley Theatre, which had previously produced* Short Eyes. *So successful was its run that the Back Alley plans a revival for the Spring of 1979. According to WRC-TV (NBC) critic, Ron Heldon, " 'Cool' is every bit as powerful, as supercharged with emotion, and as true to life as* Short Eyes *was, only this time, the ex-cons are on the street, shucking, jiving, and plying their trade." Of the production by Back Alley, under Frederic Lee's direction, Chip Berger of the* Unicorn Times *wrote that "The creative interweaving of music, the simple yet amazingly appropriate costuming, and the almost mimed and magical qualities of the body itself all contribute to a sensuous celebration of being alive — even if you are a pimp, prositute, or numbers runner. The play has a satin and sequin gloss, which, when mixed with the corresponding coarseness and expediency of the afterhours world, demands participation of the audience. Participation of the heart, of the blood. Red is the color of* Cool."

While The Sun Always Shines for the Cool *will always be compared with* Short Eyes *it is different in intent and, to some extent, style.* Short Eyes *projects the sterility and nakedness of men thrown together against their will in prison and thus lacks the spectacular appeal of* Cool *which is a rich mosaic of cocky male and female characters "strutting their stuff," with the glitter, glamour and confidence of vaudevillians. They entertain us with their jive talk, their disco dancing and song.* JUSTICE'S *tavern, more than a mere "players' bar," is a stage; it offers the spotlight to the people who play their* lives out on the streets as they come in and perform for each other as well as the audience which is invited, no hustled, in the Prologue of the play. Piñero brings us along to see through their act and perceive the humanity in these creatures of the night who, one after another step into the spotlight, the midnight sun. Those who overplay their role, like CAT EYES, are doomed to shame, ridicule and ultimately death on this stage where one must bet his life on his performance. And Piñero maintains that constant, suspenseful undercurrent of impending violence until the fateful climax when CHILE GIRL must see through the glitter and hip talk as VIEJO unmask the hustling CAT EYES. Cool deals with the very substance of theatre and society: masks and costumes, acting, conning, hustling . . . playing for all one is worth. Do not be blinded by the spectacle that Piñero has created for you, for he is once again only underlining that eternal theatrical message: life is but a stage.

The Sun Always Shines for the Cool

CHARACTERS:

VIEJO	DIAMOND RING
JUSTICE	SATISFACTION
CHILE GIRL	LEFTY "G" GORILLA
CAT EYES	VIVA, *pianist*
PHEBE REED	JORGE, *bass player*
WILLE "B" BODEGA	BAM BAM BOY
KAHLU	SALESMAN, *john*
JR. BALLOON	A JOHN
ROSA	

Underscored by rock music with heavy bass overtones. Lights up to a dimlit street scene with male pimps upstage in a grouping and prostitutes downstage, spread apart, nearer the audience. All are frozen. With music pimps turn, heads only, to each woman (one at a time) which come to life, move and refreeze. When pimps look at main prostitute they refreeze. After signal from main prostitute, the others come to life and walk about the stage as if on the street. Again with a signal from the main prostitute, the others proposition the audience as the pimps come to life and move back and forward, still in grouping, watching over prostitutes. The main pimp (could be DIAMOND RING) advances from group and with cane, signals to women. Women stop, look at audience and retreat behind the other pimps and go off stage. Pimps go off stage leaving main pimp — who crosses to center stage, points at audience with cane, turns and strides off stage as lights dim.

ACT ONE

SETTING: *a dimlit bar in a large city, the time is NOW . . . it's about midnight and the place is preparing for business. This is a place for the Hustlers and the Players of the city. All the People are extremely well-dressed. There's soft jazz coming out of the jukebox. There is a large sign in bold letters over the bar . . .*

PUSHERS IF YOU ARE BUSTED PUSHING IN HERE
YOU WILL BE PUSHED INTO YOUR GRAVE

Once in a while a john will come in to pick up a trick.
Onstage: LEFTY, CHILE, VIVA *and* SATISFACTION. LEFTY *and* PHEBE *at bar.*
    CHILE *and* VIVA *are running through a song at piano.*
PHEBE: You know something, Lefty, for an old motherfucker you got a nerve to talk to me.

174

LEFTY G.: Hey lady just watch what you say.

PHEBE: Hey baby pick up the tempo.

CHILE: Phebe . . . Bitch a table or the bar, but not here.

PHEBE: Fuck you, you pseudo nigger . . . I know more about the song than you do.
After all I inherited it. (*Crosses back to bar.*)

LEFTY G.: Listen, get your back off the bar . . . you know better than giving your
back to the bar.

CHILE: Why not run the bar on the sap, Lefty? Teach her a lesson.

PHEBE: Why don't you mind your own business?

CHILE: Child, this is my business, and if you open up them painted bubble gum lips of
yours again . . . I'll shove that blond wig down your throat, bitch.

PHEBE: Ohhh go bitch, go on . . . come from behind that bar . . . come, that's right,
just one step more across the threshold.

LEFTY G.: Put that razor down, woman, or they'll be putting a tag on your big toe
tonight . . . you hear me . . . you hear me, woman.

JUSTICE: Hey. What the hell is going on here?

LEFTY G.: This bitch with the razor . . .

JUSTICE: Woman, what you doing with that razor in your hand? Put that thing away
as of this minute. Lefty, she's drunk, but not that drunk . . . Lefty, I want you to
count to ten, and if that thing ain't on the floor, I want you to put a hole in her
head.

LEFTY G.: Right. (*Begins to count.*) seven . . . eight . . . nine . . . (*Enter* BAM-BAM
with dishes.)

PHEBE: Hold it . . . hold it. O.K., there. Justice, she ain't got no right calling me a
sap.

CHILE: She was going to cut me.

LEFTY G.: She had her back to the bar . . . I told her to get off it and she ignored me.

PHEBE: I heard you loud.

LEFTY G.: Then why did I have to tap your shoulder? Chile said I should run the bar
on her to teach her a lesson.

CHILE: She was going to cut me with that razor.

JUSTICE: It's your stroke . . . stroke it.

CHILE: Come, bitch, now let's get it on with our hands . . . me and you on a fair one.
I'll whip your tight little ass like I own you . . . Bitch . . . (*Pulls off wig, throws it to
Lefty. They begin to fight.*)

BAM-BAM: Mátela, Chile . . . mate la cabrona, mátela . . . (CHILE *pulls* PHEBE'S
dress over her head.) . . . Ooooh, pantaletas sucias . . . bien chingada.

JUSTICE: Okay, Chile Girl, that's enough — you proved your point . . . Bam-Bam,
get your ass in the kitchen. (*Exit* BAM-BAM *followed by* SATISFACTION *who
laughs and ad-libs with* LEFTY G.)

CHILE: Next time you pull a razor on me, I'll cut you from your throat down to your
trick filled pussy . . . bitch.

PHEBE: You called me a sap.

JUSTICE: That's just what you are . . . a sap . . . You disrespect my place, and then
you pull a razor on my girl, and you goddam well knew you wasn't going to use the
damn thing . . . cuz you ain't ready to die.

PHEBE: Please, Justice. I'm sorry.

JUSTICE: Sorry, didn't do it . . . Phebe Reed did. Who's your man now?

PHEBE: Cat Eyes. (CHILE *crosses to her.*)

JUSTICE: Cat Eyes, huh?

LEFTY G.: A young Latin brother . . . a mean youngblood, Justice.

JUSTICE: Run the bar on her.

LEFTY G.: Ain't nobody here, Justice, but Viejo.

JUSTICE: Viejo . . . Where is he?

LEFTY G.: He's in the bathroom taking a shit.

JUSTICE: I don't need all the detail, Lefty. Why didn't you tell me he was here?

LEFTY G.: I couldn't . . . not with that bitch giving us all this static.

JUSTICE: Run an hour on her.

PHEBE: Cat Eyes will kill me. He a mean man, Justice . . . please.

JUSTICE: Should of thought of about it first. He ain't gonna kill you, just touch you up a bit . . . the very thing you need too. Chile, tell Cat Eyes I wanna see him when he come in.

PHEBE: Please, Justice, give me some. (PHEBE *crosses to barstarts, ad libs with* LEF-TY *about getting another drink.*)

JUSTICE: O.K., you got some justice . . . next time. (*Enter* VIEJO.) Hey, holy shit-balls . . . Viejo, you fowl, stink-breath, low lifed, high-living son of a street walker. How the fuck you been?

VIEJO: Hey, toiletbowl mouth, long time no see, man.

PHEBE: Justice, this motherfucker 86 me.

JUSTICE: I already told you, you copped. Right? Now kindly vacate these premises and do not enter again thru them doors, unless you are accompanied by your man or a john. Is that clear?

PHEBE: Thank you.

JUSTICE: Put an egg in your shoe and beat it!

VIEJO: Qué pasa with her?

JUSTICE: Violate numero uno house rule.

VIEJO: Still the same rules. Huh?

JUSTICE: Oh, fuck you . . . and get your back off the bar, you greyass, high-yellow, Puerto Rican nigger.

LEFTY G.: Want me to run the bar on him, Justice?

JUSTICE: You could if you wanna . . . but I think Chile Girl will crack your skull for you if you do.

LEFTY G.: Blood is thicker than whiskey.

JUSTICE: Viejo, it's now been . . .

VIEJO: Eighteen months, two weeks and three days.

JUSTICE: You been in, huh? I thought so. For what, man?

VIEJO: For the same reason she got her ass kicked.

JUSTICE: Violation, huh? What?

VIEJO: The shit is so bad, I don't even want to say . . . no visible means.

JUSTICE: He musta really wanted you bad, to pull that one.

VIEJO: As soon as he found out his wife was pregnant.

JUSTICE: What's so bad about that?

VIEJO: He's sterile.

JUSTICE: Beautiful.

VIEJO: How's things been going?

JUSTICE: Not bad. On Saturdays I make as much money from the undercovers — plainclothes and provocateurs — as I do from the players.

VIEJO: Tap?

JUSTICE: The whole joint.

VIEJO: Bad scene.

JUSTICE: It's them so-called revolutionary, loud-mouth militants . . . using places like these to make their meetings. Then the pushers come in after the law come out . . .

LEFTY: Sons of bitches.

JUSTICE: . . . made things worse for all. See the sign? Don't think I put that up. All those that signed it did . . . and let me tell you, it's been enforced more than once. Believe me.

VIEJO: I see no reason not to.

JUSTICE: I don't mean it that way. Everybody knows that when you fell into dealing drugs, it was because of . . .

VIEJO: Everybody knows?

JUSTICE: Well, everybody that counts.

VIEJO: Chile?

JUSTICE: Yeah . . . I guess she got ears.

VIEJO: She not?

JUSTICE: No, she's cool. Goes to college in the day, works here at night . . . she been like a daughter to me.

VIEJO: And you've been like a father.

JUSTICE: As much as a father as you would've been.

VIEJO: What's she taking up?

JUSTICE: She going to be a social worker, but they got a fancy name for themselves.

VIEJO: Poverty Pimp.

JUSTICE: Social Worker.

VIEJO: Vaya, that's cool.

JUSTICE: You're off for good? No extra change hanging around somewhere . . . is there?

VIEJO: Nothing hanging loose. Everything is tightened up.

JUSTICE: Max-out? All of it?

VIEJO: Every dime of it, that includes delinquent too.

JUSTICE: Well, that's really good to hear . . . Lefty G. . . .

LEFTY G.: God listens to those who speak.

VIEJO: And the devil listens to those who whisper.

JUSTICE: You remember, huh?

LEFTY G.: Two points for El Viejo.

JUSTICE: Lefty G, put a tab up for Viejo.

LEFTY G.: You got it. (*Crosses back to bar-returns with gun wrapped in napkin, gives to Viejo.*)

JUSTICE: Had a chance to cop some combo with Chile?

VIEJO: Negative, that thing about the cracked skull was cute, but I get the feeling it would have been my head and not Lefty G's.

JUSTICE: You sell yourself too short.

VIEJO: Perhaps, quizás, pero I still feel it.

JUSTICE: It's all in your mind. You know every time someone comes out of the joint it's paranoid time.

VIEJO: Run that shit under somebody else's belt, not mines.

JUSTICE: I'll prove it to you.

VIEJO: Later . . . right now tell me why the streets are so empty of players.

JUSTICE: There are players in the streets, just that things change. Some players are not into the same kinda thing we were into. You looking for a game? Or are you gonna shoot your regular?

VIEJO: I'll do some scouting first . . . before I go into the field.

JUSTICE: Yeah, after 18 months.

VIEJO: Two weeks, and . . .

JUSTICE: I know, I know . . . three days. Hey, Chile, come here.

VIEJO: I told you later.

JUSTICE: But I thought . . .

VIEJO: You shouldn't think for me . . . I'm capable of doing my own.

JUSTICE: O.K. What the matter? Why the rocks?

VIEJO: I haven't any rocks. Look, all I wanna find out is how is everything and everybody doing . . .

JUSTICE: Well, let me put it to you this way, Viejo. (*Enter a john, looks around and goes to bar.*) Everything is everything . . . and everybody is either breathing or not. You're scared?

VIEJO: Me? No . . . Well, O.K. damn it, I am.

JUSTICE: Why?

VIEJO: Look. What am I supposed to say to her? "Hi, I'm Luis Rivera. I'm the spick who turned your mother into a whore and dragged her down into drug addiction with me, into prisons, and hospitals, and abandoned you to a players' bar?" I never gave her anything worth having . . .

JUSTICE: Wait a minute. If I remember correctly . . . there was a ten thousand dollar bank account in her name when you left her in my house.

VIEJO: Your memory is beautiful, but that was only material things.

JUSTICE: What are you talking about "material things?" What else is there?

VIEJO: There's things that money can't buy, something of value . . . from the soul of love . . . something spiritual . . .

JUSTICE: (*Laughing.*) From the soul of love . . . Are you for real? You are for real, aren't you? Where the hell were you? In some prison, or a Mahariji Guru retreat? What's gotten into you? This isn't the Viejo I know or knew.

VIEJO: Sometimes I wonder myself . . . I guess it's age and time. You know something? The first time I went to the joint . . . nothing . . . time slipped by so fast and I was swift and clean with my mitts . . . copped what I needed, and kept something extra just in case I ran out. This time the bit put a hurting on my ass. This bit really got to me . . . I guess I woke up to find a very rude awakening waiting for me in the mirror. (*Looks at reflection in glass.*)

JUSTICE: O.K. (*Takes glass away.*) You woke up to a certain fact of life, that once meant shit to you, and means the same to millions of others . . . but she is your flesh and blood . . .

VIEJO: Jake, I don't know if I can handle it.

JUSTICE: There's only one way to find out. Right? Well?

VIEJO: Don't go too far.

JUSTICE: Fuck you . . . now straighten yourself up . . . Chile, you got some time for yourself.

CHILE: Good, I'll go get something to eat . . . I hate the food here. (*Begins to leave.*)

JUSTICE: That's not what I meant . . . (*She returns.*) Viejo would like to talk to you.

CHILE: He has nothing to say . . . anyway, not to me, Justice.

JUSTICE: He's your father.

CHILE: In name only.

JUSTICE: He needs you Chile. He's old.

CHILE: I needed him when I was young.

JUSTICE: Chile . . . don't do that to him.

CHILE: He did it to himself. And if that's why you gave me some time for myself off . . . I'll go back to work.

JUSTICE: Go back to work . . . he's a customer. Treat him like one . . . his table is lonely . . . his glass is empty.

CHILE: Yessum bossem . . . (*Cross to* VIEJO.)

VIEJO: Hi.

CHILE: Your glass is empty.

VIEJO: Sí, yo sé. ¿Cómo está, mi hija?

CHILE: Sorry I don't speak Spanish.

VIEJO: Chile . . . (*Enter* JR. BALLOON *with* ROSA.)

JR. BALLOON: Why is there no music in this place?

JUSTICE: Cause we was all waiting for the rhythm to arrive.

JR. BALLOON: I am here.

JUSTICE: And there's the box. It takes dollar bills. (*Motions* ROSA *to juke box.*)

CHILE: Customers . . .

VIEJO: Chile.

CHILE: Customers . . . see you around sometime. (*Music begins.* JR. BALLOON *dances with* CHILE *and* ROSA.)

JR. BALLOON: Hey, Justice . . . What do you think about this girl putting a make-believe beauty mark on her face, without my permission?

ROSA: But baby, I did it for you.

JR. BALLOON: I was talking to Justice. Girl, you been beginning to take too many liberties . . . girl, you keep that mouth of yours running when it should be closed, I'm gonna have to run you down to the East Village with those transvestites.

JUSTICE: The beauty mark adds essence to her beauty, Jr. Balloon.

CHILE: She should have something black about her. (*Serves drinks to everybody.*)

JR. BALLOON: Good . . . good, give the young lady two points. She's learning too much from you, Justice.

JUSTICE: Like father, like daughter. That's what some fool said.

JR. BALLOON: Go find us a nice table, Rosa.

JUSTICE: All the tables are nice, Jr. Balloon.

JR. BALLOON: What would you do without my business? (*Enter* WILLIE BODEGA *with* KAHLU.)

JUSTICE: Celebrate!

WILLIE BODEGA: Lefty . . . Hey, What's going on? Junior Balloon . . . Justice . . . (KAHLU *and* ROSA *sit at table together.*)

JR. BALLOON: Well, if it ain't the talking gringo . . . Hit any grocery stores lately?

WILLIE BODEGA: Funny . . . funny . . . you got a nerve talking. You look more like an advertising for an Orchard Street clothing store.

JR. BALLOON: Poorly. Who writes your material?

WILLIE BODEGA: Your money's calling you.

JR. BALLOON: Yeah, but there's no police 38's coming from that moneymaker. (JR. BALLOON *and* WILLIE *sit at table together.*)

WILLIE BODEGA: Lefty, let me have . . .

LEFTY G.: You can have anything and as many as you want . . . the tab is on Cat Eyes.

WILLIE BODEGA: Well, in that case, let me have a bottle of your best champagne.

JR. BALLOON: You mean to tell me you had let me put money on the counter?

LEFTY G.: Jr. Balloon, you always said you got it like the Feds . . .

JR. BALLOON: Yeah, but when it's free? And the competition is paying? Well, that's another story all together.

JUSTICE: You should never acknowledge competition, Jr. Balloon; can slow you down worrying about it.

JR. BALLOON: Who worries? The way I see it, there's enough for everyone that can handle it.

WILLE BODEGA: No one gives Jr. Balloon any compo.

JR. BALLOON: You tell 'em whitey. June, the month of love. Love, the bug you just can't slap away. (*Enter* LEFTY *and* CHILE *with champagne and glasses.*)

WILLIE BODEGA: California? This is the best? How we gonna toast with grape juice? (JUSTICE *with various ad-libs.*) Here's to the hustle.

JR. BALLOON: And the hustlers.

VIEJO: And to the suckers.

WILLIE BODEGA: The suckers.

VIEJO: Who without there would be no hustle . . . or hustlers.

JR. BALLOON: Suck my left nut. Am I seeing who I'm seeing? Viejo.

VIEJO: Jr. . . Willie . . . long time. I see you two are still on each other's cases.

JR. BALLOON: Can't shake the snake charmer loose.

WILLIE BODEGA: You and your brother should have never taken my lunch money.

JR. BALLOON: Justice, you ain't shit. You stand there, knowing the old man is in town, and don't let up on it . . . Shit . . .

JUSTICE: The toilet is to your right.

JR. BALLOON: What are you doing, old man?

VIEJO: Well, nothing as of yet, just looking over the store.

WILLIE BODEGA: You got ends?

JR. BALLOON: How's your collar?

VIEJO: Got enough to see me over any humps . . . my collar is tighter than a pimp's hatband.

JR. BALLOON: I'll have it loosen for you tonite . . . Rosa, come here, mama. (*Cross* ROSA *to* JR. *who motions, turns her towards* VIEJO. ROSA *crosses to* VIEJO.)

ROSA: Hi.

JR. BALLOON: This here is one fine, moneymaking 'hoe . . . most of the bread I made with her head. Just give her your address and she is yours for as long as it takes . . . but remember, just for that long, not longer than that.

VIEJO: She young.

JR. BALLOON: She old enough. Can you handle it, mama?

ROSA: Anything you say . . . but he old.

JR. BALLOON: Don't let snow fool you, there plenty of oil in the basement. (*Laughs.*)

WILLIE BODEGA: Jesus H. Christ! Jr. Balloon, you tell the corny's jokes . . . and then he laughs at them too. I don't see what they see . . .

JR. BALLOON: Mama, tell this near-sighted fool what you see in Jr.

ROSA: June.

JR. BALLOON: And that's all they wanna see, cause they don't wanna see the winter in me . . . O.K., mama, go back there and look pretty.

ROSA: Old man, when I get through with you, you'll be in your second childhood.

JR. BALLOON: That's why you could never make it as a Mack . . . you never let a woman see what she wants to see, but what you want her to see. This way, she is always looking for something to see.

VIEJO: "I see," said the blind man . . . to his deaf daughter.

WILLIE BODEGA: I know this payroll clerk who's given me all the details of his route. He has pocket money for both of us . . . ten G's apiece.

VIEJO: Is it a two man job? Your word?

WILLIE BODEGA: No, not really, but you know things sometimes happen, and . . .

VIEJO: No thanks . . . I don't play alarm clock.

WILLIE BODEGA: Just trying to be helpful.

VIEJO: I know, thank you, but I am not looking for welfare. (*Leaves table to counter. Cross* JR. BALLOON.)

JR. BALLOON: Why be like that, old man? He only trying to be helpful . . . he's a heist kid, that's all he knows.

VIEJO: You're right, I don't know where my head was at there . . . Excuse me, I'll go apologize . . . Willie, look, I didn't mean to sound like that. (CHILE *crosses to piano. Signals* VIVA *to play* CAT EYES *music.*)

WILLIE BODEGA: That's O.K. . . . I was out of line, but you did teach me everything I know about the business.

VIEJO: Let me buy you a drink. (CAT EYES *enters with* PHEBE.)

WILLIE BODEGA: Haven't you heard? The drinks are on Cat Eyes. (VIVA *plays rousing fanfare.*)

CAT EYES: Hold it! Hold it! Wait a minute. Now . . . what's this about the drinks on me? I don't remember ever inviting you to drink with me.

JUSTICE: Well, you invited everybody for an hour of free drinks tonite.

PHEBE: They are running the bar on you, Papi.

CAT EYES: Running the bar on me? Justice, you must be clear out your mind . . . I ain't paying for nobody's drinks . . .

JUSTICE: Cat Eyes, there are many unwritten rules in the game that you play . . . this is a hustler's place . . . all my customers are players, and they go with the rules . . . the same ones that are out in the street apply here. One . . . the major, is respect . . . you don't disrespect the place . . . if you turn your back on the bar you disrespect me . . . and if you disrespect . . . you pay.

CAT EYES: I have never placed my back on the bar.

JUSTICE: She did . . . she's yours . . . you're responsible.

CAT EYES: You didn't tell me this. You embarrassed me in front of all these people. (*Pulls wig off and pushes her toward the door.*) Get out . . . and I don't want to see you at home, I want you in them streets until your soles waste. Get out. Beat it . . . (*Turns to* JUSTICE.) Here's a couple of hundred, Justice, this should cover it.

JUSTICE: Man, goddam you young. Look here, brotherman, it has nothing to do with the bread, can't you get that through your head? You ain't cool at all, are you? I mean, you need some type of schooling, man. If you don't get your head together, you gonna end up with a teacher.

CAT EYES: Yah, who?

JUSTICE: Me . . . I make a good principal, brotherman.

CAT EYES: And I never made a good student.

WILLIE BODEGA: That's why you a dropout in the players' game.

JR. BALLOON: Pendejito . . .

CAT EYES: Oye, tú no me conoce a mí.

JR. BALLOON: Y I don't really want to either, bro.

WILLIE BODEGA: Man, you ain't got no kind of class, do you?

CAT EYES: Who the fuck is this fucking gringo talking to?

WILLIE BODEGA: Unless you a wall, motherfucker, I'm talking to you.

CAT EYES: Better dig yourself, mister.

WILLIE BODEGA: You do right calling me, mister. (CAT EYES *reaches inside jacket.*)

JR. BALLOON: Better not go for it, kid.

WILLIE BODEGA: Guess at your age you wanna call it a game of cards.

JUSTICE: Willie Bodega . . .

WILLIE BODEGA: Yah, Justice, I'm cool, man, I'm cool.

CAT EYES: He better be, or he be dead soon. You dig?

WILLIE BODEGA: (*Going for gun. Everyone clears.*) Now, where have I heard that rap before? (JUNIOR and WILLIE *act as if they're going to draw weapons.* CAT EYES *prepares for advance.*)

JUSTICE: Junior . . . Willie . . . I mean it.

WILLIE BODEGA: O.K., Willie B. ain't gonna cause you no damages.

CHILE: Look, if you ain't gonna put no money on the tab, then book out of here.

CAT EYES: O.K., I take the tab . . . I can afford it. (*Staring at* WILLIE.)

JUSTICE: You can't afford it.

LEFTY G.: Well, what you gonna do, youngblood? You stare real hard.

WILLIE BODEGA: He must practice . . . in front of the mirror.

JR. BALLOON: Come on . . . sit down already, Willie . . . leave the dude now.

WILLIE BODEGA: I ain't bothering him.

CAT EYES: Your breath is.

WILLIE BODEGA: Oh my, oh my . . . next thing he gonna do is talk about my mother. Oh my, oh my . . . I feel so rotten, boo hoo . . . I'll weep for days behind that statement.

JR. BALLOON: Willie . . .

WILLIE BODEGA: Yah, O.K., Junior.

JR. BALLOON: Man, it ain't you I'm worrying about, man, it's Justice's place, man . . . You know the place is getting hot.

WILLIE BODEGA: Look, man, I'm gonna squash this here bullshit between me and you, kid . . . but I just wanna drop something on you before I do squash it.

CAT EYES: Make it short.

WILLIE BODEGA: As short as it takes, man. Man, if you wanna be a player, you got to realize that everything that jumps your way ain't threatening your manhood, brotherman.

CAT EYES: Look, man, I was in the joint and no one ever . . .

WILLIE BODEGA: Not that kind of manhood, brotherman.

CAT EYES: A whitey that raps like a nigger. Ain't that something?

WILLIE BODEGA: No, that ain't nothing, man. I just rap this way cuz that the way I raps . . . but what I wanna tell you is this, youngblood, . . . the man been in the game before you crawls out of your mama's cunt, and this man told you, rightly so too, that your lady disrespected the place, and there was no kind of shit jumping your way, man. All you had to do, if you really think yourself as being what you are, a man, is, man, that you apologize to the place and accept the play, man, to you . . . that's all. No big thing . . . no big money coming out of your pocket . . . no big thing being taken out of your hustle, man. Nothing, man, nothing at all . . . but you gotta jump stink right quick on the place, because you think everybody is out to make you or take something away from you. That's too bad, man, . . . cuz you ain't never gonna learn to trust, man, and that's real bad . . . cuz if you can't trust, then you can't ever relax and enjoy the stings you make. Can you dig it, man? And you wanna know something? The run of the tab on you was just a way of Justice letting you know that you blew it in here with him and that you should be aware of it. Like on the streets a knife in your gut or a bullet in your head would have been the respond and I guess that's what you think that you are supposed to respect, the Force, and fuck the rest of the real attitude. (*Cross* ROSA *to juke-box.*)

CAT EYES: Man, you talk too much.

WILLIE BODEGA: I guess that I do, cause I like you and your motherfucking arrogance. (*Jazz music begins.*)

JUSTICE: Man, brotherman, you better believe that he likes you for reasons known only to him.

CAT EYES: Maybe he's a faggot.

JUSTICE: You want your table?

CAT EYES: Yah.

CHILE: It's ready. (*Cross* LEFTY *with drinks on tray.*)

JR. BALLOON: Hey, Lefty. Can you dance, man?

LEFTY G.: Sure. (LEFTY *dances pathetically.* JUNIOR *and* WILLIE *try to teach him steps.* JUSTICE *tries,* LEFTY *gets angry and leaves.* JUSTICE *dances with* KAHLU, *then* ROSA *ad-libs "hot stuff."* JR. BALLOON *"that's gonna cost you".*)

VIEJO: So that's what out here on the streets making the money, huh?

JUSTICE: Yah, that's what out here, man. That ain't nothing. Wait till you see the rest parading around, man. (*Enter* DIAMOND RING *with* SATISFACTION, *arguing with a man.* JUSTICE *crosses to see what's the matter and calm things down.* SATISFACTION *leaves.*)

DIAMOND: Man, Justice, I . . . I . . . man, tell me something quick, man, like . . . like this dude, man, . . . I'm gonna waste the motherfucker, I'm gonna waste the motherfucker . . .

MAN: That'll be the last motherfucker you'll ever try to waste too. (DIAMOND *angri-*

ly heads toward man, but JUSTICE *restrains him.*)

JUSTICE: Man, calm down, man, calm down . . . like, what the hell, man. (DIA-MOND *calms down a bit and walks around acknowledging everyone.*)

DIAMOND: Who that?

JUSTICE: This here is Viejo, man, a really down to the . . .

DIAMOND: That's the dude you be rappin' about, man? Hey, what's happening?

VIEJO: Right now you're what's happening, brotherman.

DIAMOND: Thank you.

JUSTICE: Now, who is this that you gonna kill this time, man?

WILLIE BODEGA: He's always killing somebody.

DIAMOND: No, this time I'm for real, Willie, really for real, man. You know what this dude did outside to me . . . to me, Diamond Ring, the baddest Mack-o-roni that ever jumped out of the cooker. This dude out there sold me a motherfucking . . . (*Takes hat off and* ROSA *and* KAHLU *exit to ladies room.*) a motherfucking ticket in front of my woman, man, in front of my ladies. See, Willie? This time is serious business . . .

WILLIE BODEGA: Yah, man, real serious.

DIAMOND: Him and his boys.

WILLIE BODEGA: You ain't got no piece, man?

DIAMOND: Have you ever known me to wake up without brushing my teeth with my three roscoes?

WILLIE BODEGA: Then why are you in here rappin about it?

DIAMOND: Man, this dude, this punk, called me out in front of the motherfucking cops . . . in front of the cops, man. That's why I'm here, man, cuz or else . . . you know what it all about, man. Man, I got to get my feelings out here, or else I be out there with these two dudes dead at my feet, facing the motherfucking police, man, and you know about me, man, I hold court in the streets, man, I can't do no time.

CAT EYES: That's why people worry about him knowing too much.

DIAMOND: You talking bout me?

JUSTICE: That kind of talk is not allowed here, mister.

CAT EYES: It's a free country.

JUSTICE: Since when?

WILLIE BODEGA: Be cool, Diamond. He's a little hot cuz Justice is running the bar on him.

DIAMOND: Give me four bottles of the best champagne that you got, Just.

CAT EYES: That's the only way you can get it . . . when it's free.

DIAMOND: Make it eight.

JUSTICE: No, man, you can't do that.

DIAMOND: Why not?

JUSTICE: You ain't gonna drink them, man, that's why . . . and I hate seeing good champagne going to waste.

DIAMOND: I'll drink them, besides, I got friends that will help me. (*Everyone tinkles their glasses.*)

JUSTICE: Oh, shit, here we go with another drunk . . . Lefty, give Diamond a bottle of champagne.

LEFTY G.: Right.

DIAMOND: Oooh come on, Justice, my pockets grow hungry out there. I mean, if you gonna give away welfare . . . give me some.

LEFTY G.: (*Brings bottle of champlagne.*) Hey, Diamond . . . you did right, man, walking away. There will be another time.

JUSTICE: There always is, remember that, there always is another time.

DIAMOND: I will, cuz I believe it, man.

CHILE: Your table is ready, Diamond.

DIAMOND: Thank you. (*Looks at* CAT EYES *and kisses* CHILE.) Show me the way. Hey, old man, care to drink with me? (*Enter* KAHLU *from ladies room.*)

VIEJO: No thank you, youngblood.

DIAMOND: Suit yourself. (WILLIE *and* KAHLU *join* DIAMOND *at his table.* JR. BALLOON *goes and gets* ROSA *from ladies room and they dance.*)

CAT EYES: Hey, baby.

CHILE: My name is Chile.

CAT EYES: Come here, girl.

CHILE: What do you want, sir?

CAT EYES: Hey, man, come on . . . don't do that to me.

CHILE: The way I see it you are doing it to yourself.

CAT EYES: Come on, baby, be nice.

CHILE: Have you ever seen me be mean?

CAT EYES: What do you call what you are doing to me, being?

CHILE: Natural.

CAT EYES: Hate to see you in the mornings.

CHILE: Really?

CAT EYES: Now, what the hell did I do to receive this treatment?

CHILE: You don't know?

CAT EYES: Girl, if I did I wouldn't be asking, now would I?

CHILE: Can never tell about you.

CAT EYES: Now, what is that suppose to mean?

CHILE: Just what I said, that's all.

CAT EYES: Come, baby, sit down for a second with me, let's rap this here thing out between you and me real nice and quiet like.

CHILE: I'm working.

CAT EYES: Take some time off . . . a few minutes. (*Caressing her breasts.*)

JUSTICE: Chile, you gonna host or you gonna play the host?

CHILE: I have some time for myself, remember you said so.

JUSTICE: Yah . . .

CHILE: What you got to say to me? It better be good.

CAT EYES: Now why does it have to be good? You act like I'm supposed to always drop a line on you if I want your attention.

CHILE: Your behavior tonight was enough to grab anyone's attention.

CAT EYES: Oh, is that it?

CHILE: Yes, that's it.

CAT EYES: Listen, I can't let these older dudes try to run over me. Most of them think that cause they been out on this thing longer than god, man, they think they are self-appointed teachers of the play. Everyone and their mother wants to run a school for P.I.'s. Ain't that a kick in the ass?

CHILE: But they know.

CAT EYES: So do I . . . come on, let's drop it now.

CHILE: Carlos . . .

CAT EYES: Don't call me Carlos here . . . I'm sorry baby.

CHILE: That's O.K., Cat Eyes.

CAT EYES: Come, baby. Why the ice? . . . melt, baby, melt on me . . . I get enough cold weather in them streets, baby, don't you start snowing on me too.

CHILE: I'm sorry, baby.

CAT EYES: How about a kiss?

CHILE: Not in here . . . Justice will blow a fuse.

CAT EYES: You said he ain't your father . . . not your real father.

CHILE: Oh, but he is . . . as real as any other girl's father is to them.

CAT EYES: O.K., baby, but I don't like playing high school boyfriend.

CHILE: I ain't asking you to play anything at all.

CAT EYES: Let's squash the whole thing and let me rap to you seriously, baby.

CHILE: I'm always listening to you.

CAT EYES: Like I told you last time, baby, I want out but I need me to make me some money. I don't wanna work in no place for some lousy weekly salary that costs you your fucking life, baby, that's not for me. No, I needs something more of value than that, baby . . . I need to go on for about a year. And then you know what I wanna do, baby? I wanna open up something like this, to be cool just like Justice is. I mean something that brings you respect as well as a decent living, as I know living to be; like you know what I mean, baby? Do I make any kind of sense to you, baby?

CHILE: Yes, you do, Papi.

CAT EYES: It's important to me. Like my old man didn't leave me shit when he drop out of this miserable world that he created for me and moms. Like he was a jerk and a full time drunk wino who kissed his bottle goodnight first, then he come and tucked in our pockets for loose change that me and my brother hustled . . .

JUSTICE: Chile . . . Chile Girl, I'm calling you.

CHILE: I hear you.

JUSTICE: That one hell of a break you taking, girl.

CHILE: Why are you complaining? I never complain when you ask me to work overtime. Do I?

JUSTICE: Sorry honey . . .

CAT EYES: He always on your case. Ain't he?

CHILE: Shit yah, that's cause he loves me . . . he always say, "Chile Girl, to me your shit smell like perfume."

CAT EYES: He a nice old man . . . I kinda like him too.

CHILE: I know that he don't like you at all.

CAT EYES: You can't please everybody, baby.

CHILE: That the God's truth.

CAT EYES: It's a simple man's truth.

CHILE: You sound like Viejo.

CAT EYES: The Viejo?

CHILE: That's him over there.

CAT EYES: Shit, a legend in person. You know him?

CHILE: Yah, I do.

CAT EYES: Shit, now from him I wouldn't mind being schooled, . . . though he don't look like much to me.

CHILE: People change their ways over the years, Papi.

CAT EYES: So I've been told.

CHILE: Baby . . .

CAT EYES: Yah, you know him, huh? Maybe you could introduce me to him, real cool like. You know what I mean?

CHILE: Baby, I don't want to introduce you to somebody like that.

CAT EYES: A minute ago you sounded like you admired him.

CHILE: Maybe I do, but I also hate him with a passion . . . I wish he were dead . . .

CAT EYES: That's kind of a strong wish for a beautiful girl like you.

CHILE: Well, maybe not dead, but in the joint doing life where he belongs.

CAT EYES: You only wish for the best.

CHILE: Baby, let's drop him. Let's talk about us. (*Kisses* CAT EYES.)

CAT EYES: Yah, we never get enough time. Baby, I . . . I wanna open up a classy stable of girls that'll make these guys eyes pop out of their mother fucking . . . (*Cross* JUNIOR *and* ROSA *to their table.*) Skulls. You know, girls with style . . . a private business . . . and I can do it, but I need your help, baby, I really need your help, baby. Please don't do that, baby, listen to me. Don't turn off on me . . . please, baby, listen to what I got to say first.

CHILE: I'm listening.

CAT EYES: No, you're not.

CHILE: Make it quick.

CAT EYES: I'll make it short . . . good-bye.

CHILE: What?

CAT EYES: I said, "I'll see you around sometime, baby."

CHILE: Carlos.

CAT EYES: Later, baby, later. (*Cross to* VIEJO.) Hi . . . Cat Eyes is my name.

VIEJO: Hi.

CAT EYES: Can I buy you a drink?

VIEJO: You already have.

CAT EYES: Yah, that's right . . . you're welcome.

VIEJO: I didn't thank you.

CAT EYES: No, you didn't.

VIEJO: And I wasn't planning to either.

CAT EYES: What's the matter? You don't like me or something?

VIEJO: It's not a matter of whether I like you or not. Even if I didn't, would that make a big difference in your life?

CAT EYES: Not one bit of a difference, I was around before I met you and I'll be around after you hit that grass in Long Island cemetery. You wanna blow?

VIEJO: No thanks, man, really. I just got out and I'm trying to figure something out in my head for myself, first, before I make any kind of moves in any direction that ain't considered legal by the state of New York. Dig what I mean.

CAT EYES: Yah, that you is leary like a motherfucker.

VIEJO: That's a good lesson for a youngblood like you to learn. When you are leary, you are careful . . . if you're careful, you survive in this here planet. If you take that into your brain for a moment each day, youngblood, and with a little bit of luck, you might live to be my age.

CAT EYES: I hope I never get that old. (*Crosses to his table.*)

VIEJO: That's just the same thing I said a long time ago. (*Cross JUSTICE to* VIEJO'S *table. Sits down.*)

JUSTICE: So you met Cat Eyes.

VIEJO: No, he met me.

CAT EYES: That's what they all say.

DIAMOND: You know something, Junior? Like, some people think they are players, you know what I mean? They really think they can do this here thing that we call the game . . . like they get themselves a couple of Junkie broads, put them on the corner with a million kinds of diseases dropping out of their eyes . . . like gonnorhea, syphillis . . . (*Stops, takes off his hat.* CHILE *crosses to bar.*) . . . like I was saying, a million kind of diseases dropping from their eyes, as well as their cunts. They buy themselves a flashy suit, from some wholesale store on the bowery, and they jump into the scene calling themselves P.I.'s. Man, they ain't never even seen a pimp unless they were shining his motherfucking shoes.

CAT EYES: Fuck you, punk motherfucker.

DIAMOND: What's with the kid? Oh, you want to fuck me, kid? Maybe I should be out on the corner. (*Various other ad-libs.*)

JR. BALLOON: How should I know, man? Maybe he's crazy or something.

DIAMOND: Must be.

LEFTY G.: You O.K., Cat Eyes? (*Crosses to men's room.*)

DIAMOND: He probably had too much to drink . . . you know these young dudes, can't handle the firewater.

186

JUSTICE: Chile, get me a drink. Will you?

CHILE: Can't you get it yourself?

JUSTICE: Yes, I could, but I asked you. Didn't I?

CHILE: You lazy motherfucker, you fat lazy . . . (*Various other adlibs-crosses to table.*)

JUSTICE: Shut up already, will you. Man, all day you been quibbering with the jibbering. Girl, I mean like, I don't know where you get all that from cause it don't come from your papa, that's for sure, and it don't come from your mama and you can ask your papa about that.

CHILE: How would he know?

VIEJO: I did love her, Chile, in my own way, I loved your mother.

CHILE: Sure, I bet.

JUSTICE: How much?

CHILE: His life . . . here . . . (*Slams drink on table.*)

JUSTICE: Thank you . . . maybe if you banged it a little harder it could've broken and then you could start . . .

CHILE: Up yours.

JUSTICE: Is that for my health or my death?

CHILE: Either way you want it.

JUSTICE: Strong girl, ain't she?

VIEJO: Yah, she is a strong woman.

JUSTICE: See you in a little while, I'm gonna talk with her.

VIEJO: O.K. later. (*Enter BAM-BAM, followed by SATISFACTION. BAM-BAM gives wallet to SATISFACTION and hides. SATISFACTION takes money out of wallet and gives it to DIAMOND RING and goes to lounge. Enter a salesman, looks around and heads for lounge. DIAMOND RING follows. BAM-BAM leaves.*)

ROSA: Are you ready to go, old man?

VIEJO: In a little while, girl, in a little while. Let me finish my drink first. O.K.?

ROSA: Sure . . . (*Crosses to CAT EYES.*)

CAT EYES: You know that girl is very hip, like someday she gonna make somebody a mean money maker out there, you know.

ROSA: Her? Chile? You must be crazy, ain't a P.I. in the life got the game to pull that quail, baby.

CAT EYES: Don't be too sure of that.

ROSA: You talk a lot, that's why I'm with Junior.

CAT EYES: I wouldn't let you work for me on a weekend basis, girl. (*VIEJO laughs.*)

ROSA: You couldn't be Junior's chauffeur. He's got his here milk crate with bottle tops, he calls it a car. I'll wait for you by Junior's table. (*Enter DIAMOND and SATISFACTION from lounge. DIAMOND drops wallet on floor. SATISFACTION leaves.*)

VIEJO: O.K., girl, be with you in a second.

ROSA: Take your time . . . Junior said my only work today is you.

VIEJO: Tell Junior I really appreciate it.

ROSA: I will, old man.

VIEJO: Hey, Rosa.

ROSA: Yah?

VIEJO: Stop calling me old man . . . the name is Viejo. (*LEFTY plays music in jukebox.*)

ROSA: Viejo.

VIEJO: Right . . . (*Salesman comes from lounge. Picks up wallet. Cashes check and leaves.*)

JR. BALLOON: Come here girl, dance with me.

WILLIE BODEGA: What make you think you can dance?

JR. BALLOON: If you believed it hard enough you might be able to get up on the floor too with a young lady wrapped in your arms. Right Rosa?

ROSA: Anything you say, daddy.

WILLIE BODEGA: Man, I'm gonna have to shut this man mouth all up. Now you gonna look mighty silly, my man. Come on girl. (KAHLU *dances to* WILLIE.) Diamond, put on a record with a hustle to it.

JR. BALLOON: Man, put on some Latin.

WILLIE BODEGA: Shit, man, that don't scare me none at all.

JR. BALLOON: O.K. loosen up.

DIAMOND: Vaya, Willie will, doing it up on the floor with the Latin roots . . . must have been a spick under the wood pile. Huh?

WILLIE BODEGA: Shove it.

DIAMOND: Is that the name of a record or a dance?

WILLIE BODEGA: That's the name of the grave diggers that are chasing you.

DIAMOND: That a white joke?

WILLIE BODEGA: Racist.

DIAMOND: So was your mama . . . Hey Lefty how do you turn this thing off? (LEFTY *pushes reject button.*)

LEFTY G.: You know how this whitey got the name Willie Bodega?

DIAMOND: Yah, Lefty, we know.

ROSA: I don't.

LEFTY G.: Could I tell you then? Junior, can I tell her?

JR. BALLOON: Man, we are about to have the Latin dance contest of the century and you wanna tell her dumb thing like that . . . (*Latin music begins.* LEFTY *pushes button, music stops.*)

LEFTY G.: It ain't dumb . . .

JR. BALLOON: It's about as dumb and dull a story as you are, Lefty.

LEFTY G.: I'm sorry, I won't say anything. (*Turns music on, picks up empty glasses and goes to bar.*)

DIAMOND: Hey Lefty . . . Lefty Gorilla . . . (JUNIOR *turns music off and seats everyone.*)

JR. BALLOON: Go tell Rosa how he got his name.

LEFTY G.: You mean it?

JR. BALLOON: Of course, man, of course, man, I was just fucking with your head before . . . after you tell it, we'll have the dance contest. Is that cool with you, Willie B?

WILLIE BODEGA: That's cool with me . . . I always like listening as to how I become a spick.

LEFTY G.: You know, Rosa, before you was born we all use to hang out together as kids. Right fellas? . . . me and Justice are like that. Right, Justice?

JUSTICE: Right.

LEFTY G.: Yah, man, it was the good old days. We started together doing everything, man, it was real cool. Like Justice and me, we would go to these places. Right? In uniforms of cleaning people . . . you know the people that sweep and mop places, and nobody would say anything to us and after the place was empty we would go into the offices and Justice would yell out. "All those that wanna live, hit the floor. All those that wanna go to meet their maker remain on your feet." And the whole place be on the floor before you could blink your eyes . . . man, it was real cool. After we got some money we started doing other things. Like Justice became a big numbers man in Harlem and in Brooklyn. Man it was real cool.

JR. BALLOON: Man, I don't think Justice would like you talking like that out here in the open, man, tú sabe?

LEFTY G.: We are among friends. Ain't we?

DIAMOND: Yah, Lefty, that's true . . . but you know walls have ears and you guys did a lot of shit that ain't accounted for yet.

LEFTY G.: Yah, that makes sense. Yah. Well, you Rosa . . . sometimes you are traveling so high on the hog that you forget where you are or who you are and how you got to where you are. That's what happened to all of us within a couple of years; we were doing it so hard in those days that we forgot to be cool about ourselves, man, like we just didn't think and the next thing you know we all in jail almost like if it was a sickness running around . . . Going to jail was like a fever, it spread fast, and for many of our friends, may they rest in peace, the fever was real hard and they just didn't get the medicine in time. The medicine is the experience of the streets, not just the streets but the good doings of the streets. Anyway, we were all in Attica on 36 gallery. The fuck ups . . . that's what they say, man, we were getting over, wasn't we? . . . we sure was, man, we sure was. I use to cook and play bodyguard to the fellas and their young chickens, you know. These dudes were doing it up. Anyway hard time always fall on all of us, sooner or later hard times are gonna fall and at that time we all looked out for one another. Right fellas? We sure did, all the time. I remember the time we had to throw this guy off the tier becuz he thought we were fooling with him. Man, he swam in the air just like people swim in the water. It was really funny. Hey, remember the time Viejo threw that game into those new hacks and they fainted? Ah aha. Man I had some real nice times in the joint in them days . . . I sure did. I had better times and friends in the joint than I ever did in the streets . . . in my life . . . in any place I ever went. When hard times fell on us we would look out for one another and all you had to do was say, "Hey, hard times are here for the brother," and we all knew better days would come . . . we all knew better days would come . . . and better days would come . . . right around the corner. And you know . . . I was never . . . No, that's not what I want to say. (*Begins to leave.*)

ROSA: Lefty, Willie . . . Willie. (*Everyone coaxes him on.*)

LEFTY G.: Willie . . . Willie . . . oye Willie, mira Willie . . . let me cop some sugar . . . Willie me and you on the sandwich, man . . . Willie you got some matches? And Willie would say, man, you think this is welfare . . . Willie, you making some cool aide tonight? Me and you bro, just like it always been, me and you brother, me and you. And Willie say, "You motherfucker must think I'm a fucking BODEGA."

WILLIE: Goddamn corner store.

LEFTY G.: Willie "Z GALLERY" Bodega. Willie Bodega that's how he got his name. (*Everyone begins to get up.*) Me and Willie, we use to play handball for money. Money is cigarettes, you know, or he would have me fight some dude in the yard for money. You know? I use to fight real good, I could have been pro . . . you know I could have been pro. Right Willie? . . . that's what they all said, I could have been pro. (*Fights with DIAMOND RING. Gets out of hand. JUSTICE stops him.*) Yah, those were the good old days. Justice says we now are into the good new days. That's funny, ain't it? I mean the way Willie Bodega got his name.

DIAMOND: That's funny, Lefty . . . that's real funny.

LEFTY G.: You know something, I wasn't going to say this before, but I will now. When I was in the joint with them . . . I was never lonely . . . (*Crosses to bar.*)

CHILE: Viva . . . play number six. (CHILE *sings ballad to* LEFTY. *At end of song they both go to bar.*)

DIAMOND: (*In at end of song as they go to bar.*) Let's have the dance. (JR. BALLOON *turns music back on.*)

CAT EYES: Man, that dude is a head blower.

VIEJO: Know something, Cat Eyes? Your experience is very limited.

CAT EYES: What is that suppose to mean?

VIEJO: Just what it's suppose to mean. There's no hidden meanings in anything that comes out of my mouth . . . I am a very simple man when I address people.

CAT EYES: You got the same type of attitude the rest of these niggers have. You think you know it all.

VIEJO: I know that there's a lot I don't know . . . and I also know that the only way I am going to learn the things I need to know is if I admit that I need to know these things.

CAT EYES: You sure must have done a lot of time in the joint. When I was in the joint, all the long time doing, motherfuckers talk like you talk, man.

VIEJO: And how is that?

CAT EYES: Like they see things.

VIEJO: That's becuz they did. And I bet you saw nothing in what they saw. Right?

CAT EYES: Right. They all talk nonsense.

VIEJO: That's too bad. That why you think the way you do now.

CAT EYES: I think all right, and I do all right too.

VIEJO: Not in the circle you don't, I can feel it and I am here fresh off the banana boat.

CAT EYES: Look, man, I don't care what them motherfuckers think about me and my game, I'm getting over. That's what counts. I pay my bills and eat good food . . . and I fuck everynight.

VIEJO: So does the warden.

CAT EYES: Man, let me tell you something.

VIEJO: Something I don't know? . . . something that has meaning? Or the "I told the hoe to sell the kid but keep the Cadillac cuz I need the wheels to move," kinda shit?

CAT EYES: You see them dudes? They think they got it made.

VIEJO: Don't you?

CAT EYES: They got some of it made, but not all of it. They got themselves years ahead of me in the game . . . plenty of time in the life to learn much experience. But me, I came fast Viejo, faster than any of them. That's why they don't like me, cuz they all know that I'm swifter than any of them were at my age, man. I am a youngblood fresh off the doctor's mitts. You know I still have the smell of the afterbirth hanging about me . . . but I'm swifter than those people who call themselves "folks," and have the smell of death in the breath. Me? I am new life, Viejo, I am new life. You think I don't know they are jealous of me and my fast talking self. Man, I know that. Shit, that why I talk to them the way I do cuz I know that. You think I may be wrong, but I'm not . . . I'm not . . . Viejo, my rap is strong and my words are never wrong. I'm young and faster than a streak of lightning and a ball of heat . . . and I always land on my feet, ever since I could remember. I never touched the floor with my knees. You see that girl, Chile, they all wanted her but they all fear Justice and Lefty Gorilla, but not me cuz their time is up on the earth. I know that this is a jungle law . . . (*Enter* BAM-BAM *and* SATISFACTION.) and I'm steaking my name to that game. She is gonna make me a very wealthy man, my man. She is gonna put me on the mack map of the year . . . every year until dooms day.

VIEJO: Are you saying what I think you are saying? You gonna turn her out?

CAT EYES: That's right, mister. I'm gonna turn her sweet ass out.

VIEJO: I can't let you do that.

CAT EYES: What you mean you can't let me do that? Who the fuck are you? Oh, you wanna turn her out there for yourself. Is that it? Listen, with your experience and my rap we got it made all the way.

VIEJO: You don't seem to understand. She isn't going out to the way of all flesh.

CAT EYES: You don't seem to understand you can't stop me, cuz she loves me . . . and beside . . . Why the fuck are you telling me some shit like that, if you don't want her as a pimp? Why the fuck are you playing boy scout?

VIEJO: I'm her father . . . (*Activity of bar takes over, dancing, ad-libs, music building to end of act one.*)

ACT TWO

Scene One: *A small hotel room.*

ROSA: Come, Papi . . . get it on. Oh, Papi, get it on . . . come on, baby. Shit, wait a fucking minute, man . . . What's happening, old man? We been in this damn bed for a half an hour and all you be doing is slobbering all over me . . . and your johnson ain't even hard. What's the matter, man? Are you too old to get it up any more?

VIEJO: Shut up, bitch.

ROSA: Oh, now it's shut up bitch routine. Huh? What you gonna do, old man? You know if it hadn't been that Junior ask me to lay you, I'd be with some real man who gets it up when he lays down next to a woman. Ha . . . look at this . . . it's as dead as a corpse in the city morgue. You were supposed to come in here with me to take care of business. Now what you gonna do, Mister Viejo? . . . the master of the hustle . . . What you gonna do? Hey, what's the matter? The cat got your tongue? You lost your voice as well as your strength to do it? Shit, I lay in the bed and I get a tongue bath . . . man, I can dig a little tongue but too much of it makes me horny, honey, and you shouldn't be out here giving up all this tongue if you can't give up anything else . . . I don't wanna be sucked off like a lesbian, I wanna be fucked like a woman.

VIEJO: Bitch, I told you to shut the fuck up once and I ain't gonna say it again. Now I can't fuck you cuz I can't get it hard and that's that . . .

ROSA: What's the matter, old man, don't you like girls anymore?

VIEJO: You going too far with your mouth, hoe.

ROSA: Not as far as you went with yours, old man.

VIEJO: Stop calling me old man. You know my name.

ROSA: Yes, Viejo, which means old man in Spanish. Right?

VIEJO: That's right . . . in Spanish not in English.

ROSA: Does that rule also go for your fucking abilities?

VIEJO: What you talking about?

ROSA: That you can fuck in Spanish but not in English? (*Grabs her trying somehow by violence to retain his sexual potency. She fights then lays back and laughs.*)

VIEJO: Shit . . . god damn it . . .

ROSA: I guess that it's true what I hear the folks rappin' about men who spent most of their lives behind bars. They become nothing with their dicks. No dick Ricks . . . can't get it uppers . . . unless the other person is a young boy like Cat Eyes, huh? I saw the way you stared at him before we left the bar . . . I bet if he was in this room with you, you'd be jumping with joy . . . happier than a faggot in Boys Town. What's your score, old man . . . little boys or little girls . . .

VEIJO: Shut the fuck up, bitch. I said shut the fuck up. (*Grabs pillow beats her.*)

ROSA: Go on, hit me some more . . . That's your speed, you like beating up on women . . . Now, look, it ain't even hard . . . ah . . . aha . . . oh, that's not your speed either. Is it? Maybe you like being whipped. Look in the closet . . . you'll find a nice leather whip. I'll look. Here. What you want me to wear, freak? . . . black rubber suits? . . . silk stocking? . . . leather boots? . . . What? I got it all in here. What ever is your pleasure I can do it . . .

VIEJO: Sit the fuck down.

ROSA: Maybe you want me to freak off with you . . . I would like to, but I wonder . . . hey, that's not a bad idea . . . I never had it done by a limp dick before.

VIEJO: Why the fuck are you so down on me? . . . Don't you understand?

ROSA: Sure, I understand . . . I understand that you pretend to be what you ain't, a bad motherfucking player . . . a pimp of the old guard . . . Hey, I got an idea. Should I piss in a bottle or maybe shit on your chest? . . .

VIEJO: (*Grabs her by the throat beginning to choke her.*) Bitch, I'll kill you . . . nobody speaks to me like that and lives, man or woman. I'll kill you.

ROSA: Please . . . don't . . . you . . . Sorry . . . please . . .

VIEJO: Oh, God. What the hell is wrong with me? I . . .

ROSA: Please . . . please don't kill me. I'm sorry. I'm sorry . . . please don't kill me, I wanna live. Please don't kill me.

VIEJO: Why the hell did you talk to me like that for? Who the fuck do you think I am? A motherfucking trick you picked up on the streets? I'm VIEJO . . . VIEJO. Say it, bitch, say VIEJO . . .

ROSA: Viejo . . . please, I didn't mean nothing . . . I only thought that you might be like Junior in bed.

VIEJO: What the hell are you talking about?

ROSA: Junior.

VIEJO: What about Junior?

ROSA: He can't do anything unless you insult him . . . unless you make him feel like he ain't shit . . .

VIEJO: That's Junior, that's not Viejo. Viejo is Viejo. Junior is Junior. If Junior is a freak for shit like that, that doesn't mean that every player in the life is the same way. Now get that thru you head, cuz the next man you do that kinda of shit to may not be like Viejo. I'm a nice guy. I try to be a nice guy but I don't like being talked to or treated like if I was a piece of shit. Do you understand, bitch? Do you understand, bitch? Answer me.

ROSA: Yes I understand . . . I understand, Viejo.

VIEJO: Cuz it don't mean shit to me to take you off the census . . . you be one less the pussy posse will be missing on their rounds on 'hoe stroll. You get me?

ROSA: Yes, I do . . . please don't kill me.

VIEJO: I ain't gonna kill you . . . just lay back and shut the fuck up. I don't wanna even hear you breathe hard.

ROSA: Yes, Viejo, whatever you say.

VIEJO: Yes, Viejo, whatever you say. Now I'm the law, huh? Now I become god to you becuz I was willing to ice you, huh? You ain't even worth fucking if I could get it up, bitch. I ain't gonna run you the this is the first time this happened to me story, cuz it ain't. You're young and you don't understand that it's the blood that makes it hard up.

ROSA: I learned that in Sex Education.

VIEJO: Well, they should've educated you to the terrible shit you could do to a man's head by pulling that, "you can't get it up" shit on him . . . You can ruin a man that way. Don't Junior teach you any compassion for the tricks that can't get it up?

ROSA: All Junior is interested in is how much I make.

VIEJO: That ain't the Junior I knew . . . that ain't the mack I grew up with.

ROSA: He's trying to make enough money to retire like Justice did . . . like Lefty Gorilla did. He wants out of the life and he's taking me with him. That's why I work more tricks then any of the other girls . . . that's why I know he gonna make it, cuz with me it's real feeling that pour out of him in bed. I am the one who gets it hard for him before he fucks any of the others girls, cuz I know what makes him make it move. I know him . . . and I am the youngest of the stable . . .

VIEJO: You wanna drink? (*Gives bottle to* ROSA *who drinks it straight down.*)

ROSA: Thank you . . .

VIEJO: What you know about the kid, Cat Eyes?

ROSA: Wow, for a minute there you sounded like a cop.

VIEJO: Forget about what I sound like, just talk to me.

ROSA: O.K. I'll talk to you . . . but answer me one thing and I'll answer your questions about Cat Eyes. Why do you want to know about Cat Eyes? I'll answer them regardless of the answer you give. Even if your answer is to mind my own business and answer your questions.

VIEJO: What different would it make then, since you just gave me the right to advise you to go fuck yourself or to give you a lie?

ROSA: The difference would be up here, in my head, and here in my feelings about myself. You see, Viejo, no matter what I am, how I get over . . . I like feeling good about myself . . . and if I do or say something which might make me feel bad about myself, I become very upset and I can't work. And I need to work to make that money so that Junior can retire young enough to be a part of a world that left him behind.

VIEJO: And you say that to say what? Am I expected to bring tears to my eyes and a light touch in my face?

ROSA: I don't like being a rat.

VIEJO: Yah . . . right . . . O.K. . . .

ROSA: So ask me all you want and I'll answer all you need to know, but . . .

VIEJO: May have to kill him.

ROSA: You may have to stand on line.

VIEJO: You can't see the truth. Can you?

ROSA: It may be the truth, but there's plenty of feelings like that around him.

VIEJO: No . . . those feelings are nothing more then just that. Feelings of hate and anger . . . but there's no feelings with me. I mean serious business when I talk of killing someone . . . There's nothing cheap about life, Rosa . . .

ROSA: He's my brother . . .

VIEJO: Your brother?

ROSA: Yes, my brother and he was my pimp and my lover . . . until Junior came into my life.

VIEJO: I have nothing to ask you.

ROSA: He's not bad. He's not mean . . . he's like little Bam-Bam that hangs around Justice's place . . . he is trying to make a hustle. Ever since he saw Mom fucking with the welfare investigator . . . ever since then, he always jumped on what came his way and I was naturally in the world that was in his way to put to use. A very simple story of life is what Cat Eyes is about. A what can I call it? A ghetto fairie tale that came true.

VIEJO: I have nothing to ask you, because whatever is the case, I know what I must do.

ROSA: Are you going to kill Cat Eyes?

VIEJO: Yes, I am going to kill Cat Eyes . . . the pimp . . .

ROSA: You're going to kill him . . . you're going to waste him . . .

VIEJO: I'm only going to do what man has done for centuries and what others have avoided doing . . . what every player and hustler know what they must do when they enter a new town or a new prison. You stop the action before it starts . . . you go for broke in any situation that threatens to take control of your game, or take control of something you consider valuable enough to fight and live for. You never trade what you need to feel good in the morning about, for a friendly smile from the next player becuz that's what keeps you going . . . what makes everything in the streets . . . the hustle, the stake . . . everything . . . worth throwing yourself under the gun everyday. Every player is a poet . . . an actor . . . statesman . . . a priest . . . but most of all he's a player, making up rules as he passes the next car on this highway. You go out there on that street and you meet the world of suckers . . . the world of greed and whatever other names have been defined for those that seek something outside the acceptances of their society . . . and you stand with your ball exposed in this jungle of fear . . . and you battle . . . and you fight the hardest fight of your life, each day out there in them streets that demand blood to nourish its own energies . . . today and tomorrow, and all the todays and tomorrows that are left inside your soul. And it's all dragged out, no holds barred. Kick . . . punch . . . scratch . . . spitting . . . screaming. Fight. And when it's over, and the streets are soaking up the blood, you smile and know that you just won another day with yourself. He's trying to take the only real thing I dream of . . . the reason for my surviving. I live with the dream of seeing her smile at the sound of my name. I won't let him destroy that dream . . . I won't let him. Yah, I'm going to kill me a pimp. (*Lights.*)

Scene Two: JUSTICE'S *bar. The scene is jumping.*

Everyone enters into JUSTICE'S *place dancing to modern disco.* JUNIOR *dances with* CHILE, DIAMOND *with* PHEBE, WILLIE *with* KAHLU *and* CAT EYES *with* SATISFACTION. CAT EYES *takes* CHILE *from* JUNIOR. BAM-BAM *enters and dances downstage. Everyone clears floor and watches.* BAM-BAM *challenges* SATISFACTION *to dance. He makes advances to her breasts and privates with his mouth.* SATISFACTION *at first astonished, then cooly dodges his advances, and finally surprises him by putting her leg between his and grinds with him. They dance for a while and all of a sudden she kicks him in the balls. Everyone cheers her and she bows and crosses to bar. Everyone laughs at* BAM-BAM. BAM-BAM *gets up, looks around, looks at* SATISFACTION *and dances to her.* CHILE *turns off music.*

CHILE: Show time . . . I like singing . . . I like to make people feel good . . . and since I ain't a player I can only talk about the players . . . so, I'd like to sing this tune which by the way I wrote with my own little two hands. That's right, don't laugh, I can write. I go to school. And the name of the song is "The Sun Always Shines For The Cool." Maestro, por favor . . . and by the way, this is dedicated to Cat Eyes.

> OOOOOOOO LA LA LA LA LA LA LA
> Wake up in the morning and find your dreams behind.
> Every kind of rainbow in every color scheme.
> It's the players golden rule . . .
> That the sun always shine for the cool.
>
> (*CHORUS*):
> So wear your eternal high
> As you hustle to get by.
> Sport your fancy clothes
> And let the whole world know,
> That you belong to that school
> Where the sun always shine . . . for the cool.
>
> OOOOO LA LA LA LA LA LA LA
> But when the neon lights are dark,
> That's when you shed your player's heart
> Being free to fall in love with me.
> Until then I'll remember, the players golden rule
> That the sun always shine for the cool . . .

(*CHORUS*)

OOOOOOOO LA LA LA LA
You belong to the school
Where the sun always shine . . . for the cool

CHILE: Thank you . . . thank you. (*Gives mike to* BAM-BAM *and cross to bar.*)

DIAMOND: Go, Chile girl, with your badself . . . walk on girl. Girl . . . man, that girl does harder than a broke dick dog. Oh shit, you know . . . there is too much sunlight in here . . . let me fish out my shades. (*Cross* CAT EYES *to bar.*) Yah Willie . . . Yah man be cool . . .

WILLIE BODEGA: The drinks are on Diamond Ring, so drink, sing, dance and be merry . . .

DIAMOND: Wait a second, Willie, I never said anything about buying the whole house a drink.

WILLIE BODEGA: What, man? I just asked you and you said "Yah, Willie, yah, Willie, be cool."

DIAMOND: Shit, man, I didn't know what the fuck you were talking about, man. You a jive motherfucker. You sure there wasn't a nigger in your family somewhere? Cuz you about the niggerest nigger I know, and you ain't even black.

WILLIE BODEGA: Do I take that as a compliment or an insult?

DIAMOND: Willie, as bad as we are, you take as you want.

WILLIE BODEGA: Shit, I ain't even gonna rap on it.

JR. BALLOON: Hay, Bam-Bam. Come here. (BAM-BAM *dances downstage to* JUNIOR.) You dancin' fool . . . you got the racing forms with you?

BAM-BAM: Yah, first the bread.

JR. BALLOON: Shit, if I didn't know you were a Rican . . . I think you be a Jew motherfucker.

BAM-BAM: You wanna shine?

JR. BALLOON: You're crazy man, you probably ruin the motherfuckers for the goof . . . Hey, what number came out? ¿Tú sabe?

WILLIE BODEGA: Man, you still play those fucking numbers, man?

JR. BALLOON: Sure, man. Why not? It's the only thing that keeps me close to the streets as I knew them once to be. ¿Tú sabe?

BAM-BAM: 614 . . .

WILLIE BODEGA: Shit, man, I blew by one fucking number.

JR. BALLOON: You still play those fucking numbers, man . . . dig this motherfucker.

DIAMOND: I told the whole place how jive this whitey is and no one listened.

WILLIE: That's cuz you was lying.

DIAMOND: Diamond Ring never lies.

CAT EYES: That a fucking lie.

DIAMOND: Man, I don't remember asking you for a comment.

CAT EYES: Well you got one . . . so what. (DIAMOND *lifts hat and* KAHLU *crosses to other women gathered near lounge.*)

DIAMOND: Man, when I was a kid and I wasn't wanted around . . . I knew. Some people you can't hint them away because of their hard face. You know what I mean, man,?

JR. BALLOON: He must be from Vajado . . . el pueblo de los cara duro.

CAT EYES: I'm from la Pela, pa' que te lo coma con leche, cabrón.

JR. BALLOON: Vete a coger por culo mamao.

CAT EYES: Oye, lo tuyo viene por ahí.

JR. BALLOON: Hey, did you guys hear what jumped down with Tito Pan Doblao?

WILLIE BODEGA: Tito Fold Bread?

JR. BALLOON: Yah, man, you know the hiest kid from out of the east side.

WILLIE BODEGA: Oh yah, yah . . . I remember him.

JR. BALLOON: Man, I don't know what get into people sometimes, tú sabe? Pero like this dude had a good thing going with himself. Tú sabe, like he was out here making a good dollar doing the simple shit he do . . . ¿tú sabe? . . . like this dude was on parole man, ten years on the motherfucking paper. Dig? And el chamaco goes out and does his thing, fronting a job in a store he practically owned. Tú sabe. (*Women cross to bar leaving* CAT EYES.)

SATISFACTION: Hell, I don't remember the very first one. Well, I remember the first trick I turned. Guess who. My elementary school principal. Really . . . this one is something else . . . I was about eleven . . .

CHILE: Eleven!

SATISFACTION: No . . . seriously. I was taking a smoke in the girls' bathroom . . . no, not marijuana . . . tobacco, just plain tobacco. Well, school was out and I didn't hear the bell ring . . . so there I was, by myself, in the john, smoking a cigarette and Mr. Sanders, that was his name — never can forget it . . . Anyway, he comes in and stands there looking at me. Now, at the time I was sleeping with my brother . . . no, not fucking, just sleeping . . . and in the morning he would get up and try to cover his "thing" but I could always see that it was hard . . . I found out later that most guys wake up in the morning with it hard . . . anyway he caught me smoking, right . . . you know, an infraction . . . so he starts giving me this lecture and I pretent to be sorry and all ears to everything he's saying. So he puts his hand on my shoulder, right, comforting me and all that shit. But I see this bulge in his pants. Now, like I told you, I slept with my little brother and he use to have this friend that would take him to school in the morning and I would pretend I was sleeping and he would feel me and jerk-off all fast kind of business . . .

PHEBE: You know, you sure take a long time to get where you're going. Tell me about the principal.

SATISFACTION: Oh, yah . . . him . . . well anyway, my brother's friend used to alway say, if I ever wanted to make a little money, just let him know and he would give me the whole wallet . . .

PHEBE: I bet he would.

SATISFACTION: So, the first thing that came into my head, while Mr. Sanders was feeling me, was to ask for a dollar. So, he pulled out his wallet and gives me a $20 . . . pulls me into the toilet stall . . . and he's a big guy and I'm kinda small . . .

CHILE: Kinda?

SATISFACTION: Well, I'm not a midget. This was really freaky here. We are in this small space . . . oh well, then he pulls it out and I let out with a WOW — and he starts shushing me quiet, "please, we'll get caught." Man, it was big and fat.

CHILE: Spare me.

SATISFACTION: Well, you asked. He couldn't fit the place, right, and for the both of us it was tight. He sat on bowl and let out this big fart . . . man it stunk. (*Cross* KAHLU *to bar.*) We're in all these weird positions trying to settle on the right angle. Anyway, nothing works and he gets really pissed off . . . he takes me by my neck, pulls me down to my knees and tries to put it in my mouth . . . but you know I wasn't into that and that's where the money is, you know? Anyway, he came in my hair and shits on himself (*Cross* KAHLU *from bar, turns and goes back.*) and I'm thinking he's catching a heart attack, and all he kept saying was, "cold water . . . cold water . . . put cold water in your hair." Anyway, they found him the next morning with a hard-on . . . but DEAD. (*Cross* CAT EYES *to bar with other men who cross back downstage.*)

JR. BALLOON: . . . that's the way these people make you go, you know. Like even when he was going great legal, the role man jumped on his case, tú sabe. Well, the dude is doing alright, tú sabe . . . and he does this stupid shit the other day . . . hey,

Bam Bam. When did you tell me about Pan Doblao?

BAM BAM: Friday . . . I got the news clipping. You wanna see it?

JR. BALLOON: Yah man let me have it.

BAM BAM: I sell it to you for a dollar.

JR. BALLOON: Man, dig this motherfucker here.

WILLIE BODEGA: Hey man . . . I'll buy it.

JR. BALLOON: He a sucker for kids.

WILLIE BODEGA: Anyone that tries to sell you a newspaper clipping got to really be out here hustling his motherfucking ass off . . . Yah man, you got to give it to him. He tries harder than Satan.

BAM BAM: That's cuz I'm god, nephew Willie.

JR. BALLOON: Go on, kid, tell him how much of a sucker he is. He don't know nothing. Right kid?

BAM BAM: Willie knows a whole lot. He even teaches me math in his house. (*Cross to* VIVA *at piano.*)

JR. BALLOON: You do Willie?

DIAMOND: Not bad, Willie B.

WILLIE BODEGA: Yah, so what? So I know a little bit of math.

JR. BALLOON: Nothin ma, tú sabe, just asking. (JUNIOR *and* DIAMOND *cross to lounge.*)

PHEBE: With me it was in a car . . . I was hitching a runaway . . . where I was going I didn't know, but I was leaving where I was coming from . . . this guy pulls up and lets me in . . . white dude, a farmer . . .

CHILE: Why was you running away from home?

PHEBE: It's a long story . . . one *thing* was my father. He was well, *hard* to describe. He was a slob . . . a *real* slob . . . *always* fighting with my mother . . . and well, once he found out that I *screwed* his brother. *Actually it was the other way around. He* screwed me cause I really didn't know what I was doing being just 8 years old. And my father instead of *fucking* up his brother, *he* took some money from him and kept quiet about the *whole* thing. I heard them in the living room . . . and my father was saying, well she *might* as well *learn* to make money out of it. Like one day the family went out to do some *shopping* and I stayed home. It was hot so I was taking a shower and he came into the bathroom and took off his clothes and *jumped in the shower with me and he started telling* me how he *fed* me, *clothed* me *housed* me, the *whole* number. And then he did the *same* thing that his brother did and told me not to say *anything* to mom. I then knew that what we was doing was *something* that was not right. But as the years went by, he stayed away from me, but I just couldn't stand to be around him. So one day I just got what little things I had and split . . .

SATISFACTION: Like you said . . . you take a long time to get . . .

PHEBE: O.K. . . . O.K. . . . well this guy *pulls* over and *tells* me that he *knew* that I was a *working* girl and I thought that he meant that I had a job . . . then he asked me for a job . . . and I told him I *can't give* you a job. *I didn't owned anything for him* . . . and he said *come* on woman you *understand* what I mean. Maybe where you come from they have *another* name for it, but I want a *blow job* . . . so I start blow air at him . . . then he said, "Oh, I see, money *takes* the action with you, huh? O.K. . . . *here.* Pulls out ten dollars, hands it to me. Pulls out dick, *shoves* it in my mouth and when it over, he had to *pull* me away cause I didn't know when he wanted me to stop. He tells me that I work out *good* and what was my regular place of work. I told him I didn't *have* any and he took me to meet this woman who ran a bar. Well, from there on I just said to myself, "well, this is *one* way of living and it's *easy* and I *really* get down to it. I kinda enjoy the work in a way . . . Well, a few years back I came up North and here I am. . .

SATISFACTION: Boring.

PHEBE: Chile, did you ever . . . turned someone . . . did you ever . . .

SATISFACTION: Naw, she still a virgin . . . at her age too . . . ridiculous . . . really girl, sex is sound of mind . . .

CHILE: I am not a virgin . . .

SATISFACTION: I'm shocked.

PHEBE: I think I'm gonna faint . . . hold me somebody . . .

CHILE: Well, my name isn't Mary of Nazaretn . . . it's Chile Girl . . . (DIAMOND and JUNIOR *enter from lounge.*)

DIAMOND: Oh shit man, he got busted for that? Wow, like why would he do some dumb shit like that. Wow, that's some strange shit ain't it?

WILLIE BODEGA: Weird, man, weird, all kinds of weird people in this world.

JR. BALLOON: Like the dude had all this thing going for him, tú sabe, and a couple of mamis that were put on him, tú sabe. What would make a dude that got all this shit going for him go out, pull a robbery and then rape the bitch too . . . I mean he was asking to get taken off the count the way I see it , tú sabe . . .

CHILE: Bam Bam Boy, come here. Listen go to the kitchen and get Jorge some shot glasses.

BAM BAM: Momentito . . . Oye Willie . . . let me have my money.

WILLIE BODEGA: Here, I don't want it . . .

BAM BAM: Cuz you already read it.

WILLIE BODEGA: That's right, son . . . like anytime you got something to sell, never let the person you selling it to get a hold of it without the cash up front. You know money talks . . . bullshit walks . . .

JR. BALLOON: That's part of your math lesson from the Street University.

CHILE: Go on hurry . . . we need the glasses fast, Bam Bam . . . He cute, ain't he?

WILLIE BODEGA: If that type turn you on, I guess so. He's not my type, you know.

CHILE: Go hump yourself . . .

WILLIE BODEGA: I will, thank you, Chile Girl.

JR. BALLOON: But I tell you, man, tú sabe, that shit with Pan Doblao is really fucking too much, man, too strong.

WILLIE BODEGA: Yah, I never expect him to come out of a bag like that, like that don't sound like him at all. Right?

DIAMOND: Man, you never know anything about anybody until the shit comes out in the wash. You know what I mean?

WILLIE BODEGA: Yah, all of it comes out in the wash, man, all of it . . .

JR. BALLOON: Man that old man should have been back by now . . . Two hours with the girl.

WILLIE BODEGA: What you expect, man? He got a collar on him.

DIAMOND: Yah, man, he got a collar on him.

JR. BALLOON: Queso Jones coming down and out of his helmet tonight.

WILLIE BODEGA: What the fuck is a "queso jones"?

JR. BALLOON: You know a Hundred Fires? The mack from downtown? Hundred fires to light up any woman's desires. Well, he say that since come is milk and milk take the form of cheese, so when a dude ain't seen un pelo for a long time he gets a cheese cake in the back of his neck, you know. ¿Tú sabe? So cheese is queso, man . . . he got a . . .

WILLIE BODEGA: Queso Jones . . .

JR. BALLOON: Good for you. You learn Spanish sooner or later. (*Enter ROSA and VIEJO.*)

WILLIE BODEGA: It's a bilingual city, my man . . .

JR. BALLOON: Hey, man. Qué pasa with that dude with the pure shit? ¿Tú sabe? That dude is full of baby shit, man. He is supposed to have something nice for us tonight and like he ain't showed up yet, man. Tú sabe, me . . . I feel a little shakey around a dude that ain't got no sense of time.

WILLIE BODEGA: He be here, man, he be here. Give him time. He might of got a flat tire or something, you know . . .

DIAMOND: The only other whitey that I knew that had a sense of time beside you, Willie, was your brother, Billy Boy.

JR. BALLOON: Yah, he was a good man . . . Why don't your woman talk, man?

WILLIE BODEGA: She a mute, my man . . . she can't do that thing with the tongue.

VIEJO: Hey, man, Willie, I forgot to run it on you earlier, man, but like, I'm sorry to have heard about your brother man . . .

WILLIE BODEGA: Yah, thanks a lot Viejo . . . you know he thought a great deal about you, man. He dug you a whole lot . . .

VIEJO: I dug on him too . . .

WILLIE BODEGA: Yah . . .

VIEJO: Was you there when the shit jumped off?

WILLIE BODEGA: Yah man, I was there, but there was nothing that I could have done, man. You know, like he gave me the out, man. He would've have been really sore at me if I would have fucked around and blew it. You know how Billy was, man. Let me tell you something Viejo. I'm sorry he dead, dig, but I'm proud at the way he went, man, real proud at the way he went. Like, that's the way we should all go when the times comes that we have to say it's a game of cards . . . holding court in the streets . . . guns smoking, man, that's the way to do it when you got to do it. Becuz when you play it that way, and you don't want to end the game that way, then you should never had played anyway, right? . . . right! Like, that what's it all about, ain't it, man? Going with your head held high and your trigger fingers aching . . . man. Viejo, you know that I would have stayed with him if he wanted me to. I would have gone with him to shake hands with Satan. Shit, I bet he lonely down there . . . get all the heat . . . man that's what he always got a lot of, fucking heat. Ever since I could remember man, our old man played it to the bitter end with us. He played it so tough that we never learn what it meant to be a little warm inside ourselves. But man, the time were like hard candy in a cheap soda shop. But like that day, man, like that day, I should have remember, "When a cross eyes mark get in your way, don't play," cuz it's bad luck . . . when you speak like you ain't ever gonna see day light again, man, that's the time to spend in bed with pussy smelling pillows in your face. You know that the time to hit the invisible man scene in the life, man, but he knew all that too . . . he knew all that too, but he went anyway, man. Viejo, he knew that too. You taught both of us that shit way back then. You remember, right? . . . the roof top, shootin' coke bottles off the edge. Man, I was mean with a pistol and so was he . . . but that day he spoke like he wasn't going enjoy the bread from the sting no matter how much it was. It was like he knew that there was a jinx in the air for him that day, but he went. He insisted in making the hit anyway . . . it was like he had what you call a bad ju ju, there was like no wind in the air . . . man, no taste in our mouth, no feeling in our pulse, no beating in our hearts man. The train didn't even make noise for us that day. The lights were all red in every corner that we came to, but he wanted to go to the hit anyway . . . He was going for broke. I should have known that. Well, guess that I did know it man, but I didn't know how to put a capper on it. You know what I mean, man. He wanted to go for broke. He was tired I guess, like so many of us get tired with this whole thing out here. Remember the way he held his guns in his holsters, real close to his heart, man. But that day he held them down around his waist like if he wanted to put his head and heart out there for the buzzard in blue. He wanted to die, man. Viejo, he wanted to die and I didn't want him to . . . but like that his right to go if he wanted to. I see him running, man. He was running. The first cap was booked into his leg man. He fell, got up and booked a cap into the man . . . they came out of nowhere, man. They came out of nowhere blasting them 38's his way. He was next to the building. They blew right thru the door, and he came out as they walked his way where he was suppose to have been laying dead. He came out blasting caps into their asses, man. They ran, they ran and those that didn't laid down dead on the streets, were laid down dead. They laid down dead and I laugh cuz I knew that he was badder than all of them in the shining blue uniforms looking like semi gods. He was a rebel. He was Satan in heaven fighting God for a piece of the action man. That's who he was, Lucifer, fighting God for a piece of the action. That's what he looked like. He looked like a young god taking his anger out on the fucking world. And he was mean-looking in his walk, in the bullets that flew out of his power. That was his power. That's why they had to kill him three times over after he was dead . . . but they should have known, man, that he was alive . . . he was more alive than they will ever be, cuz he was a rebel in the middle of them all, and he would have never hanged up his gloves . . . they were on his mitts for good and he wore them tight . . .

JR. BALLOON: El chamaco estaba en algo. ¿Tú sabe?

DIAMOND: Man, the collar loosen up now. Hey, Viejo?

JR. BALLOON: Look like you lost some weight up there, Viejo.

VIEJO: In the joint?

JR. BALLOON: I ain't talking about no joint, motherfucker.

VIEJO: You can't be talking about nothing else.

JR. BALLOON: Pérate. She did take care of business with you. Right?

VIEJO: Oh, that. Yah man, she took care of business . . . thanks for looking out . . .

JR. BALLOON: That's what friends are for. Ain't it? Shit, I don't need me no friends when I am doing good. Right, bro?

DIAMOND: Right. Solid on the wallet . . .

WILLIE BODEGA: Solid on the wallet? What kinda of shit is that?

DIAMOND: Regular shit, my man, just plain ordinary shit.

WILLIE BODEGA: Sounds like it too . . .

JR. BALLOON: Oye, cut that shit out, man. You guys are beginning to bore me today with all this wolf-ticket selling that's going on around here. Shit, I feel like I'm at the garden and not in Justice's joint having a good time with the folks. Viva, play me a tune.

WILLIE BODEGA: Guess that kid got me on edge all day, selling me a ticket, man. I should have cashed it for him, but man it's not worth it. He be out of the life a lot earlier than I thought he be . . .

DIAMOND: Yah, he got on my nerves today too . . .

JR. BALLOON: Squash that shit too man . . . forget about that nonplayer . . .

WILLIE BODEGA: Viva, play me a little "Misty."

VIEJO: See you guys later . . .

JR. BALLOON: Viejo, the kid's alright, you know . . . it's that sometimes he comes across like bad medicine . . . like a laxative. You know what I mean? ¿Tú sabe? (*Everyone dancing on dance floor.*)

VIEJO: Yo sé . . . later . . . Lefty, rum and coke . . . easy on the coke, heavy on the rum, no ice . . . What can I get you, Cat Eyes?

CAT EYES: Me? You gonna buy me a drink?

VIEJO: Yah, why not? The enemies of two armies were at one time sitting together in the same room talking about which is the best way in which to kill men in wars . . .

CAT EYES: Freaky kind of shit. Ain't it?

VIEJO: Yah, I guess some people would look at that as freaky, weird . . . fucked up thinking, but you know after they made up the rules they went out and had themselves a great big war to test out the rules and see which of them play fair . . .

CAT EYES: Who played fair?

VIEJO: Nobody ever plays fair when it involves the heart or the pocketbook . . .

CAT EYES: Look, old man, you kind of old to be talking like you mean to do something to somebody, you know, like the thing you said about your daughter . . . if she is your daughter.

VIEJO: She is my daughter . . . call her . . . ask her . . .

CAT EYES: Chile Girl . . . here Cat Eyes . . .

CHILE: Yah, what can I get you?

CAT EYES: Some questions answered . . .

CHILE: Like what?

CAT EYES: Like this man said that he's your father. Is that true?

VIEJO: You can deny it if you wish, nena, pero tú sabe en tu corazón that lo que pasó, pasó. Don't hold the world of yesterday against me, nena.

CHILE: He's the man that fucked my mother and created a child who he named Chile Girl Rivera. Yah, if that's being a father, I guess he my father. Then it means nothing to me at all.

CAT EYES: Vaya, I guess that you want to say something to me on your own that ain't got her approval.

VIEJO: Her approval isn't needed in this case, young man.

CHILE: Are you two discussing me and my life . . .

CAT EYES: Seems that your old man doesn't approve of me going out with you . . .

CHILE: It's no business of his, whatsoever.

CAT EYES: He thinks I am going to turn you out.

CHILE: That's because he sees himself in you, but you're different than he ever was with my mother. At least you can tell me the truth . . . even if it's in the dark. (CAT EYES *kisses* CHILE.)

VIEJO: You have a beautiful smile, Cat Eyes . . . you have the smile of a man that just got over like a fat rat . . . (*Shoves him.*)

CAT EYES: Hey, man. What the hell you doing? Get off my dick. Are you a faggot or something?

CHILE: What are you doing?

VIEJO: Shut up, both of you . . . not another fucking word, you hear me, not another fucking word, from either of yous . . .

CAT EYES: Man, you better be cool . . .

VIEJO: Punk, I got a 357 magnum eight-inch barrel sticking in your balls and if you don't be cool I'll blow them off.

CAT EYES: Man, be cool with that thing, man, be cool, please.   ·

CHILE: Are you crazy? Haven't you done enough to me.

VIEJO: That's just it, mi nena linda, I have done too much to you and I never have done anything for you. Now I'll make it up to you, tonight baby . . . tonight . . . right here.

CHILE: By killing my man?

CAT EYES: Talk to him, baby. He looks crazy, man . . . he looks crazy. Talk to him, baby, talk to him. Please, Viejo, man, shoot anywhere else but there, please man.

VIEJO: Chile, I ain't out to kill your man but to kill your would be pimp.

CHILE: What are you talking about? You are crazy.

CAT EYES: Come, baby, don't get him madder then he is.

VIEJO: She gonna have a man . . . not a pimp like you are, trying to be like I was . . .

CAT EYES: Man, I ain't her pimp, man, I love her. Believe me, I do.

VIEJO: You lying punk son of a bitch . . . get up . . . up . . . faggot, up . . . get your yellow ass up in the air. Get it up, punk. (DIAMOND *crosses from dance floor.*)

DIAMOND: Oh shit. What the fuck is Viejo doing? (*Everyone gathers around.*)

WILLIE BODEGA: Oh shit, he gonna kill that kid . . . Viejo.

201

VIEJO: Shut up, all of you . . . keep out of it . . .

WILLIE BODEGA: Man, you just got out . . . if you wanna waste him let me take care of it. That's my shot, man, not yours . . .

JUSTICE: Viejo . . . don't . . .

CAT EYES: Please don't kill me, please . . . don't kill me.

VIEJO: Punk, I ain't going to kill you, but you gonna wish that I had.

JUSTICE: Viejo, man, you gone crazy, man? What are you trying to prove, man? He's a punk kid, man, just a punk kid.

VIEJO: Is he right? Man is he right that you ain't nothing but a punk kid? They fucked you in the joint . . . they fucked you in the joint? Is that what he is saying? Answer me.

CAT EYES: Yah, man, I ain't nothing but a punk kid.

VIEJO: You gave it up in the joint. Didn't you?

CAT EYES: Yah, man, I gave up my ass in the joint . . .

JR. BALLOON: Man, Viejo, what you think you gonna get after this shit, man?

ROSA: Carlos, please do what he says . . . he's crazy.

CAT EYES: Man, what have I done to you? Man, I ain't done nothing to you, man, nothing . . . I don't even know you.

VIEJO: But you know my daughter. Don't you motherfucker? And you wanna turn her out. Don't you? That's what you told me. Didn't you?

CAT EYES: Yah, man, but I didn't mean it.

CHILE: Did you say that?

CAT EYES: Yah, baby, but I was only kidding, baby, believe me.

VIEJO: Liar!

CAT EYES: O.K. . . . O.K. . . . I did mean . . . but man, let me go and I won't even look at her anymore. I mean it, man, really.

VIEJO: Why should I believe you, man? You lied to her . . . you lied to me . . . you lied to everybody, you bullshitting punk.

CAT EYES: Man, I mean I wouldn't do anything.

VIEJO: Rosa . . . Rosa, tell Chile what you are to this thing here?

ROSA: I . . . I . . .

CAT EYES: Rosa, Rosa . . . cállate, te corto tu cuello. Rosa . . .

VIEJO: Shut the fuck up, faggot. Go on, Rosa, tell her.

ROSA: He's my brother . . .

VIEJO: (VIEJO punches CAT EYES in his stomach.) See, baby? I know punks like him, I known them all my life . . . You love him and you don't believe . . . but it's the truth, baby, the truth . . . he put his own sister out on the corner to hustle. He sold her to Junior Balloon. Ain't that the truth, Junior?

JR. BALLOON: Yah, man, that's the truth . . .

ROSA: We had to survive . . .

VIEJO: There are other ways to make it out here, in any of the games of the fast . . .

WILLIE BODEGA: Man, he started out on his own family, man, that's out . . .

DIAMOND: He needs to die.

CHILE: No man needs to die.

VIEJO: Baby, this is one scumbag that needs to die.

CAT EYES: I don't wanna die, man, please, don't do it . . . take pity.

CHILE: Shut up! (Slaps CAT EYES.) Die if you have to, but don't beg for pity.

CAT EYES: Fuck you, you ain't the one that gonna get killed. Viejo, listen man, I give you a share of all my shit, man. Please don't waste me, man.

VIEJO: I ain't gonna waste you . . . you gonna do it to yourself. Your skin becomes soft, your voice will become pitch high and . . .

CAT EYES: Oh my God, please . . . kill me . . .

VIEJO: No, man, you got to go slow man, you got to know your mistake everyday that you are gonna live . . .

CHILE: Punk . . . Punk . . . (*Crosses toward pay phone.* JUSTICE *holds her.*)

JUSTICE: Stay right where you are, Chile . . . stay right where you are . . . (VIEJO *makes* CAT EYES *strip to his underwear.*)

DIAMOND: Sissy ass motherfucker had the heart to sell tickets . . . shit . . .

JR. BALLOON: Shut up, Diamond.

DIAMOND: Fuck you.

WILLIE BODEGA: Lefty . . . cool this will you . . .

LEFTY G.: No, man, you guys cool it. (*Pulls gun.*)

VIEJO: Get down on your knees, punk . . . down on your knees.

PHEBE: Cat Eyes . . . baby . . . don't . . . baby . . .

DIAMOND: You're mines now bitch . . . so get over here and enjoy the show . . . Move! (PHEBE *places pillow on floor in front of* CAT EYES.)

VIEJO: Get down on your knees, faggot . . .

WILLIE BODEGA: Get down on your knees, man . . .

JR. BALLOON: Get down on your knees, maricón.

CAT EYES: Man be cool, please be cool . . . I getting down.

VIEJO: On your knees, mariconcito . . . down . . .

CHILE: Cat Eyes . . .

JUSTICE: Get down boy, if you wanna live . . .

VIEJO: Now beg . . . motherfucker, beg . . . Lefty, la puerta . . . (LEFTY *locks door.*) like you wanna live I want you to beg me like if you wanna stay alive as bad as you wanna live, that's as bad as I wanna hear you beg. Am I God?

CHILE: No, papi, no . . . no, Carlos . . .

CAT EYES: Yes, you are God . . .

VIEJO: I see there are tears in your eyes . . . cry motherfucker, cry . . . scream out . . . scream out your tears, motherfucker, scream them out, you no-good-low-life son of a whore. (CAT EYES *begins to scream and cry, hold on to* VIEJO'S *legs.*)

VIEJO: Kiss my shoes punk, kiss them. (CAT EYES *complies with all of* VIEJO'S *wishes.*) Everybody back, back, every motherfucking body get your ass away from here . . . move you son of bitch, move.

JUSTICE: Viejo . . . Viejo . . .

VIEJO: You too, you ugly motherfucker, move back . . . now you sit in the chair right there . . . come on crawl over there . . . go on crawl . . . sit . . . stop crying already, motherfucker . . . you would-be king of the pimps. Listen to what I got to say punk . . . You think that playing a pimp makes you a mack. Punks like you are marks in the game. You get by cause people don't wanna deal with shit. You a player? You ain't never played nothing, creep . . . you couldn't play a dime off a blind man in a dark alley. You think you got it all in the cap . . . you ain't got nothing. Sucker, you got about as much sense as a split mustard seed. You ain't never played beyond the footlights, where the action is you and you alone . . . on the corners . . . on a roof, the blacktop streets of the jungle . . . Lefty, you only think you done it . . . becuz on the street the game is staying alive and you don't know how to stay alive . . . you don't know how to survive because you put your-self in a position to die . . . like right now, sucker . . . like right now you are going to die, Cat Eyes the pimp . . . Cat Eyes the pussy . . . you a player? A player is a survivor of a constant struggle to do it hard . . . to play it to the bitter end . . . to the bitter end. Faggot, don't you know that out here in this jungle if you are caught acting you are one dead player? Out here you go for broke . . . you take it to the streets on all levels and you took it to the level that's gonna cause your death. This ain't the semi-truth world of the tennis hustler or the pro golf pusher . . . this is the real world of the dreamer strung out . . . but you can't understand that. Are you listening, Chile Girl? He ain't shit. He's a phony being, a fake . . .

even his lies are false. You blew this the minute that you thought you were the only player in town that the rules made. I invented the game, and so did your mother. You can't hustle off a hustler. You can't play on a player. You gave yourself no out. You put yourself in solitary confinement, baby. They tell me if you don't open your mouth when you are dying, you don't need any questions answered about death. Motherfucker, I told you and you closed your ears; now you close your life. I won't let you get away with it, not me. I won't let you motherfucker . . .

CHILE: No, no lo mate, papi, no tire . . .

JUSTICE: Viejo . . . (VIEJO *shoots himself and goes to bar. At sound of shot* CAT EYES *falls back searching for a wound crying and screaming for* CHILE . . . *everyone rushes to* CAT EYES *thinking he is shot.*)

DIAMOND: You ain't shot . . . he ain't shot, man, look, he ain't shot.

WILLIE BODEGA: Oh shit, Viejo played it . . . it was his play and he played it.

JR. BALLOON: The motherfucker was a blank . . . (KAHLU *screams,* VIEJO *falls . . . dead.*)

JUSTICE: Girl, what's the matter with you . . . Viejo.

CHILE: No papi . . . no (*Rushes to* VIEJO. *Everyone rushes toward* VIEJO . . . JUSTICE *holds* CHILE, *faces her toward* CAT EYES.)

JUSTICE: He played it . . . to the bitter end.

EPILOGUE (*Music and lights.*)

Set to Rock music in prologue. There are five flash-back freezes. CAT EYES *on his knees.* DIAMOND RING'S *entrance.* WILLIE BODEGA'S *entrance.* JR. BALLOON'S *entrance.* PHEBE REED *and* LEFTY *and* THE MAIN PIMP *with cane pointing at audience who then strides off as lights dim.*